Tithe & Other Records of Essex & Barking (to the mid-19th century)

A guide for local and family historians and teachers

Herbert Hope Lockwood

ESSEX RECORD OFFICE

Published by the Essex Record Office
Wharf Road, Chelmsford, Essex CM2 6YT

© Essex County Council 2006

All rights reserved.
This book may not be reproduced, in whole or in part, in
any form without written permission from the publishers.

A catalogue reference for this book
is available from the British Library.

ISBN: 1 898529 24 8

Essex Record Office Publication No. 000149

Cover illustrations: Wyfields House, near Cranbrook by Edward Sage.
Map of Eastbury Tithing in Ripple, 1831 (ERO D/SH 17).

Contents

Foreword by Professor Roger Kain		2
Acknowledgements		3
'The Yearly Distress'		5
Introduction		6
Chapter one:	Tithe in general	9
Chapter two:	Tithe documentation	20
Chapter three:	Origin of the Barking tithe circuits	
	Part I: Before the Dissolution	28
	Part II: After the Dissolution	33
Chapter four:	Thomas Cartwright and the evolution of Barking documentation	40
Chapter five:	Barking tithe documentation	
	Part I: The system in the 18th century	48
	Part II: Isaac Johnson's survey and commutation	54
Chapter six:	Other Barking tithe related documents	62
Chapter seven:	Documents complementary to Barking tithe surveys	70
Chapter eight:	Research potential of the Barking documents	85
Appendix:	Notes on the provenance of principal Barking sources	110
Notes		118
Bibliography		136
Index		144

Foreword

In this, his last work, now published posthumously, Herbert H. Lockwood leaves a fine testament to his scholarship.

Tithes and Other Records of Essex and Barking is a most valuable contribution to the understanding of tithe documentation, both that specific to Barking and that which illuminates issues of the tithe in the country generally. The author's deft handling of the subject matter successfully highlights some of those forces which have shaped the landscape in which we now live. His work on the 'indelible tithing' is particularly noteworthy in this respect.

Whilst the elucidation of the exceptionally fine collection of tithe records that Barking possesses is, in itself, of great value to the student, Herbert Lockwood's tenacity in identifying and seeking out those records deserves praise too. By his own admission, the research that finally became this book started some four decades ago, at a time when attitudes to the keeping of historical documents were very different. His tireless pursuit of tithe and other documents has, without doubt, made available to other researchers a collection that might otherwise have been lost or not recognised.

This book is the culmination of many years of passionate research; a work of great detail, yet one that engages the reader by its argument's clarity. It is a real privilege to be invited to write a Foreword to such a valuable book.

Professor Roger Kain,
Exeter University

Acknowledgements

This particular volume was conceived whilst preparing a lecture delivered to the Barking branch of the East of London Family History Society in 1997. But much of the material content of the work derives from sources discovered long before when I was seeking material for an uncompleted doctoral thesis on the evolution of the settlement pattern of Barking. So my then supervisor, G.A.J. Hodgett, and many of those mentioned in the appendix and notes to the present work like Harold Wand, James Oxley and Kenneth Glenny helped to lay the foundations of a building not yet planned.

Amongst them also are Dr Cyril Hart and Raymond Powell – still active in retirement – who both provided much inspiration and encouragement in the earlier period. The late Derek Emmison and the institution which he founded and nurtured, the Essex Record Office, has continued to play a key role in this production with the help given by Vic Gray, Ken Hall, Janet Smith, and – latterly – Deborah Peers. There has been similar continuity of assistance from the Barking and Dagenham Library and Museum Service at Valence, from John O'Leary and James Howson through to Sue Curtis, Mark Watson and, most recently, Linda Rhodes and Judith Etherton. The excellent new Local Studies Centre there could help only in the final stages, so I wish to say a special thank-you to staff in Valence Library, particularly to Meredith Myears, who searched patiently for books and documents.

Throughout most of the historic times covered by this volume Ilford was part of Barking, so the holdings of the Redbridge Library Service can bear no comparison with those of the above institutions. Nevertheless, their Brand Collection has been very useful and those who followed Peter Wright in the reference library and local history room – particularly Ian Dowling – have given whatever help they could. I would also like to thank Bill George, now serendipitously translated from Ilford to Valence Library, for his help in tracking down references and obtaining books.

Material of importance to this book is in the private collection at Hatfield House. Most of my investigations there were also carried out before the present work was envisaged, but the helpful attitude of Lord Salisbury's archivist, Robin Harcourt Williams, has continued to be appreciated. My debt to the Public Record Office is obvious from both text and endnotes. My thanks are also due to the British Library, Dr William's Library and the National Portrait Gallery, whilst the Guildhall Library and the library of the Antiquarian Society have proved agreeable places to study.

I offer my sincere thanks to the Friends of Historic Essex for their generous financial contribution which enabled the inclusion of coloured illustrations in this volume.

The generosity of Professor Roger Kain as a leading authority on the subject in reading through the first draft and commenting favourably was an important incentive. I was also encouraged by the comments of the late Dr Stuart Mason, whose knowledge of Essex maps and surveyors was unique, and of Ken Neale. And I cannot praise too highly the expert assistance given by Alan Hooker with computerisation of text and illustrations: nor the patient expenditure of time by Michael Wand in preparing the index. Finally – sincere thanks to my wife, Dorothy, for support and criticism throughout.

Herbert Lockwood

Herbert Hope Lockwood B.A.(Hons) A.K.C. F.S.A. 1917-2004

This work now stands as a testament to the scholarship of the late Herbert Hope Lockwood, it encompasses his extensive knowledge of, and particular interest in, Barking and places it in the wider context of the county of Essex and beyond.

Ever mindful of the student, this is for those who will study and research the subject in the future. It is hoped that many will be encouraged, enriched and inspired by his accomplishment.

The Yearly Distress.
Tithing Time at Stock

Now all unwelcome at his gates
The clumsy swains alight
With rueful faces and bald pates
He trembles at the sight.

And well he may, for well he knows
Each bumpkin of the clan
Instead of paying what he owes
Will cheat him if he can.

One wipes his nose upon his sleeve
One spits upon the floor
Yet not to give offence or grieve
Holds up the cloth before.

Oh, why are farmers made so coarse
Or clergy made so fine?
A kick that scarce would move a horse
May kill a sound divine.

Then let the boobies stay at home;
'Twould cost him I dare say,
Less trouble taking half the sum
Without the clowns that pay.

William Cowper
(Dedicated by the poet to his friend,
W.C. Unwin, Rector of Stock, c. 1835.)

Introduction

The primary purpose of this book is to describe the exceptionally full tithe records of the old parish of Barking – particularly those prior to the Tithe Commutation Act of 1836 – and illustrate their potential for research in conjunction with other records. Some description of these other records – manorial and fiscal – will be an important secondary consideration. The opening chapters are intended to illuminate the nature of tithe in a wider context, particularly of Essex parishes, of which Barking (which then included Ilford) was amongst the largest.

Those who want to use the Barking archives solely as a source of information upon an individual topic, such as a family name, may prefer to skim the first three chapters before entering into detail. Yet, past experience has shown that the way to unlock the full potential of historical documents is to understand the purpose for which they were originally created.

Moreover, although this work does not pretend to be an exhaustive study of the pre-1836 tithe records of other Essex parishes, a sufficient sample has been made to offer an introduction helpful to those wishing to use the wealth of material in the Essex Record Office and elsewhere.

Survival of records

Unfortunately for some parishes few, if any, tithe records before 1836 still exist. A survey of the 1,200 or so parishes in Norfolk and Suffolk published in 1980 revealed only 48 parishes in Norfolk and 40 in Suffolk then had tithe books dating from before 1836, although the indications were that more might be discovered in other collections or remained in private hands.[1] For whilst the imminent prospect of official commutation of tithes and the general substitution of cash payments stimulated the production of earlier parish and private records in support of claims, the completion of that process destroyed most of their legal value long before the invention of county record offices could ensure their preservation as historical documents. The survivors are worth seeking, but the balance of survival between tithe and other records differs widely between parishes and, in practice, most lines of research will need to draw upon more than one class of document – national, parochial, manorial and otherwise.

Alan Macfarlane, who between 1973 and 1981 conducted an intensive joint research project involving analysis of all surviving records of Earls Colne in Essex and Kirkby Lonsdale in Westmoreland, stressed 'interconnectedness', for "to understand the records and hence the history of England it is necessary to consider the records as a whole".[2] For a more recent computer based study of two Yorkshire manufacturing townships, Pat Hudson employed the phrase, "multiple record linkages" which expresses the concept more dynamically.[3] Macfarlane also admitted the problem of "differential survival"; indeed he gave virtually no attention to tithe records because none appeared to survive for Earls Colne prior to 1757 and the remainder were but bare lists.[4]

So attention has been given in the latter part of this book not only to the tithe records of Barking, but also to other records and their combined potential for research. A good idea of the range of local documentation can be obtained from *Essex in London: a guide to the records of the London Boroughs formerly in Essex deposited in the Essex Record Office*.[5] When using this invaluable guide the extensive administrative changes of the 19th and 20th centuries must be borne in mind; thus, although Ilford is now a major portion of the London Borough of Redbridge, the bulk of earlier documentation is to be found under the London Borough of Barking and Dagenham. Also, it is as well to realise that the whole of the ancient parish of Barking, including Ilford, is now covered with suburban housing; a landscape transformation over little more than a century which presents both a challenge and an opportunity to the local historian.

Further reading

It must be reiterated that this book is principally concerned with tithing and its documentation *before* the Tithe Commutation Act of 1836, but the subsequent tithe commutation award with its accompanying map of a parish will be the necessary starting point for most researchers. However, so much has been written in the last few years about this Act and its implementation that the enquirer will seldom lack assistance at this stage. For an introduction the reader is referred to *Tithes, Maps, Apportionments and the 1836 Act: a guide for local historians* by Eric Evans and Alan Crosby.[6] More detailed guidance is available in a yet more recent work, *Tithe Surveys for Historians* by Roger J.P. Kain and Hugh C. Prince.[7]

For further reference, *The Tithe Surveys of England and Wales* by the same authors is recommended.[8] Although this also deals primarily with the use of records resulting from the Tithe Commutation Act of 1836, its opening chapters can be relied upon to answer many questions about earlier systems, whilst later chapters amply illustrate the potential for research of tithe documents in general. Unfortunately, this work is now out of print. *The Tithe Maps of England and Wales: a cartographic analysis and county-by-county catalogue* by Roger Kain and Richard Oliver usefully lists every official parish map in the Public Record Office covering every county, including Essex, dating each award and summarising the essential facts concerning its map.[9] A typescript list of the Essex maps with an introduction by Dr Stuart Mason is also filed at the Essex Record Office, Chelmsford, under reference T/Z 438/1. The Essex Record Office has copies of these mid-19th century awards and maps and, thanks to a scheme which they launched some years ago, they have numerical indexes to many awards prepared by local volunteers.

Chapter five of *Church Court Records: an introduction for family and local historians* by Ann Tarver exemplifies tithe procedures and documentation before 1836.[10] And, in regard to earlier tithe material in the Essex Record Office, Dr Emmison's essay, 'Tithes, Perambulations and Sabbath-breach in Elizabethan Essex', deserves to be better known. This was prepared for the second volume of his important trilogy *Elizabethan Life*, but actually published in *Tribute to an Antiquary: essays presented to Marc Fitch*.[11]

Chapter one: Tithe in general

Nowadays it may be difficult to realise that for many centuries most clergy of the established church were principally dependent for income upon the tithe which they themselves had to collect from their parishioners. In theory, tithe (*decima* in Latin) represented a tenth of all produce; in practice, mainly of agricultural produce – the tenth sheaf of corn, the tenth animal born, etc. The payment was not voluntary, the obligation to support the church in this fashion had existed in common law from Saxon times, although the mode of payment was often influenced by local custom. In the words of one authority, "no tax in the history of Europe can compare with tithes in length of duration, extent of application, and weight of economic burden".[12] And, as Eric Evans said in his so aptly titled work, *The Contentious Tithe*, the "assessment and collection were based on an amalgam of custom, precedent and case-law complex enough to baffle even the lawyers who waxed fat on the numerous disputes."[13]

Although its scriptural basis was not indisputable, the moral imperative to render tithe was seldom in dispute; medieval wills often included bequests to the parish church to cover tithes 'negligently forgotten'. But in the course of time many discontents reinforced the natural reluctance to pay taxation, like the early practice of granting portions or blocks of tithe from a parish to support distant institutions such as monasteries and colleges. For example, in 1078 William, Earl of Warren, endowed the newly founded Cluniac Abbey of Lewes in Sussex with the great manor, or honour, of Wakefield, Yorkshire which included the rectorial tithe of the extensive Pennine parish of Halifax; "owing to the difficulties of transport… the monks appear to have encouraged the landowners to commute their tithes into money payments… [and] a system of farming out their tithes and other rents was instituted by which the prior sold for a fixed sum the right to collect the moneys due to the priory."[14] Shortly before its dissolution by Henry VIII, the doomed monastery sold this lease to an ambitious Halifax family who secured the connivance of Thomas Cromwell, the King's Vicar-General, by a substantial bribe. Their subsequent attempt to take tithes in kind precipitated a violent dispute resulting in a lawsuit and even a murder.

Having obtained possession of the tithes the appropriator normally appointed a vicar (Latin, *vicarius*, 'a substitute') to minister to the parish who was entitled to receive only the 'small tithe' for his maintenance. Halifax is a glaring example, but in Essex Prittlewell Priory near Southend, a daughter house of the Abbey of Lewes, was "for its size, unusually rich in church spoils", for it held, appropriated at various times, no less than a dozen Essex churches, including Clavering with Langley in the opposite corner of the county, together with portions of tithe from four other parishes.[15]

Further reluctance to pay followed the Reformation and the Dissolution of the Monasteries in the mid-16th century when many such appropriated tithes passed to lay impropriators to be treated as private property separated from any religious or charitable purpose. Perhaps a third of all great, or rectorial, tithe – that on main crops – in England and Wales thus passed into the hands of laymen.[16] In the case of Waltham Holy Cross, one of the largest parishes in Essex, the Denny family obtained from Henry VIII both great and small tithes together with most of the lands formerly held by Waltham Abbey. They thus became lay rectors as well as lords of the manor, but with no legal obligation beyond paying a 'donative' curate the sum of £8 per year to minister to the parish. This, it must be admitted, was a somewhat exceptional case arising from the fact that Waltham Abbey had been a house of Augustinian canons, who, being priests, had served the parish themselves without instituting a vicarage.[17]

Abortive puritan attempts to put tithing upon a voluntary basis during the period of the Commonwealth (supported by independents and Levellers in the ranks of the New Model Army, but resisted by the Presbyterian majority in parliament) were finally defeated by the Restoration. However, ministers reinstated in the 1660s met increased problems when reclaiming their benefices.[18] The Rector of Belchamp Otten, a small parish in north Essex, left an instructive account of his experiences, which a subsequent incumbent put into his own tithe book –

> I was instituted and inducted into this Living in [December, 1665]... my Predecessor, Mr Bird had been ejected out of this place in the time of the long Rebellion, [and] was restored again in the year 1660, who continuing but a few years before left a very imperfect accompt to me his Successor of his perquisites and tithes belonging to this Rectory: Whereupon, being a Stranger, I had no other way to understand what appertained to me, than by taking in the limits of our parish by Perambulation; and then consulting the Tax Rate, and the Overseers Rates, I did make a probable and conjectural Estimation of what belonged unto me." [He describes] the fierce contention and opposition which several of the chief inhabitants as well as farmers by their clashing and skrewing of each other made...and seeking to...reconcile their affections each to other by composing differences, with as many persuasions and encouragements as I could use upon such occasions, at length a settlement of the rates in an equal proportion to each others charges put a period to these discords, tho', they did not much unite their affections to each other.[19]

Nor perhaps to their rector – for it is difficult to know how far the "fierce contention and opposition" here were actually religious or anti-clerical – although a later rector reported only "1 Anabaptist family" in the parish in 1764. For 30 or so years after the 1660 Restoration, despite the failure of the Savoy conference in 1662 and the wholesale expulsion of dissenting ministers by the subsequent Act of Uniformity, many Dissenters still clung to the hope of a more comprehensive Church of England and attended services at their parish church as well as meetings addressed by Presbyterian or Congregationalist preachers.[20] Nevertheless, by the end of the 17th century the growth of dissent and some easing of the law had resulted in the formation of congregations with their own meeting houses and ministers independent of the official church. This swelled the numbers who resented the compulsion to support the established Church of England, even if they were not prepared to join the Quakers in outright refusal to pay tithe.

But even loyal Anglican farmers were aware that since the 16th century law had followed practice in acquiescing in the difficulties of collecting personal tithe from merchants and shopkeepers (householders in towns like London escaped with a small rent-charge), so placing almost the whole burden upon the shoulders of the agricultural community.[21] Furthermore, on the evidence of 18th century episcopal visitations alone, it is plain that Anglican clergy in many Essex parishes in this 'age of negligence' were not providing value for money in respect of frequency of services, administration of the sacraments, instruction of children, or pastoral care in general. In some at least, pluralism, lay impropriation and clerical poverty were at the root of the trouble.[22]

Practical problems attended even collection of tithe from the farmer. The difficulties of taking the tithe in kind are evident. In the case of the great tithe (that on growing grain crops or grass) the collection needed to take place at a time shortly after harvest or haymaking convenient to both producer and tithe-owner. Although the former was responsible for fairly laying out the sheaves or haycocks (incentives were sometimes offered to ensure greater co-operation), the latter had usually to arrange for the necessary cartage, labour and storage (and possibly marketing) of the produce. For an article in 1954, R. Lennard assembled evidence showing that during the Norman period lords donating blocks of tithe to religious institutions sometimes also granted the services of a peasant responsible for collecting the tithe. Among Lennard's examples were grants in some nine Essex parishes made by Eudo Dapifer to Colchester Abbey at the beginning of the 12th century.[23] In early 14th century Barking the carters who drove the 'gadercart' collecting tithe, and their attendant pitchers and stackers, were being paid in money or in allowances of corn.[24] And still, in 18th century Lexden (one of the parishes, incidentally, in Eudo's grant) we find charges for cartage entered in the rector's accounts under "Expended on Tithe".[25] A large barn would be a further capital expense if all tithes of grain and hay were taken in kind. The term tithe-barn is now popularly misused for any large and ancient barn; in practice it can be difficult to discover if one were a tithe barn proper, built or even employed mainly for that purpose.[26]

Produce that could be used immediately, or readily marketed locally, might be taken in kind at any period. Where available, tithe wood was a valuable benefit often, but not invariably, classed as great tithe. This was due only on occasions when cutting took place, but many Essex parishes were well wooded and the product would not be difficult to sell because the tenant of the woodland would have notified dealers before felling. The Vicar of Wimbish in north Essex recorded "Tithe Wood sold" for every year from 1755 to 1759.[27]

Fig. 2. 'The Tithe Pig' by Thomas Rowlandson (1756-1827).

The small tithe of animals and animal products presented its own problems when taken in kind. The occasional tithe piglet, so beloved of 18th century cartoonists, was no doubt welcome in the parson's kitchen or even in his pigsty if he had one.[28] The same could be said of poultry, and it was not uncommon for particular tithe agreements to specify the provision of a fat goose to the parsonage at Christmas. But larger numbers of tithe animals would require pastoral care of a sort unwelcome to many clergy. The difficulties were even greater in the case of perishable products such as eggs and milk: it is difficult to know what the Vicar of Great Dunmow did with the hundreds of eggs he was receiving in the 1660s; although it is not difficult to understand why in the 1730s the Dean of Bocking usually took tithe in kind from the 20 hop grounds in his parish when we learn that he did his own brewing![29]

By the end of the Middle Ages all parties were beginning to realise the convenience of collecting tithe in cash rather than in kind. The earliest tithe survey in the Essex Record Office is that for the parish of Writtle (one of the larger parishes in the county) for 1597-98, and cash payments already predominate.[30] The names of farmers paying tithe are followed by detailed lists of small tithes received from each: the numbers of tithe lambs, calves, goslings, pigs, the pounds of wool, bushels of fruit etc., and the amounts of money paid over for each item, based apparently

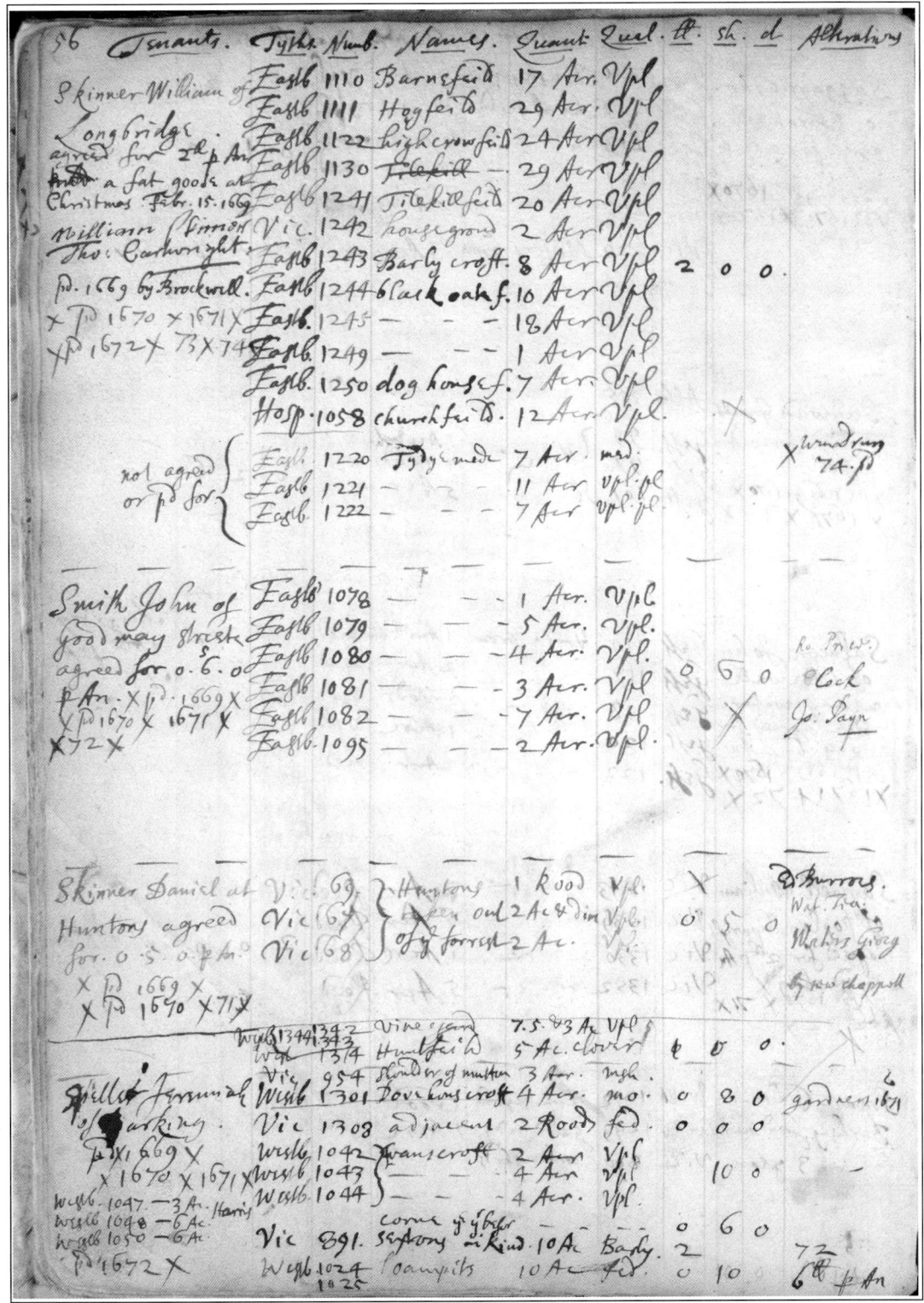

Fig. 3. Barking Tithe Book, 1669, p.56 (ERO D/P81/3/110). Top is a typical entry for William Skinner of Longbridge Farm; but note the agreement with the vicar to provide a fat goose at Christmas, as well as the composition of £2 p.a.

upon a standard tariff. These are followed by the total sum paid. Writtle was only a vicarage, but the records of Rayne and Widdington, which were rectories, follow much the same pattern during the first half of the 17th century.[31] For example, at least one tenant (William Pamphlin) in Widdington is shown as paying most of his tithe in the 1640s and '50s – including items for hop grounds and wood felled – in cash, but also rendering tithe wool and pigeons in kind. Even in the 18th century there were incumbents who kept detailed annual accounts of this type (Great Parndon and Wimbish are examples), but these involved a great deal of repetitive paper work on the part of the incumbent.[32] So where similar cash totals were being recorded on successive years, an agreement or composition to accept a single fixed sum for a period was the obvious next step.

In fact, such agreements had a long history and took several forms. Earliest of all was the *modus decimandi* or fixed annual payment in lieu of tithe upon an estate or farm which could not be varied either by the owner of the property or the incumbent. Most dated back to the Middle Ages or to the Dissolution. According to a judgement by Mr Justice Hardwicke in 1747, "a modus is nothing more than an ancient composition between… the owners of land in a parish, and the rector which gains strength by time". Impervious to inflation or to increases in output, moduses were as much valued by tenants as they were disliked by clergy. In the parish of Loughton, for example, a total of 1,052 acres which comprised the demesne of the manor of Loughton Hall (formerly part of the possessions of Waltham Abbey) was covered by a modus of only £3. 7s. per annum.[34] Barking, as we shall see, could provide similarly striking examples.

Ordinary compositions usually terminated with a change of incumbent and in any case most parsons were careful when making such an agreement to try to ensure that the tithe potential of the land was correctly estimated and the period limited; three years was a common term. An agreement between the Rector of Debden and John Perry in 1689 illustrates a common method of setting a standard charge per acre to cover the great tithe.[35] This leased,

> *All the Tythe arising… out of the farm called Tendrings …* [viz] *for every acre of tylth crop* [the main arable crop, usually wheat] *at four shillings & so for a lesse quantitie, and for every acre of each corne* [etch corn, the secondary or 'after-crop'] *two shillings the acre… for every acre of hopground ten shillings… his custom hay four pence… for six cowes two shillinges and six pence a cowe… for tythe lambes five shillinges …*

The rector reserved the right to send someone in to measure the land.

A *terrier*, or field-book, setting out the acreage of the individual fields of farms might result, as in the adjoining Widdington tithe book of 1664.[36] Plainly the crop yields were seen as the most profitable source of tithe revenue and also the easiest to forecast. One difficulty with measuring the small tithe from animal husbandry is well illustrated by a note left by a Vicar of Witham

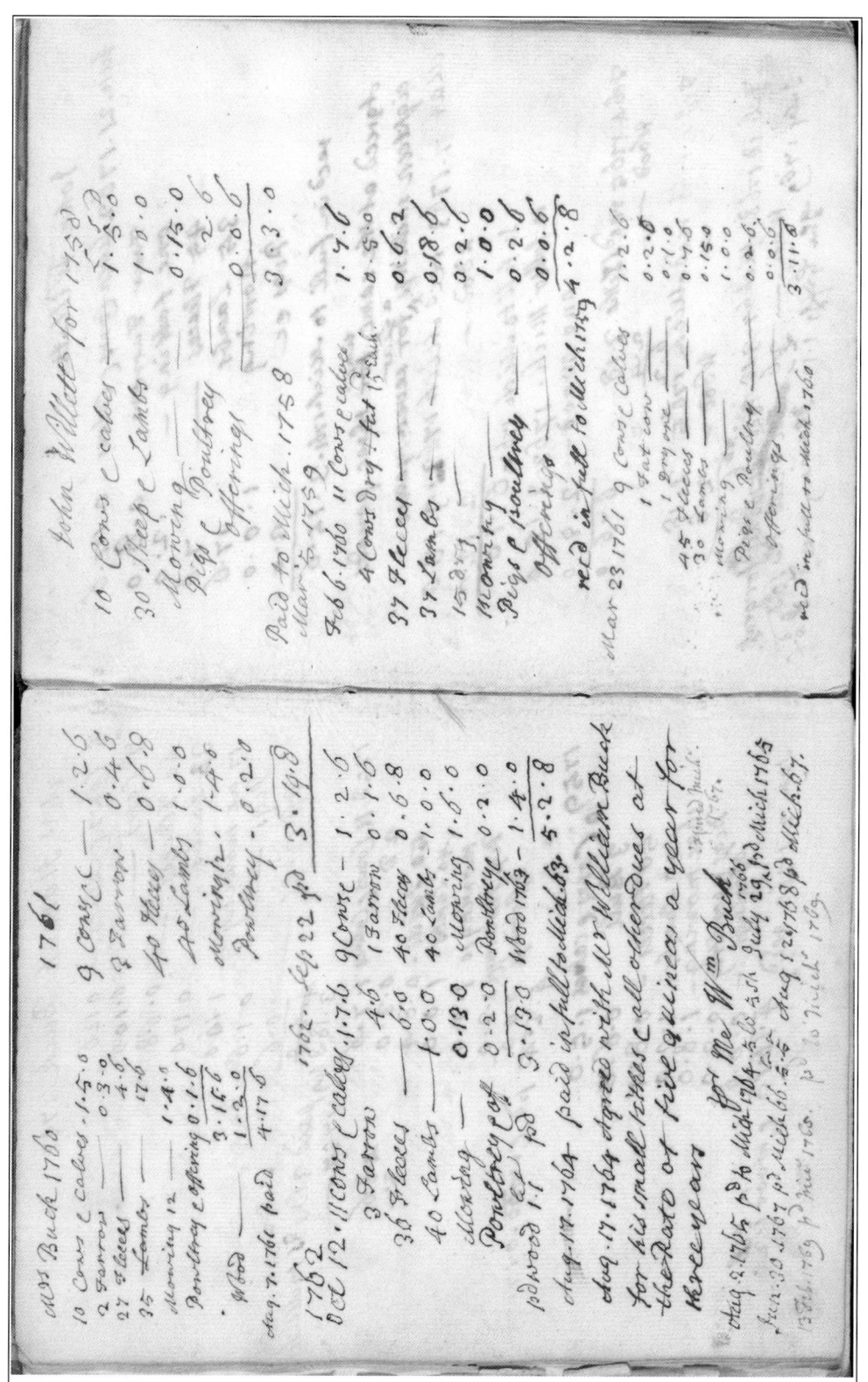

Fig. 4. Wimbish Tithe Accounts, 1757-69 (ERO D/P313/3/1). Details of small tithes can be seen here; note the three year signed agreements.

concerning one of his farmers in the mid-18th century, "He has other farms in his own occupation [some in other parishes] the tithe therefore is not so easy to settle with him as he may change the stock from one farm to another. This he gives me to understand he generally does."[37]

By definition, a rector was entitled to great and small tithe, a vicar only to small tithe. In practice the distinction might be less clear. The Vicar of Wimbish, mentioned above, was not alone in claiming tithe wood, but the legal position was complicated and local custom often prevailed. A generous lay impropriator could augment a vicarage; in 1710 Thomas Middleton, Lord Mayor of London, who owned the rectory of Stanstead Mountfichet, specifically devised the tithe hay to the vicar.[38] In 1659 the lay rector of Earls Colne, Richard Harlakeden, gave his vicar, Ralph Josselin, the more profitable great tithes of corn and grain to induce him to stay in the parish. Although Harlakeden reserved the tithes of his demesne together with the mill, hop grounds and woods, the vicar's tithe income was increased by some 50%. In other cases, as at Witham, Navestock, Great Baddow or Barking, the vicar was allowed to lease all the great tithe belonging to the rectory.[40] As a general rule, however, records kept by rectors tend to give most attention to the great tithe because of the predominance of arable farming; those kept by vicars record more detail concerning animal husbandry.

We saw how the Reverend Robert Poole, "being a Stranger", set about estimating the rectorial tithe of Belchamp Otten in 1665. Overseers' rates (valuations of property for the statutory poor rate) continued to be one favoured method because most occupiers already accepted these as reasonably equitable. The rent that the tenant-occupier paid to his landlord could be another practical basis for valuation, providing this information was available to the incumbent. The tenant-occupier was usually required to sign the written agreement in the tithe book, or to set his mark thereto. Sometimes the composition was put into full legal form as a lease.[41]

A conscientious clergyman anxious to obey the injunction to "maintain and set forwards, as much as lieth in you, quietness, peace, and love, among all Christian people, and especially among them that are or shall be committed to your charge" could scarcely indulge in continuous altercations with his flock concerning tithe.[42] Even the less conscientious were usually aware of the costs and inconveniences involved in taking tithe disputes to court and so were ready to accept compositions which guaranteed less than the tenths to which they might feel legally or morally entitled.[43]

Besides individual agreements based upon common tariffs, some agreed terms at general meetings of parishioners (e.g. at Wickford in 1822, 1823 and 1825).[44] In 1704 the Vicar of Newport (Essex) agreed with the Newport Vestry to commute all small tithes in exchange for the proceeds of a sixpence in the pound rate.[45] And in 18th century Bocking, compositions are specifically stated to have been agreed "at a meeting of the Vestry".[46] A composition with a new Vicar of East Ham in 1756 in respect of potatoes and turnips is recorded in the East Ham Vestry minutes.[47] Indirectly a parson was open to pressure from the vestry because tithes, like lands and houses, were liable to poor rate and, subject to an appeal to the Quarter Sessions, a vestry could increase his assessment if they could prove that the parson had substantially increased the yield from his tithes.[48]

Free food and drink were often an added inducement to pay at the time set. Those who have read the 18th century *Diary of a Country Parson* and recollect the quantities of beef, mutton, pork and "plumb puddings in plenty" as well as "wine, punch and ale" which Parson Woodforde dispensed each 3 December in Norfolk at "My Frolic for my People to pay Tithe to me" will hardly be surprised that the Rector of Wickford paid out £8. 2s. 6d. for "Dinner at ye audit" in 1823.[49] It was probably more effective than the annual tithe sermon preached by the Vicar of East Ham.[50] It would be fascinating to know to what extent resident clergy used a tithe collector; a task which in Barking was often performed by the parish clerk.[51]

The alternative method mentioned earlier in this chapter concerning Halifax, namely farming out the right to collect the tithe in return for a fixed annual sum, continued to be used for convenience by absentee rectors and impropriators at a distance from the parish concerned. For example, the prebendaries of St Pancras in St Paul's Cathedral were the sinecure Rectors of Chigwell from the 15th century to 1848, and from the Tudor period onwards the Chigwell rectory and glebe were leased out to tithe-farmers for terms of 31 years. In 1800 the reversion of the lease was offered for sale for no less than £13,000.[52]

Of course, the tithe issue was only one of many affecting the Church of England in the late 18th and early 19th centuries, which could be regarded as a period almost as traumatic as the middle years of the 17th century had been. The growth of Methodism, which at once revitalised Nonconformity and produced the powerful evangelical movement within the Church of England itself, had repercussions upon the tithe issue. So obviously had the related movement for reform in state and church — the revolt against the age of negligence. At the same time the radicalism associated with the American, and more particularly the French, Revolutions often manifested an agnosticism and antagonism to official religion which added to existing anti-clerical feeling. By the 1820s the radical press had become vehement in their criticisms of the 'state-church' and by the 1830s "many leading churchmen and politicians, such as Sir Robert Peel, saw reform or disestablishment as incontrovertible choices".[53] That reform had to include changes in the tithing system.

Yet the forces most directly responsible for bringing about the Tithe Commutation Act of 1836 must be sought in the practical world of agriculture, in the prolonged evolution which we still refer to — for want of a better title — as the agricultural revolution. The valuable tithe yielded by hop grounds has been mentioned above in examples from Bocking, Widdington and Debden, but numerous other examples could be cited from Essex. However, hops were by no means the only new commercial crop introduced from the 16th century onwards. The Witham tithe book for 1749-61 also includes tithes from clover, rye-grass, turnips, cole-seed and peas.[54] In southwest Essex, under the influence of the London market, garden crops like turnips, peas and potatoes expanded over fields by the 17th century. By 1626 their liability to small tithe had been firmly established in the courts, but rates of payment continued to cause friction.[55] Moreover, together with seed grasses, clover and sainfoin they resulted in new crop rotations, or 'courses of husbandry'. In East Ham, the vicars had such success in extracting tithe from market gardening and also for "herbage or feeding" that, by the time the Commutation Act took effect, the vicarage was valued at £1,001 and the rectory only at £320.[56]

So, by the later 18th century, some clergy complained about the increasing difficulties of securing the tenth of production to which they were justly entitled. Farmers, on the other hand, complained that incumbents and other tithe owners were seriously hampering progress in agriculture by effectively taxing improvements. Many landowners and most political economists sided with farmers on this issue. After 1815 the situation was exacerbated by the agricultural depression which followed the end of the Napoleonic Wars and which persisted for a couple of decades. The tithe burden was generally held to be a significant contributory factor in this depression, and played an important part in the Swing Riots at the beginning of the 1830s. Before 1836 all parties had agreed that a change in the law was inevitable.[57]

The Tithe Commutation Act of 1836 substituted an annual rent-charge upon each property in place of tithe. The initial payment was to be based, where possible, upon a voluntary agreement between the landowners and tithe-owners in each tithe district (usually a parish); this amount would then be varied in future years only on the basis of the seven-year average price of wheat, barley and oats. In the event of the parties not being able to reach a voluntary agreement, an assistant commissioner appointed under the Act could intervene and award initial rent-charges which reflected the average tithe collected over the previous seven years. So farmers were now subject to a uniform system of payments in lieu of tithe and increased agricultural productivity was no longer taxed. Yet at the same time the tithe-owner could also benefit from any improvement in corn prices.[58]

The 1836 Act required a professional survey and valuation in order that the agreed tithe rent-charge could be apportioned to each plot or parcel of land, which was given a reference number on the accompanying map. Blank pro-forma schedules were provided for valuers with ruled and headed columns so that *apportionments* should be on a uniform pattern.[59] It was permissible to adapt earlier maps for the purpose provided these were approved by the assistant commissioner assigned to this task.[60] Some parishes, as hinted above, already had tithe surveys which foreshadowed these apportionments in form as well as content and some, like Barking, also had maps linked to terriers. Further consideration will be given to such documents in succeeding chapters.

The Act of 1836 applied to all parishes where tithes existed and had not been commuted or extinguished already by previous, usually enclosure, Acts.[61] Such exceptions were rare in Essex compared to the midland and northern counties where the survival of large areas of open fields and common pasture had resulted in many parliamentary Enclosure Acts.[61] The extent of the undertaking in Essex is demonstrated by the recent analysis of Kain and Oliver who list 397 tithe award maps in the county.[62]

Chapter two: Tithe documentation

The inscription on the cover of one 17th century tithe book reads:

> Dr Thomas Carter's account of Tithes For the Parish of Debden. Very necessary to be kept and so particularly recommendable. Richd. Chisnell Jnr. Esq. ... procured them from the Executors... on his decease.[63]

A century later a tithe book of Lexden begun in 1792 contained the explicit memorandum:

> Whereas I am possessed of two tythe-books of Mr Skingle my immediate predecessor, and one tythe-book of Mr Cuffley immediate predecessor to Mr Skingle, which books I have found useful; It is therefore my desire that my family or Executors will deliver the three fore-mentioned books together with this my own tythe-book into the hands of my successors, and not into any other hands who may have an interest in altering or suppressing accounts.[64]

Both of these cases illustrate two vital points: tithe documents were the personal property of the incumbent, and yet a new parson could be in serious difficulties if he was without access to the records of his predecessors. We have already noted the post-Restoration minister of Belchamp Otten in the first chapter, while the new Rector of Moreton in the 18th century wrote an ingenuous "Memo: To ask all who pay money who were the former occupyers of the land, the names of the lands and the number of acres."[65]

But tithe-payers were equally at the mercy of the system. John Savill, Bocking baymaker, noted in his diary for August 1802, "This year the Bishop of St Davids, Lord Geo. Murray, now Dean of Bocking, took the tythes of this parish in kind, which afterwards brot a heavy expence on the parish for measuring, valuation, etc."[66]

The tithe account is the most common document in its class and in its simplest form may consist only of a list of tithe payers for a particular year and the amount of composition paid by each of them. An occasional farm or field name may be included. One can even find such information on loose sheets, as at Loughton for 1664 and 1710-13, but inclusion in a book was obviously the safer method.[67] Earls Colne, mentioned in the introduction, provides examples of this common form from the late 18th century. Additional information in succeeding years might include notes concerning changes of tenure or land-use, or an occasional payment in kind or default. Sometimes the acreage of a farm is given or a note on livestock, and sometimes landlords are listed as well as their tenants. Even routine accounts may yield the odd nugget of historical information; for example the Chelmsford 'Composition Book Commencing 1710' has an entry on page 82, "cherry garden against the white house at Widford… in 1735 there was about a Rood of ground sold from ye cherry garden upon which was a windmill erected in 1735."[68]

In parishes where compositions had only been agreed for some farms, tithe accounts needed to be more detailed, with farmers' names followed by lists of payments in kind or of sums paid in lieu of particular items. Several of these were cited in the first chapter, such as the small tithes for the Vicar of Wimbish.

Not infrequently the tithe account book was used as a general account book, so including other items of clerical income and expenditure; Easter offerings, fees, glebe accounts, land tax, even some household expenses. Curious items also occur: the Lexden tithe book quoted at the beginning of this chapter concludes with recipes for "Horse cures", and a Barking account book for 1690-1711 contains a nauseating prescription for "Madde dogge or bitten by one".[69]

Some tithe books, like that of Witham for 1749-1761, may more accurately be classed as *tithe surveys* with a page, or pages, given to information about each farm.[70] The entries vary in length and detail, but generally include occupier, landlord, rent, total acreage, some field names and particulars of crops and livestock, together with the amounts usually paid. Bocking has 'An Account of Tithes and Rent' c.1730 providing similar information – some in columns – for around 40 properties, but including land tax and poor rate for comparison.[71] It contains various interesting incidental items in regard to mills and tenter-fields and, respecting Robert Wood's ten acre field adjoining the White Hart, informs the reader that he "usually lets the after pasture of this field during Braintree Mich[aelmas]s Fair to Scotch Drovers by which he gets £9 in that week only."

Tithe surveys were most likely to be made following the arrival of a new incumbent or in consequence of a dispute. At the opposite end of the spectrum to the simpler tithe accounts are measured surveys, for example that for Colne Engaine: 'An Estemation… Taken by Owen Swan' in 1767.[72] Each tithe-payer's name (1 to 27) is followed by a terrier of his farm set out in columns showing field names and the acreage of arable and of pasture in each. At the foot of each page is added the acreage of any woodland and hop ground. Tithe accounts follow, giving the tenants and compositions paid for each succeeding year from 1784 to 1825. Another survey was made in 1796, but it is only a revision of 1767, using the same acreages etc.[73] Edward Swan was clearly a professional surveyor and an incumbent would have to consider carefully before incurring such an expense. Not surprisingly, surveys once made were usually expected to serve as a basis for tithe accounts for a number of years.

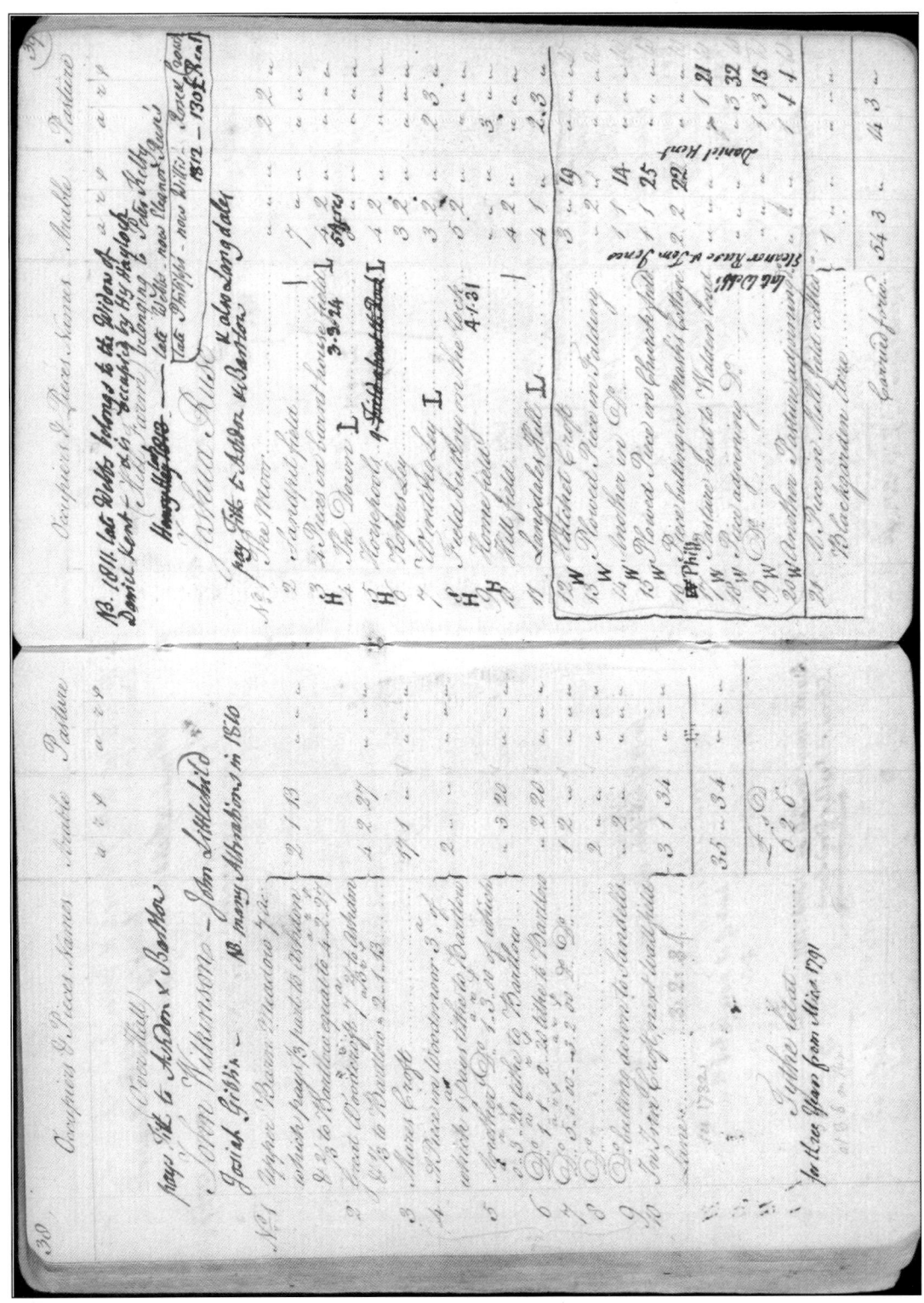

Fig. 5. *Ashdon Tithe Survey, 1796 (with alterations of 1812) (ERO 18/3/102). Note the detail for each parcel of land and the division of tithes between the rectors of Ashdon and Bartlow.*

Although it looks like the work of a professional surveyor, the archivist and local historian, Angela Green, ascribes the meticulous tithe survey of Ashdon parish in 1796 to the rector, John North.[74] He had been the bursar of Caius College, Cambridge, and had access to a large corpus of earlier tithe documents including a survey of 1730.[75] He probably also had access to the estate map prepared for Lord Maynard in 1793-4, which covered many farms in the parish.[76]

The structure and content of the Ashdon survey is much the same as that of Colne Engaine, and a similar pattern is followed in other parishes such as Chigwell (c.1800) and Widford (1814).[77] In the last two examples the owner (landlord), as well as the occupier, is named and the actual crop in each field stated. Twinstead, unusually, had a full professional survey made by John Kingsbury in 1800.[78] In 1817 another professional, William Downes, updated this, producing 'Survey, Valuation and Report of the Great and Small Tithes and Glebe Lands of the Rectory of Twinstead'.[79]

Was the Rector of Twinstead, the Reverend Robert Gray, anticipating legislation on commutation? It is not inconceivable since the agricultural reformer, J.C. Curwen M.P., had raised the issue in the House of Commons as early as 1816.[80] As noted in the first chapter, the official form prescribed for the apportionments awarded under the 1836 Act had similar categories to surveys just described, but with a valuation for each field or parcel of land. The tithe award schedule provided two columns for this to allow for a division of the tithe rent-charge between two recipients of tithe (vicar and impropriator). Manifestly the assumption was that in most parishes there would be either one or two tithe-owners. This would be the case in most Essex parishes, although the tithes of Ashdon were divided between the Rector of Ashdon and the Rector of Bartlow in the adjoining county of Cambridgeshire (see figure 5).[81] Those of Bures Hamlet were owned by two impropriators.[82]

If the situation were more complicated, the tithe award schedules contained a column without a heading which could be brought into use. The hamlet of Sewardstone, which formed the southern part of the parish of Waltham Holy Cross, totalled 2,984 acres (including 869 tithe-free) yet is shown as having no less than 16 impropriators. One was the Lord of the Manor of Sewardstonebury but the remainder (including one holding only 4¼ acres) seem to have leased estates from him complete with tithe in the late 18th century which were converted into freeholds early in the 19th. His power to treat both great and small tithes as a simple adjunct to real estate totally unconnected with the original purpose of tithe sprang from the sale of Sewardstonebury by the Dennys in 1664 and so dates back to the terms of the royal grant of Waltham Abbey possessions to the Denny family referred to in chapter one.[83] This latter-day creation of impropriators presents a curious counterpoint to the case of Barking parish – to be explained later – where multiple tithings were created in the medieval period mainly by investing certain farmers with the collection of tithe, requiring the lands so tithed to be carefully distinguished by all later surveys.[84] Yet in both cases the form of monasticism prior to the Dissolution appears to be the original determinant.

It might be expected that a map would accompany a measured survey, but before 1836 parish tithe maps are not so common, perhaps because of the additional costs involved. Doubtless some have been lost; the 1800 survey of Twinstead (noted above) refers to a map no longer extant.[85] However, most pre-19th century parish maps were really estate maps paid for by a landowner who happened to possess all or most of the land in the parish (this did not, of course, prevent their being used in conjunction with contemporary tithe records).[86] The Essex Record Office has an unusually early example of such in a map of Earls Colne made by Israel Amyce to accompany a manorial survey of 1598.[87]

But most date from the late 18th century. In 1997 the Waltham Abbey Historical Society published *A Survey and Plan of the Titheable Lands in the Manor of Waltham Holy Cross in the County of Essex. Taken by the Order of Sir Willm Wake. By B. Waddington. A.D. 1776*.[88] This map survived in a reduction made in 1815 by John Doyley now in the Northampton Record Office. The Wake-Jones family had acquired the remaining lands of Waltham Holy Cross and its tithes from the Dennys in the late 17th century. Although some of the former Abbey lands, including Sewardstone, had been disposed of earlier in the century, and although substantial portions of Sir William Wake's estates were excluded as tithe-free (mainly former demesne of the Abbey), the map and survey still covered some 3,000 acres of this large parish. It includes field-names, occupiers in 1776 and 1800, and land-use.[89] Another example dates from 1783 when the governors of Christ's Hospital, London, who had been given the rectory of Clavering with Langley in 1596, commissioned detailed tithe surveys with maps of the twin parishes, all of which survive.[90]

A fine parish map of the large parish of Southminster was made by the Colchester surveyor William Cole in 1790. The governors of Charterhouse, major landowners in the parish, probably shared the cost of this. Several other parish maps followed, some also by Cole. Those for Great Tey and Great Horkesley were subsequently used as the basis for pre-1836 tithe surveys.[91]

One for Gestingthorpe in 1804 was "Taken by the Order and at the Expence of the present Rector, The Rev. Chs. Hughes … by Isaac Johnson, Surveyor, Woodbridge, Suffolk".[92] The following year Johnson was engaged on making a new tithe survey of Barking.[93] In 1838 his Gestingthorpe map was reused as the tithe award map.[94] A tithe map of 1819 for Bures Hamlet (together with some tithable lands in the adjacent Mount Bures) appears to have been paid for by the two lay impropriators and this too was "modernized to the year 1838", with some adjustments of field boundaries and a new numbering system.[95]

A map (10 inches to 1 mile) also accompanies the detailed survey and valuation by H.C. Wright of the parish of Widford in 1814 which includes particulars of the crop in every field.[96] This was made for the Reverend William Warner who became rector in that year. A different numbering system was used here for the tithe award map of 1841.[97] Rawreth also has a tithe map of 1830 linked to a briefer survey.[98] Here the same numbering system was used on the award.[99] There is, in addition, a parish map of Sturmer in 1827 copied from a manorial map of 1816 by the rector.[100] However, this seems to have been a means of locating portions of the glebe in open fields rather than a tithe map.

Following the Poor Law Amendment Act of 1834, the Boards of Guardians of the new Poor Law Unions began to authorise more parish maps for rate valuation purposes anticipating that the cost to the ratepayers might be partly offset by selling them to the local landowners for use as tithe commutation maps. According to Dr Stuart Mason, "for 46 parishes the tithe [award] map indicates its origin as an old map: a further 28 parishes are almost certainly derived from old maps."[101]

Yet it follows from the above that there are no parish tithe maps extant in Essex prior to the last decades of the 18th century except for the early vicar's tithe map of Barking which originated in 1666 and which will be described in subsequent chapters. It is interesting to note that a Barking impropriator maintained as early as 1752 that "such a Map and books have been frequently Allowed of as good Evidence" of tithe claims in the Court of Exchequer.[102] However, although earlier examples are known to have existed it is possible that the Barking parish tithe map may now be unique.[103]

The agreements between parsons and farmers are often incorporated into tithe accounts, as in the example previously quoted between the Rector of Debden and John Perry in 1689.[104] At the rear of the tithe account book of Toppesfield for 1691-1736 are some 70 agreements, accompanied by the suggestive note, "amount of the privy [small] tithes sold to those parishioners who would not buy the great ones 1694".[105] Elsewhere the agreements may be found in a separate book, like the 72 agreements made by the Vicar of Harlow in 1779, which include many interesting details of acreages mown, pastured or under clover and the livestock on particular holdings.[106] Great Chishall (part of Essex until 1895) had a book of over 200 agreements made between 1671 and 1699, some of them relating to small parcels then probably in open fields.[107]

A further category of tithe documents are those connected with tithe disputes. Tithe causes, usually initiated by incumbents or lay impropriators against recalcitrant tithe-payers, might be pursued through a variety of courts and only some of the materials engendered can be discovered in county record offices under parish or estate records. The extensive records of Ashdon parish include a dispute of 1587 which began in the ecclesiastical courts and ended up in the Court of King's Bench.[108] Another regarding tithe wool and lambs was heard in the Court of Exchequer between 1768 and 1770.[109] The Essex Record Office still has the four volumes of Hutton Wood's *A Collection of Decrees by the Court of Exchequer in Tithe-Causes, from the Usurpation to the Present time* (1798/99), which the Rector of Great Wakering purchased in 1819.[110] Now the Essex cases have been conveniently extracted and can be found in the Essex Record Office, pamphlet box 77. They include that recounted by Tate in his chapter in *The Parish Chest* on the "not very edifying history of tithes", concerning the efforts of the Vicar of Chigwell in 1678 to compel a farmer to deliver tithe-milk to the vicarage door.[111] The original documents are now in the Public Record Office at Kew.

But most tithe disputes went through the ecclesiastical courts. The Essex Record Office has a very large collection of the records of these courts including act books of the Bishop of London's Commissary Court (Essex was part of the diocese of London until 1846) and of the Archdeacons of Essex and Colchester back to the mid-16th century. One study has shown that in the Archdeaconry of Essex alone there were 484 tithe suits within the period 1571 to 1609.[112]

The original records are notoriously difficult to use, even for later periods, on account of the handwriting and abbreviated Latin. This makes the essay by Dr Emmison, mentioned in the introduction, particularly useful. It includes an appendix with detailed transcripts of depositions given in suits concerning Upminster (1586 and 1588), Kelvedon (1587), Lambourne (1581), Boxted (1588), Woodford (1589), Downham and Ramsden Bellhouse (1589), Aveley (1590), Magdalen Laver (1591) and Horndon-on-the-Hill (1600). Besides personal details, these may provide items of information on local topography and most frequently on contemporary farming. A Woodford man, for example, may have engaged in the commercial cultivation not only of fruit but also of 'damask and red roses'. Manuscript transcripts by R.H. Browne are available in the Essex Record Office for some volumes down to the late 17th century.[113]

Appeals in the Province of Canterbury were heard in the Court of Arches whose records are preserved in the Lambeth Palace archive in London. According to Jane Houston's printed index of cases heard there between 1660 and 1913, some 39 concerned tithes in Essex parishes.[114] Of these, no less than 28 were instituted by tithe-owners, mainly incumbents, in the ten years following the Restoration (1660 to 1670), which underlines the suggestion in chapter one respecting the problems of reclaiming benefices. Most remarkably, the prosecutor in 12 cases was the Reverend Thomas Cartwright, Vicar of Barking.

Perambulations were not, strictly speaking, tithe documents because the ancient ritual of beating the bounds had a practical value for all parish officers prior to the printing of 'legal' maps in the 19th century, but they are often found in conjunction with tithe surveys and accounts. William Downes in his 1817 survey of Twinstead (bordered by five other parishes) advised "As there appears much intricacy in the Parish boundaries, when they cross several fields, it is recommended that a perambulation be made of the same during the next Rogation Week, otherwise the adjoining Parishioners will encroach upon the rights of those of Twinstead."[115] Yet the intricacy of some parish boundaries was greater than Twinstead, e.g. Foxearth or Great and Little Horkesley.[116] No wonder the tithe accounts of Foxearth 1730-1818 contain a list of the boundary marks (including trees) noted on a perambulation of 1791.[117] Detached portions of some parishes added to the complications, such as the three enclaves of Bartlow End within Ashdon.

These processions were officially conducted by the minister and churchwardens of the parish and sometimes led to complaints and disputes which found their way into the ecclesiastical courts. Dr Emmison gives a number of examples from Tudor Essex in his essay noted above. Robert Pearson, Rector of Cold Norton, makes excuses for not having fetched in the bounds of his parish in 1592 claiming that he is lame and "was appointed to preach at Boreham that day" but "hath the bounds of his parish set down very directly in his register book", a not uncommon practice according to Emmison. This example was also given with many others in an informative article by the Reverend W.J. Pressey, 'Beating the Bounds in Essex: as seen in the Archdeaconry records' which includes a detailed description of the boundaries, with marks, of Heybridge in 1784.[118] Miller Christy transcribed 'A perambulation of the Parish of Chignal St James in 1797' with similar detail.[119] Much topographical detail also occurs in Dr Emmison's account of the Tilbury Ferry House dispute of 1590 which involved 13 witnesses and the boundary between Chadwell and West Tilbury.[120]

Chapter three: Origin of the Barking tithe circuits

Part I: Before the Dissolution

In a seminal article in 1953, whilst drawing attention to the private or 'manorial' origins of most Essex parishes, Raymond Powell pointed out that Barking Abbey was founded about the same time as Bishop Cedd's two minster churches of Bradwell and Tilbury and would have fulfilled a similar missionary function of converting, or reconverting, the East Saxons to Christianity. These minsters, or monasteria, were "staffed by a group of monks or priests who were responsible… for the pastoral care of an area more comparable in size with a modern rural deanery than with a modern parish".[121]

The system predates the parochial system by several centuries. As Richard Gem has shown more recently, the known early minsters of the estuarine area of Kent, as well as Essex, exhibit parallels with Barking.[122] Most were founded within a very few years of each other by royal patrons (around 70 years after the arrival in Canterbury of St Augustine's mission to England), and served pastoral areas which, though varying in size, covered a number of later parishes. Several, including Minster-in-Thanet and Minster-in-Sheppey, were associated with monasteries, probably 'double' monasteries including both nuns and male clergy administered by an abbess.

Erkenwald, later Bishop of London, whose diocese was largely coextensive with the kingdom of Essex, founded the Abbey of Barking in 666, which was generously endowed by the East Saxon royal family and its kinsmen. There is good reason to believe that the medieval manor of Barking was an estate granted to the Abbey within 20 years of its foundation by several charters from, or with the consent of, the kings of the East Saxons.[123]

Prior to 1830 the old parish of Barking still had an area of 12,307 acres (approximately 19¼ square miles). It was one of only three Essex parishes to exceed 10,000 acres; the others being Hornchurch (16,100 acres before 1784, when it included Havering-atte-Bower) and Waltham Abbey (11,017 acres).[124] There is no doubt that the parish of Dagenham (6,556 acres) had once been part of Barking, and as late as the 14th century there are references to properties 'in the vill [township] of Barking and the parish of Dagenham'. In fact the manor of Barking continued to include both parishes into modern times and their external boundaries were coterminous with those of the manor (except on the eastern bounds where 15th century gerrymandering had transferred 45 acres of the manor into the royal liberty of Havering).[125] So the extent of the original manor and parish of Barking must have exceeded 18,900 acres, approaching 30 square miles; perhaps the original pastoral area of the Abbey. It is also possible that the missionary

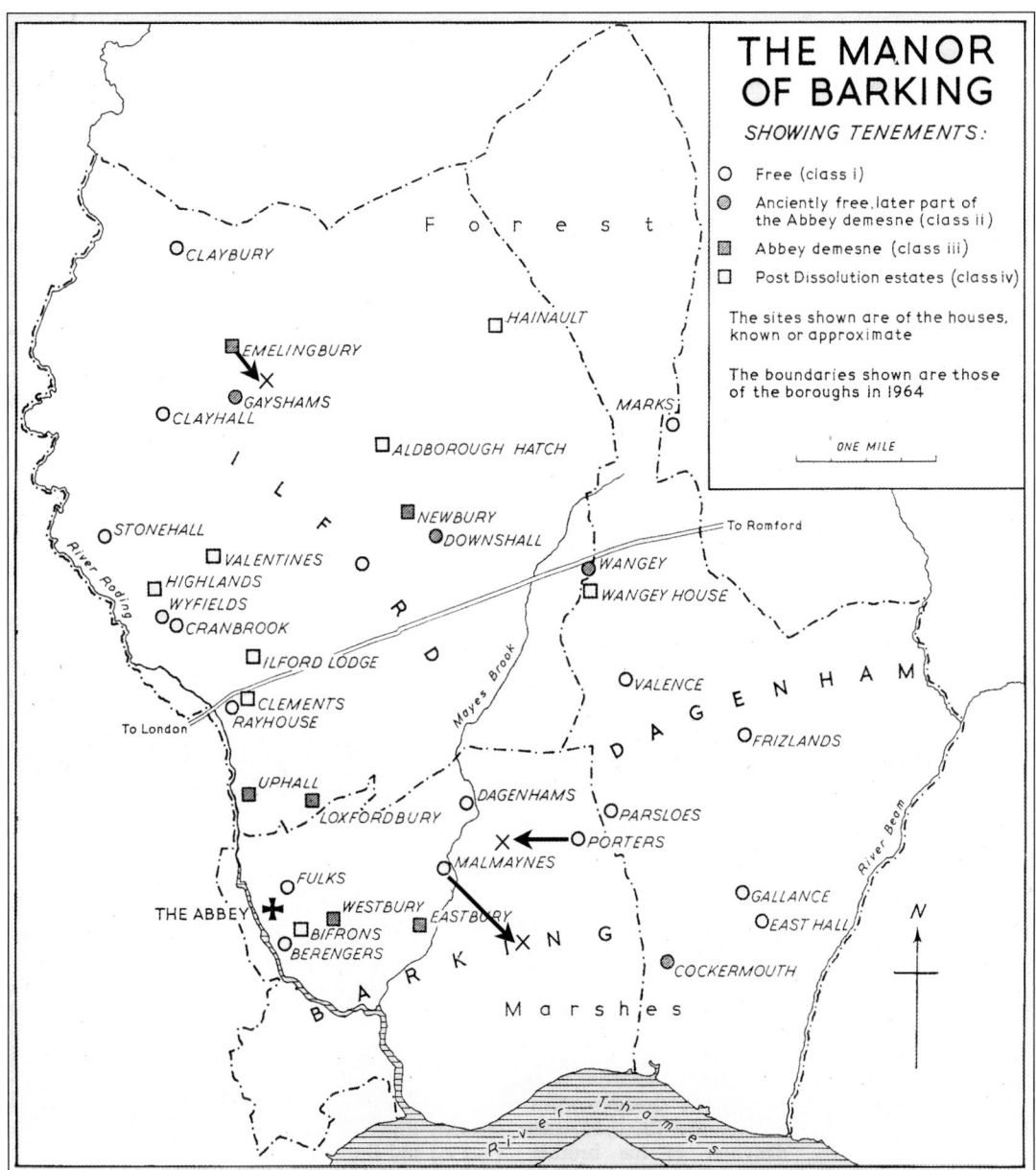

Fig. 6. The Manor of Barking. The author's suggested corrections are shown, based upon a map originally created by, and reproduced here with the kind permission of, the Victoria County History (Essex).

influence of the Abbey extended throughout the whole hundred of Becontree (over which the abbess was granted lordship in the 12th century). For it is highly probable that this hundred originated as an East Saxon royal estate administered from the royal vill of Havering, a portion of which was used to endow Erkenwald's Abbey.[126]

It has been suggested that the space given to Barking by Bede in his *Ecclesiastical History* is itself evidence that Barking was the spiritual capital of the East Saxon kingdom, whilst recent excavations have attested to its economic status.[127] Barking Abbey as described by Bede was a double monastery with male brethren, as well as nuns, both under control of an abbess (the first being Erkenwald's own sister, Ethelburga). Whilst Bede does not deal with the roles performed by the men, the probability that they included clergy would seem to be implied by the clause in Erkenwald's charter to the Abbey which admonishes future bishops to avoid interference with this monastery – "he shall govern only those things which are concerned with the welfare of souls, the ordination of priests and the consecration of the nuns".[128]

Once Bede's *Ecclesiastical History* closes in the early years of the eighth century, our sources for the history of Barking during the following three centuries are largely restricted to inferences from charters and the implications of recent archaeological investigation. We are uncertain even about the extent of destruction caused by the Danish raid of 870. The absence of any commemoration of local martyrs in the later *Barking Ordinal* (service-book), as well as the survival of earlier charters, would appear to contradict the more lurid accounts of pillage, rape and conflagration contributed by post-Conquest chroniclers.[129]

Gem points out that all minsters appear to have been targeted by the Vikings in the ninth century, but Barking seems to have recovered the most successfully. Recently discovered charters and a will, together with new archaeological evidence, confirm that restoration and extensive rebuilding of the Abbey was probably underway in the 930s and complete by 950. The restored Abbey became a nunnery under the Benedictine rule popularised in England by St Dunstan. Abbess Wulfhilda, abbess in the latter part of the tenth century, became the third Abbess of Barking to achieve sanctification (joining St Ethelburga and her successor, Hildelitha).[130] By 1066, the Abbey was in a position to entertain the Conqueror while the Tower of London was under construction and William duly confirmed their privileges and now extensive possessions.[131]

According to the Norwich valuation of 1254, the rectory of Barking had been appropriated by the Abbey and two vicarages had been created for "Northstrete" and "Southstrete" in Barking and another for Dagenham.[132] But no formal *appropriation* need have occurred in the case of Barking since the indications are that the Abbey could have taken (appropriated) the tithe from the outset while their chaplains served as parish priests. In short, there is a plausible argument for a degree of continuity in the pastoral functions of the Abbey from the missionary period and their associated claims to tithe. The parish church of St Margaret's was built within the ancient walls of the Abbey precinct and began as a chapel.[133]

Fig. 7. St. Margaret's Church, Barking c.1800 (by kind permission of London Guildhall Library).

A century earlier, when around 1140 the Abbess Adelicia endowed her new foundation of Ilford Hospital with half the benefice of the parish church and portions of tithe, she obviously assumed that the Abbey owned the rectory of Barking (and that of Warley).[134] The Abbess Maud added a considerable amount of rectorial tithe to the hospital by an agreement of 1219. This was witnessed by four chaplains; two may have been those attached to the hospital and the other two to the Abbey.[135] With Vatican approval, the two vicarages were combined after 1415, following flooding of the Thames-side marshes that seriously reduced the revenues of Southstrete.

In 1219 the Abbey had given the Ilford Hospital the tithes from three of its demesne farms or manors within the capital or paramount manor of Barking, namely Eastbury, Westbury and Loxfordbury (and added the tithes of the 'free' manors of Wyfields and Jenkins and the hospital's own enclosure of Claybury). The remaining demesne estates – Newbury, Gaysham, Uphall, Downshall and Wangey – were allowed to pay their tithes to the Abbey in the form of a modus.[136] However, most of the remaining tithes continued to be paid in kind up to, and beyond, the dissolution of the Abbey in 1539. It does not require much imagination to realise the problems that were faced in arranging for the collection and storage of produce from so many acres.

The organisation the convent developed is succinctly outlined in the Barking and Ilford section of the *Victoria County History of Essex*.[137] The editor, Raymond Powell, realised that the key lay, largely unnoticed, in a series of brief extracts from the long vanished court rolls of the manor of

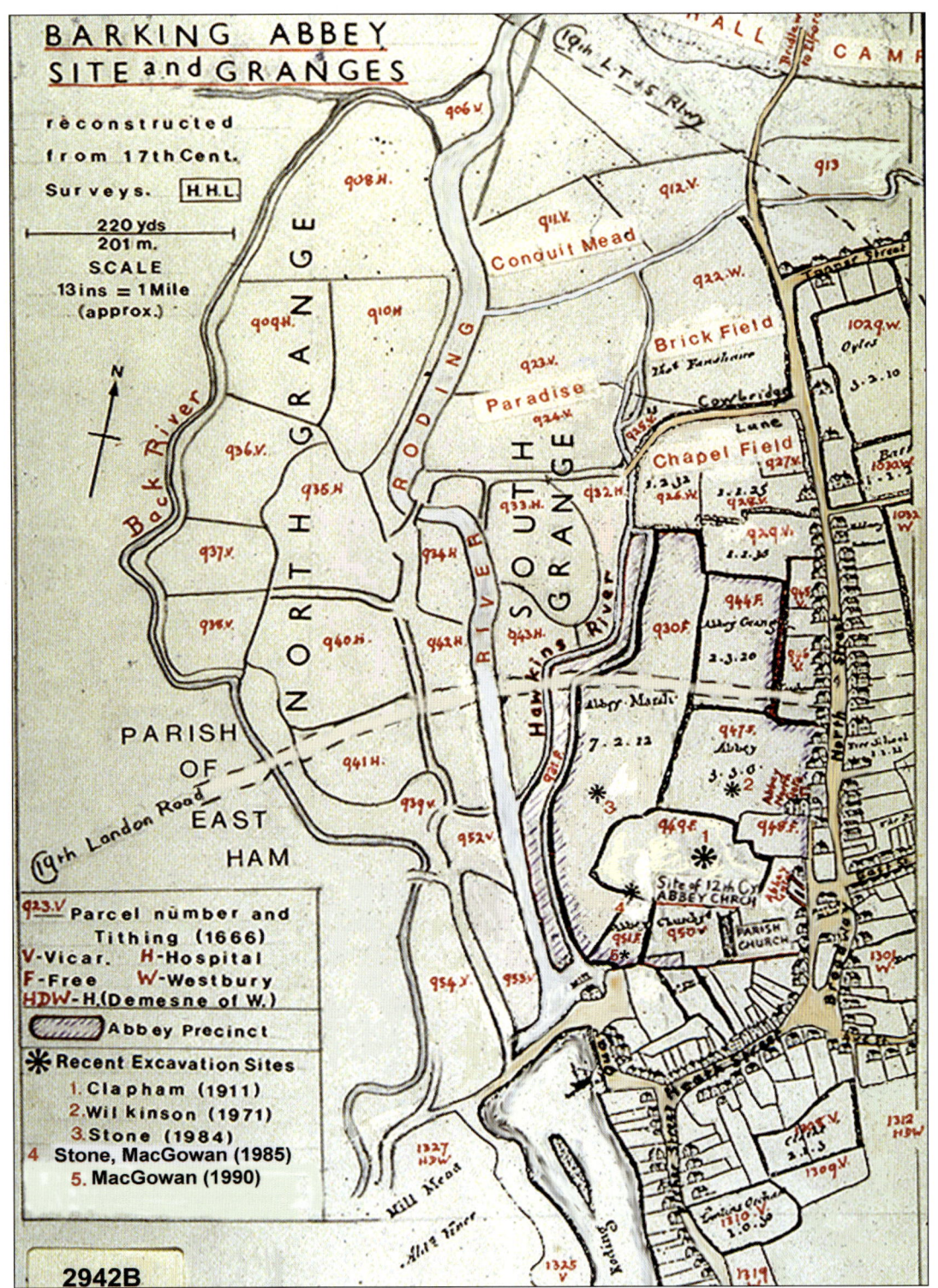

Fig. 8. *A Reconstruction of Barking Town and Abbey Site (Lockwood, 1966).* The chief base map is Luff's extract from the map of the manor, 1652-3, with parcel numbers taken from the vicar's tithe map, 1666, added with the aid of the companion.

Barking for the years between 1349 and 1469, recording the appointment of tithe collectors. These extracts appear to have been taken as evidence in certain tithe disputes of which few further details have survived, but were preserved in the Exchequer records in the Public Record Office.[138] Since the publication of the fifth volume of the *Victoria County History* documents have been found in the Local History Collection of the Barking and Dagenham Libraries (Valence House) relating to later tithe disputes, which not only confirm Powell's perceptions, but also throw additional light on the subject.[139]

It appears that by the early 14th century (and possibly long before) the task of collecting and storing the tithes not given to Ilford Hospital or covered by moduses had been divided amongst the demesne manors of Eastbury, Westbury, Loxfordbury, Newbury, and Emelingbury (this last being absorbed by Gaysham in the 1390s). Collectors – usually two – were elected regularly for each of them in the Manor Court of Barking (these demesne farms, though styled 'manors', did not have courts of their own) and the manors were expected to provide cartage and storage space in their own barns. Sometimes the tithe-payer was allowed to buy in his tithe for a lump sum; in other words, to effect a composition. In most cases, one of a pair of collectors was designated a 'riding collector' since none of these tithe circuits covered less than 1,000 acres. So far as can be ascertained, those chosen as collectors were tenants not of the demesne manors themselves, but of peripheral lands within the particular circuit, and their tasks were supervisory.

During the later 15th century the Abbey began to change its method of administration of demesne manors. Instead of putting them in the charge of managers (reeves or bailiffs) operating under the supervision of the Abbey steward, they were leased out to farmers paying a fixed annual sum for terms of years. Their rents covered not only the right to farm the land of the demesne, but also to collect the great tithe of grain and hay from the associated tithe circuit. The farmer made his own arrangements for collection and so tithe collectors ceased to be appointed in the Manor Court.[140] Thus, although the Abbey still owned the great tithe as they did the land, the demesne farmers were effectively impropriators of the tithe during the period of their lease. This was apparently convenient to the nuns and doubtless cost-effective, providing the tithes were correctly valued. Their steward attempted to secure this by using a sworn jury of local landowners and farmers appointed, presumably, in the Manor Court.[141]

Part II: After the Dissolution

The next step followed the Dissolution of 1539 when Barking Abbey ceased to exist and the crown took over all their possessions. The crown retained the manor of Barking in its own hands until 1628, but (with the temporary exception of Loxford) sold the component demesne manors including their tithe circuits to private land-owners. For several decades the mastership of Ilford Hospital, with its rents and tithes, was leased out by the crown; this was granted away to the Fanshawe family in 1572.[142] Thus the most part of the rectorial or great tithe, and part of the small tithes, had been alienated and passed irrevocably into the hands of lay impropriators before the end of the Tudor period.

For a while the crown also leased out the rectory (whatever remained of it) and the 'advowson' (the right to present the vicar), but in 1550 this was granted to Robert Thomas and Andrew Salter, merchant tailors of London, who promptly sold it to Thomas Barnes of Newbury. Finally in 1556/7 the executors of William Pownsett of Loxford, the last steward of the Abbey, bought the rectory from Barnes together with the advowson and gave it to All Souls College, Oxford, who, after some earlier challenges, have retained control to the present day. A condition of this grant was that All Souls should always allow the vicar they presented to enjoy any revenues remaining from the rectory in return for a fixed annual rent.[143]

In the closing years of the 16th century a battery of Barking disputes reached the courts principally involving the vicar (Richard Wignall, 1588-1629), All Souls College, Ilford Hospital (the Fanshawes and their appointee, Dr William Fisher), and successive tenants of Eastbury. These cases presumably helped to clarify the situation, doubtless benefited the legal profession, and certainly provided some interesting material for future historians. Reference has been made above to the recent rediscovery of case reports; these include verbatim statements by older witnesses who clearly remembered the times before the dissolution of the Abbey. John Fisher, 80 years old when questioned in 1591, explains the tithe circuits, deposing in his own words:

> "he says that before the suppression there was sundry farms in Barkinge namely Estburye, Westburye, Loxforde, Dunsehalle, and Gessames Halle the farmers whereof having the parish divided among them for that purpose did fetch in the tithe of corn sheaf and hay of the whole parish and laid the same in the barns belonging to the said several farms to the use of the Abbess. And he remembers that Eastberye fetched in the tithes in Riple ward and that Eastburye and Westburye had a tithe barn of purpose to lay their tithe in and he have threshed the said tithes sundry times in the said barns of Estburye and Westburye. And further he remembers that after the dissolution the tithes of corn and hay aforesaid were gathered by the said several farmers in the said parish to their own uses." [spelling modernised except place names][144]

The Eastbury circuit actually extended into Chadwell as well as Ripple ward, otherwise old John's memory appears good (of course, he may have been rehearsed). It might be significant that he speaks of a Downshall and not of a Newbury circuit, but these two farms had come into common ownership by the mid-century anyway.

Yet even though All Souls College had obtained the rectory and granted him the lease, the vicar was not on the face of it entitled to any great tithe. The impropriators took the great tithe from lands within their circuits whilst the great and small tithes of their demesne lands were either taken by Ilford Hospital (in the cases of Eastbury, Westbury and Loxford) or covered by a modus of only 3s.4d each. There were two minor exceptions; the vicar was anciently entitled to half of certain small tithes from the demesne of Westbury and from the free manor of Jenkins in lieu of which he claimed compositions of 50s and 6s.8d per annum respectively. There was also an ancient indeterminate claim for personal tithe from the boats of fishermen. Otherwise it would appear he could claim only small tithes from properties within the tithe circuits.

There remained a future prospect of improving the yield of some small tithes. As in the case of East Ham mentioned in chapter one, Barking was well within the ambit of the London market and market gardening was to become of some importance there by the 17th century. Similarly, during the same period, the plentiful Thames-side marsh pastures in the south of Barking were frequently used by London butchers for fattening cattle which had lost weight during long drives.[145] Whilst the hay crop was part of the great tithe, feeding and the depasturing of other men's cattle (*agistments*) were separately tithable.

Vicars were also advised that impropriators could only claim tithes specified in their original grants (*viz.* sheaves, grain and hay), which left it open to the vicars to claim tithes of wood whenever felling took place.[146] By the 1660s the parish still contained over 1,000 acres of woodland apart from the tithe-exempt 'wastes' of Hainault forest. Much of this was in private hands and whilst the laws of the forest, which covered the whole area north of the main Romford Road, permitted felling under permit, they prevented outright destruction (stubbing and grubbing) until well into the 18th century.[147] So tithe wood proved a valuable asset to the vicars of Barking, though ultimately a wasting one.

Before 1666 the vicars had gained access to other portions of great tithe. By a process whose details are still not fully known they appear to have acquired the tithes of the Loxford circuit. The matter will become clearer from the resultant list of 'tithings' in Table 1.

The demesne of Loxford, like those of Eastbury and Westbury, tithed to Ilford Hospital; but in line with the other demesne manors which had tithe circuits before the Dissolution we should also expect a Loxford circuit in the 1660s from which the landowner of Loxford would be entitled to take the great tithe. The parish tithe map of the period reveals an inner block of the estate of Loxford paying tithes to the hospital containing 153 acres which corresponds to the 152 acres of demesne in the manorial survey of 1609.[148] Yet we also find peripheral lands, particularly on the west and north, paying all tithes to the vicar; without doubt these latter had once comprised a Loxford circuit and it is not clear at what point this came into the hands of the Barking vicars.

William Pownsett had been in a unique position amongst Barking landholders following the Dissolution. Last steward of the Abbey, he became receiver-general for crown property in Barking. At the same time he continued to farm Loxford on the same terms as before the Dissolution. After his death in 1554 it passed into the possession of Thomas Pownsett (his nephew?) who obtained the freehold in 1562 as a tenant-in-chief of the crown (this crown grant was actually made in 1557 to one Thomas Powle who conveyed to Thomas Pownsett in 1562) and it continued in the Pownsett family until 1629. None of the grants or conveyances in question actually mention the collection of tithes.

Nor did the will of William Pownsett mention tithes or even contain a specific legacy to purchase the Barking rectory from Thomas Barnes for the benefit of All Souls. Pownsett's will specified only that part of the residue of his estate should be applied to "other good deeds of charity"; all arrangements were left to the executors, the chief of whom was his friend, Sir William Petre, the Queen's principal Secretary of State. Moreover, all concerned were fellows of All Souls.[149] So perhaps it cannot be a matter for surprise if the Pownsetts and the executors should have also contrived that tithes from the Loxford circuit should pass by default to All Souls College, and so to the vicar. Certainly in November 1595, the year following the final confirmation of the rectory to All Souls College, the vicar, Richard Wignal, was granted comprehensive power of attorney to collect all manner of tithe belonging to the college, specifically including great tithes of corn, grain and hay as well as timber and all other greater and lesser tithes.[150]

The stages by which the rectory of Barking passed from the crown to All Souls College must account for other apparent anomalies. Wangey and Downshall, together with Uphall, had been demesne farms of the Abbey administered by the office of the cellaress and each had paid a modus of 3s. 4d. in lieu of tithe. By analogy with the other two it might have been expected that the Downshall modus would have covered both the great and small tithe of that 'manor'. The tenant of Downshall continued to pay this sum to the vicar into the 18th century, although Downshall was absorbed into the Newbury circuit so far as the great tithes were concerned. Hence no separate Downshall tithing appears in the table. This may have been arranged during the 1550s whilst Thomas Barnes owned not only the demesne and tithe circuit of Newbury and the demesne of Downshall, but also the rectory itself before selling that to Pownsett's executors (in the interest of All Souls College) in 1557.[151]

The actual words of the deed of conveyance could be intended to cover such arrangements. Thomas Baron alias Barnes conveyed the

> Rectory, parsonage and church… with the appurtenances, <u>except and reserved</u> to the said Thomas [etc] all the tithes… arising and growing of and in the farms called Wangey, Newbury and Dunshall… <u>and also the tithes and gathering of certain tithes belonging to the said farm of Newbury</u>, which said three farms with the said tithes and gathering of tithes the said Thomas Barnes and one Bartholomew Barnes, father unto the said Thomas, did purchase to them and their heirs before he the said Thomas Barnes purchased the said Rectory. And such said farms and every of them shall be from henceforth free and discharged from paying any manner of tithes unto the said Rectory

Table 1: Tithings in the parish of Barking pre-1836 (simplified)

The acreages set down are those from the revised survey of 1805-6. Those given at the beginning of the 1669 survey are generally smaller, although showing the same order of magnitude.[152]

VICAR OF BARKING (includes gardens and woods not in demesne)	Great and small tithe to vicar	2,347 acres
ILFORD HOSPITAL (includes demesnes of Loxfordbury, Eastbury, Westbury, and 'free' manors of Wyfields, Jenkins & Claybury. Westbury and Jenkins also paid compositions for portions of small tithe to vicar.)	Great and small tithe to hospital	1,657 acres
DEMESNE OF NEWBURY	Owner pays modus for great and small*	207 acres
NEWBURY CIRCUIT	Great tithe to Newbury Small tithe to vicar	1,055 acres
DEMESNE OF GAYSHAM	Owner pays modus for great and small*	301 acres
GAYSHAM CIRCUIT	Great tithe to Gaysham Small tithe to vicar	1,584 acres
STONEHALL	Great tithe to landowner (?) Small tithe to vicar	150 acres
DEMESNE OF WESTBURY	Great tithe to hospital Composition to vicar (see above)	432 acres
WESTBURY CIRCUIT	Great tithe to Westbury Small tithe to vicar	1,010 acres
EASTBURY CIRCUIT	Great tithe to Eastbury Small tithe to vicar	1,384 acres
WANGEY	Owner pays modus for great and small*	68 acres
UPHALL	Owner pays modus for great and small*	103 acres
ALDBOROUGH	Owner pays modus for great and small†	254 acres
ABBEY PRECINCT	Exempt	31 acres
EAST HAM LEVEL (WESTMARSH)	Certain marshes also exempt because Abbey demesne at Dissolution.	43 acres

* Modus to Vicar 3s.4d.
† Modus to Vicar £1.0s.0d

N.B. The use of the word 'tithing' for areas paying tithe to a particular impropriator is more comprehensive than 'tithe circuit' and neater in the context than 'tithe district', but though justified by contemporary usage, this meaning is not noticed in the Oxford English Dictionary.

of Barking or unto the parson of the said Rectory… saving three shillings and four pence yearly to be paid unto the said Rectory for the said farm of Wangey [and the same sums for Newbury and for Dunshall], <u>providing always that if the said farms did pay any more tithes to the said Rectory than the said several payments of three shillings and four pence… within the space of three years next before the purchase thereof that then the said Thomas, his heirs and assigns and farmers of the said three farms… shall pay so much tithes as the farmers thereof did pay unto the said Rectory before the said purchase made by the said Thomas of the said Rectory</u>…" (Author's note: the underlined clauses provide scope for interpretation).[153]

This might additionally explain the mysterious Aldborough tithing. The Barnes family had also acquired Aldborough Hatch in the 1540s (where they continued to reside long after disposing of Newbury and Downshall). No separate demesne tithing for Aldborough could be easily predicted from such evidence as we possess and the apparent composition of £1 is out of line with the other moduses of 3s. 4d. (a sum equivalent to a quarter mark, a common unit of medieval reckoning). A suspicious new vicar, Dr Christopher Musgrave, commented in 1763, "The tithing now taken by Aldborough must have been included in the grant to Nubery. The claim of a modus by Aldborough must be quite novel."[155] Vicar Rashleigh was still vainly denying its existence in 1805, but it may well have been covered by the clause in the conveyance quoted above, which excepted "certain tithes belonging to the said farm of Newbury".[156] There is no doubt that in 1651, when the Aldborough Hatch estate was partitioned between the sisters Abigail (Lockey) and Hester (Stephens), married daughters of Thomas and Isabel Barnes, the deed of partition included "the tythes thereof and of divers other lands therein likewise mentioned".[157]

Furthermore, no legal challenge ever appears to have been mounted to the Aldborough claim. Perhaps the vicars took some consolation from the impropriator's acceptance that much woodland and a string of mill-ponds on the Aldborough Hatch estate were not covered by the modus. Finally, the Tithe Commissioners did, in effect, recognise an Aldborough tithing in 1847, though in several portions. One large portion was by then exempt from tithe because it had come into the hands of the crown during the early 19th century. Another small portion, White's Farm, had been acquired by a Joseph Perkins who successfully claimed the great and small tithe on this piece for himself. The award recognised the claims of Francis and Samuel Stevens, whose family had bought the Lockey inheritance in 1803-4, to the great and small tithe of the remainder of the estate.[158]

The origins of the separate tithing claimed for the 150 acres of Stonehall Farm are more obscure. Medieval evidence is lacking, and in the large grant of Barking manors made to Sir William Denham in 1545 of Stonehall with Gaysham, Westbury and Eastbury, only Stonehall is conveyed without a portion of tithe specified.[159] Subsequently, the manor of Stonehall descended with Wanstead. The tithe surveys up to 1727/8 classified its fields as part of the surrounding

Gaysham circuit, but a note in the first pages of the 1669 book says "free from Great Tythes but pay small tythes to ye Vicar". The tithe survey 1750 omits the Gaysham connection. Finally the tithe award of 1847 did recognise a separate tithing in which the interested parties were the vicar, entitled to the small tithe, and Lord Mornington, owner of Wanstead and Stonehall. No modus seems to have been involved and the most feasible explanation would appear to be that sometime during the 17th century the impropriator of the Gaysham circuit agreed that the great tithe of Stonehall should pass to the landowner.[160]

As a final point – the table does not really show the extent of land within the parish which was *exempt* from all tithe, great and small. Some 2,000 acres were exempt because they were waste and common within the royal forest. The land which is actually shown as tithe-free in the Abbey precinct and in Westmarsh was exempted under an act of Henry VIII which freed former monastic lands even when they had passed into lay ownership. According to Christopher Hill this act was widely employed for tithe evasion, but in Barking its application seems to have been restricted to land actually in Abbey demesne (and not on lease) immediately before the Dissolution; a claim by Thomas Fanshawe in 1598 that Cricklewood was exempt as demesne appears to have been abandoned.[161] The area exempted may have been increased later by the Tithe Commissioners.

Chapter four: Thomas Cartwright and the evolution of Barking documentation

Dr Thomas Cartwright, Vicar of Barking from the Restoration of 1660 to the revolution of 1688-89 was the chief architect of Barking's system of tithe documentation. No Vicar of Barking ever achieved a more prominent, albeit unenviable, position in national history, for he has long been stigmatised as one who, consumed by personal ambitions, encouraged King James II to follow that disastrous course which lost him his throne.[162] Local sources suggest that his activities in Barking may not have been entirely unconnected with his role on the national stage.

Fig. 9. Reverend Thomas Cartwright, c.1680 (copyright National Gallery). Vicar of Barking 1660-89 and principal architect of Barking's system of tithe documentation.

His father had been a schoolmaster at Brentwood. During the reign of Elizabeth his distinguished puritan grandfather, also named Thomas, had been the leader of the Calvinist faction within the Church of England pressing for government of the church by elders, or presbyters, and the abolition of bishops. Young Thomas was at Oxford during the Interregnum when the victory of Parliament temporarily ensured Presbyterian control of the church and the universities. Yet, surprisingly, when he decided to enter the church himself he sought ordination as a priest from a retired Bishop of Oxford.[163]

No doubt this stood him in good stead when, during his first incumbency as Vicar of Walthamstow (1657-1660), the Restoration took place, and he declared himself an ardent supporter of the monarchy. In petitioning for the living of Barking immediately afterwards he claimed that he had been invited there by parishioners.[164] This is credible since Barking had been repeatedly disrupted (like Walthamstow and many other parishes) by the rapid turnover of indifferent or controversial clergy during the Interregnum.

Educated and industrious, episcopally ordained, an able preacher of professed loyalty to the re-established monarchy and church, and yet with a family name reassuring to those of Presbyterian views, Thomas Cartwright appears to have been favourably received by the local gentry of various persuasions. Despite his ambitions for further promotion – or perhaps in consequence of them – he gave close attention to his parish for almost a dozen years, during which time he increased his resources by cultivating good relationships with leading families and assiduously improving the living.

At the end of November 1661 his first wife, Mary, died following the birth of their third child. The following May he married Sarah, daughter of Henry Wight of Gaysham – one of the largest landowners and tithe impropriators in Barking parish.[165] No doubt tongues wagged at the haste of this advantageous marriage. Since it is unlikely that Thomas Cartwright, the son of a schoolmaster, had much inherited wealth, this marriage may well have helped him to find the resources to launch a prolonged campaign to recover all tithe attached to his benefice.

This campaign proceeded along three lines: legal proceedings against individual defaulters, begun by 1663 or earlier; the preparation of a parish tithe map, ready by 1666; and the completion of a detailed tithe survey by 1669. Very probably the second and third stages developed naturally from the problems of amassing sufficient evidence to support court proceedings. One may speculate whether the great plague of 1665-6 slowed progress; there was a marked increase of Barking burials in 1666 and of widows remarrying during the following years.

However, in the space of the five years between 1663 and 1668 the Vicar of Barking pursued no less than 12 tithe cases into the Court of Arches. It has already been pointed out that these represent nearly half of all tithe cases originating in Essex before this court in the decade following the Restoration.[166] But how many cases must have been brought into the lower ecclesiastical courts in the first instance to generate so many appeals? And how many were settled out of court, or diverted into the secular courts by the writs of prohibition increasingly employed at this time? Dr Thomas Cartwright was certainly complainant in two cases concerning tithe known to have been running in Chancery around 1664.[167] The costs of all this litigation must have been considerable. Did the vicar, one wonders, receive assistance from any other impropriators or landowners in the parish apart from his father-in-law? During the controversies of the Interregnum many landowners had become fearful that resistance to the payment of tithes could be the precursor to a wider attack upon property rights and inclined to agree with a pamphleteer of 1654 "that landlords rent and tithe rent will stand and fall together".[168] Nevertheless, Cartwright's will of 1688 reveals that the extent of the vicar's tithe claims brought him into eventual conflict even with his own father-in-law.[169]

Undoubtedly, Vicar Cartwright received help from Thomas Fanshawe, Lord of the Manor of Barking, in the construction of the parish tithe map.[170] The Fanshawes had held property in Barking from the mid-16th century and Queen Elizabeth had granted them the mastership of Ilford Hospital in 1572. They had bought the manor of Barking from James I in 1628 – at a bargain price, so it was said.[171] Then they had sided openly with the King in the Civil War and, like many royalists, had suffered the sequestration of their property at the hands of the victorious parliament. However, in 1647 Thomas Fanshawe of Jenkins (1607-1652) was allowed to 'compound his delinquency' and regain his estates in return for heavy fines.[172] His young son, (Sir) Thomas Fanshawe (1628-1704), inheriting upon his father's death early in 1652, faced the task of rebuilding the family fortunes. He engaged a professional surveyor, William Belgrave, to construct a map survey of the whole manor of Barking in 1652-53.[173]

Not a great deal is known about Belgrave. The Civil War period was hardly propitious for estate surveys, yet as Dr Hull has pointed out in relation to map-making, "those difficult years 1640-1660 are unexpectedly active, especially in Kent", and what little we know about William Belgrave associates him with Kent.[174] At approximately 16 miles to the inch the Barking map was a large one, showing field boundaries, field names, acreages and the names of tenants. Only copies of parts of the map can now be found, although the original certainly survived into the 19th century when most of the extracts were made.[175]

Essentially the parish tithe map of 1666 was a copy of this manorial map with Dagenham excluded (indeed, it may have started as a tracing) with the addition of field numbers 1 to 1,569 (in a north to south sequence) and colours to distinguish each tithing.[176] The columns of the associated 'Companion to the Vicar's Map of Barking Parish' list the consecutive number of each parcel, the colour, the name of the tithing (indicated usually by one or more initials), acreage, field-name and owner. In the late 18th century copy of the companion, the only one to survive, entries in this last column are very incomplete, and the field-names in the preceding column need to be supplemented from the map itself.[177] On the other hand, the companion gives the size of each parcel in acres, roods and perches, instead of to the nearest acre, as do the later surveys, useful for checking and supplementing the map. Furthermore, were it not for this copy of the companion we should not know much about the colours used on the original map because the surviving copy of this latter, made probably in the mid-18th century, has only yellow tinting (mainly for tithable woodland).

One of the owners given in the companion is 'Sir T[homas] C[ambell]' of Clayhall who died in 1665, which suggests that the preparations for the companion, and most probably the map itself, were already completed by that year. The evidence in a later parish boundary dispute (undated, but probably 1795) begins, "The following are extracts from very old books in the Vicar of Barking's possession *as far back as 1666 in which the numbers refer to an antient map descriptive of the Lands and the respective Tithings.*"[178] The first tithe survey was ready in 1669.[179] We have no knowledge of who actually carried out all this work. In view of the amount of information obtained from Belgrave's survey it might have been possible to dispense with the services of a professional surveyor and Vicar Cartwright may have done much of it himself.

His situation certainly altered after 1669. In the course of the 1660s he had acquired additional ecclesiastical posts, becoming a Canon of Wells and of St Paul's and a 'chaplain-in-ordinary', which brought him to the notice of the court. In 1669 he expended £140 on a house near the top of Ilford Lane (then called Barking Lane) and close to the main Essex highway, much more conveniently situated for travelling to London, or elsewhere, than the old vicarage in Barking North-street.[180] During the following years, having leased out the vicarage, he expended a good deal on improving his Ilford house. In 1672 he agreed that Henry North, tenant of the adjoining Clements Farm, might supply oats and straw for his carriage horses in lieu of tithe.[181] In that year he had also become a Canon of Durham and, in 1675, rose to be Dean of Ripon.

Despite all this preferment he was permitted to retain his Barking benefice. However, the additional posts and increasing involvement in court politics compelled him to spend more and more time away from Barking and his now numerous family.[182] He had regularly chaired the meetings of the Barking Vestry, but after February 1672 he attended only rarely and from 1674 his regular parochial duties were covered by a succession of curates.[183] Yet, somewhat surprisingly, he took an active part in the production of another tithe survey.

A first draft of this (which could be referred to as tithe book II) was begun in 1680, in the same volume as tithe book I of 1669, but was never finished. This draft was followed by a completed survey the next year, and this 1681 tithe survey (or, tithe book III) is in the same hand as the unfinished draft. It is not certain that this is the hand of book I (the 1669 survey), although all three are in the same volume. In the early 20th century, one of the authors of the Fanshawe MSS concluded, "This vol[ume] belonged formerly to Bishop Cartwright who was Vicar of Barking and it is said to be mainly in his own script".[184] Books II and III could be in Cartwright's handwriting; the entry for Lady Cambell [of Clayhall] ends with his signature, familiar from

Fig. 10. Barking Tithe Book, c. 1750, p.40 (ERO D/P81/3/15). The entry for Henry North of Clements Farm in Ilford; note the agreement with Reverend Thomas Cartwright to stable the vicar's carriage horses.

Barking Vestry minutes. Similar agreements in book I are in the first person, though not actually signed by the vicar. However, as will be explained later, it is certain that he received assistance with the later surveys.

All the Barking surveys have the same basic structure as the measured surveys to be found in some other Essex parishes described above in chapter two. The first column contains the name of the tenant-occupier, often followed by the location or name of the estate, sometimes by a note of an agreed composition. This is followed by a terrier of the farm or smallholding in which the parcels are identified by their number on the map and usually by the field-name, and the tithing is indicated by an abbreviation. A column headed "Quantity" gives the acreage in round figures, and another headed "Quality" indicates type of land-use (information here is rather general, but market-garden crops may be named). A final column is headed "Alterations" and usually indicates changes in tenancy before the next survey.

At the front of the volume is an index to tenants' names in the 1669 survey; there is no similar index for the 1681 survey, but in the latter the tenants are entered in alphabetical order. At the back of the volume is an index to the parcel numbers in the 1669 survey, which is very useful when working from map to survey. A similar index to the 1681 survey is inserted immediately following the survey to which it refers. Finally, it must be noted that, following the 1681 survey and its numerical index, there has also been interpolated, in a distinctive hand, a copy of an earlier survey of the northern part of Barking manor in 1617. This is not a tithe survey but it is of considerable interest and will be examined in chapter six.

In the 1669 survey, the first column also records payments received to the year 1674. The inference is that no separate tithe account books were kept for these years. Tithe accounts are extant for many years following the 1681 survey. The first of these, for 1681-2, is of peculiar interest.[185] It is a small (15cm x 9cm) notebook, now coverless, with receipts entered on the left and expenses on the right in a neat secretary hand. The first page is headed "Rec'd for the deane of Rippon since Mr Bruster's accompt for tythes due for Lammas 1681 & arreares." The third item beneath is "My owne tyth for Westberry --- £2.2.0." and on the opposite page, "P'd my self & Mr Brewster for making the new tyth book and collecting the tyth the year ending Lammas 1680 --- £20.0.0." At the end of the book we find added in the vicar's handwriting, "3 Octr. 1683. This accompt I own to have receiv'd from Mr Richard Taylor of Barking, ye Duplicate wherof was signed by him 25 May 1683 and receiv'd by me then at London [signed] Thos. Cartwright – Vicar of Barking". It seems certain that, even if all the surveys were written up by Cartwright, the tithes were being collected and details supplied for the latest tithe survey by a Mr Brewster and a Mr Richard Taylor of Westbury. Who were they?

This Mr Brewster can hardly be other than Augustine Brewster, the owner-occupier of Wyfields in Ilford and one of the larger landowners in the parish. Mr Richard Taylor was the well-to-do tenant-farmer of Westbury, another large estate in Barking and Ripple. According to Edward Sage, Richard Taylor married Brewster's sister, Elizabeth.[186] One may suppose that neither was constrained to take on this work purely as a means of livelihood.

What is perhaps more remarkable is the direct evidence that Richard Taylor of Westbury was a Dissenting minister and the circumstantial evidence that Augustine Brewster was a Presbyterian sympathiser. During the Interregnum Augustine's father, John Brewster, had been a member of the parliamentary committee for the division of Essex which met at Romford and a member of the 'little parliament' (also nicknamed 'barebones parliament').[187] Under an act of this parliament in 1653 he had been made a trustee of the 'New Chapel' at Barkingside with the object of encouraging a "Godly Preaching Ministry there". The original project had envisaged a tripartite division of Barking parish with a portion of tithe for this forest side chapel beyond Fullwell Hatch. The scheme was taken over by Cartwright after he became vicar with the somewhat different object of securing an endowment of rent from a farm, also to be enclosed from the royal forest, to support a "pious and orthodox priest" to officiate there. The New Chapel was ultimately abandoned owing to differences over patronage (although the enclosures – Fencepiece Farm, Chapel Field and Chapel Piece remained). John Brewster died in 1677.[188]

A near contemporary of Cartwright at Oxford, Richard Taylor had been appointed curate for Holt in Denbigh in 1659 only to be expelled like other Dissenting ministers under the Act of Uniformity in 1662. According to Calamy, "after being silenced, he continued preaching twelve months in the church *gratis*, by connivance. He then removed to London, and at length was pastor of a congregation in Barking in Essex."[189] He appears in Barking records in 1668 when he married Mrs Elizabeth Hiett at St Margaret's. Although the author has not been able to find the evidence for the statement by Edward Sage that she was a daughter of John Brewster, it is plain that she was a widow of some social status.[190] According to the 1669 survey, Taylor was already paying part of the small tithe for Westbury at that date. In May 1670 he first appeared at a meeting of the Barking Vestry where he subsequently became a most diligent attender for the following 20 years, often signing immediately after the vicar, curate or churchwardens. He served as surveyor for Barking Town ward in 1676, and Ripple overseer in 1682-3. He was present when church rates were sanctioned and an approving witness to the gifts of communion plate to the church from the Bertie family of the Beehive.[191] The archdeacon's visitation in September 1683 mentions him specifically. Reporting on the state of the old vicarage which Dr Cartwright had abandoned for his Ilford house, the archdeacon begins, "The Vicaridge house is out of repair and lett to two Tenants, Mr Taylor *who collects ye tythes of ye Dr and lets ye house.*"[192]

And yet at the archdeacon's visitation in July 1683 Mr Richard Taylor had been the first amongst 18 parishioners charged with not receiving the sacrament at Easter and failure to attend church.[193] Furthermore, his name appears on the list of Dissenting ministers in the London area compiled in 1690-91, when a common fund was being set up by Presbyterians and Congregationalists to assist those in need, as "Mr R. Taylor – Ejected – Att Barking, has a good estate of his owne – keeps a coach." *The Victoria County History* suggests that he may have been identical with the William Taylor who in 1676 was already said to have been holding a Presbyterian conventicle at his house in Barking.[194] Nevertheless, when he died on 12 August 1697 'Mr Richard Taylor, *Clerk*' was interred in the chancel of St Margaret's, Barking, near to the pulpit, apparently without any objection from the new vicar, John Chisenhall, who had been curate under Cartwright. No wonder that William Frogley in his history of Barking erroneously suggests that Taylor must himself have been one of Cartwright's curates![195]

In the absence of more direct evidence one can only speculate upon the curious relationship between Richard Taylor and Thomas Cartwright in the light of the unsettled circumstances of the period. No doubt, like most high churchmen of the time, Cartwright favoured comprehension of moderate Dissenters, many of whom were reluctant to form separate congregations.[196] But the ambitious vicar, basking in the sunshine of royal favour, which culminated in his appointment as Bishop of Chester in 1686, was prepared to go further – in defiance of fellow bishops. He readily accepted the assurances of James II (now a Roman Catholic) that he would protect the position of the Church of England after the royal Declaration of Indulgence 1688 had granted freedom of worship to both Dissenters and Roman Catholics. So was Cartwright (the vile sycophant of Macaulay's history) simply using Taylor and others as a means of enlisting

Dissenting support for royal policy; or had the vicar's views been shaped by a conviction of the divine right of kings and by his own success in achieving accommodation with both Presbyterians and Catholics at parish level?[197]

As Anne Whiteman has pointed out, "some ejected ministers made a point of attending the parish church before, and sometimes after, holding a service and preaching either in their own house, a neighbouring property, or perhaps out of doors." So Taylor was another example of the partial conformity widespread in this period; perhaps he went further than most in accepting the job of vicar's tithe collector, as well as in the extent of his participation in the Vestry. Possibly, he regarded Cartwright as an ally, seeing royal declarations of indulgence as offering a step forward to an inclusive national church. After all, the Quaker William Penn was not the only Dissenter to believe in the sincerity of King James, even after the French revocation of the Edict of Nantes in 1685 had underlined the potential dangers of putting faith in a Catholic monarch.

In December 1688 Cartwright followed James to exile in France and died of dysentery in Dublin in April 1689.[199] In June, All Souls College as patrons installed their own warden, the Reverend Leopold Finch, as Vicar of Barking. The curate, John Chisenhall, whom Cartwright had suspended in June 1688 for refusing to read out the controversial Declaration of Indulgence in church, was re-instated (even though he had been appointed Rector of Mistley). In February 1697 he succeeded Finch as Vicar of Barking, and died in office aged 71 years on 31 March, 1724.[200]

As already mentioned, a number of tithe account books for these years have survived, but there is an hiatus during the incumbency of Finch. Two narrow volumes contain almost continuous annual accounts from 1697 to 1723 (whilst Chisenhall was vicar).[201] These typically include little additional information beyond the name of the tenant and the amount collected. A further difficulty with these books is that some later entries seem to have been made in spaces left earlier, which can create dating problems. However, the first volume actually begins with sums "p'd for Mr Finch" followed by eight pages of schedules resembling a partial tithe survey and dated 1690. Presumably these are updates on some of the entries in the 1681 survey prepared for a new absentee vicar by Chisenhall, then curate.

Judging from the frequency of Chisenhall's signature in the Barking Vestry book he spent more time there than at Mistley, but no Barking tithe accounts have survived for 1691-96. At the rear of this volume there are short lists of tenants compounding at Mistley for the years 1691-92, which are followed confusingly by another partial survey of Barking dated 1697, apparently prepared by Chisenhall when he replaced Finch as vicar. Incidentally, many entries in these partial surveys suggest that rateable values of properties were then being used in the calculation of tithe compositions.

Chapter five: Barking tithe documentation

Part I: The system in the 18th century

Following Chisenhall's death, the Reverend Thomas Machen Fiddes was installed on 5 September 1724 and a new tithe survey appeared in 1727-28, later known from its cover as 'Mr Fiddes' green book'.[202] It could be called tithe book IV, although it is only the third *complete* survey. It is constructed on the same lines as its predecessors and still employs the system of parcel numbers referring to the same parish tithe map. There is no quality column to show land-use, but in a few instances crops are stated. Like Cartwright's book, it appears to be mainly in the vicar's own hand. There is an index of parcel numbers at the rear. The 1733 tithe account book has also survived from Fiddes' incumbency; it is a careful production, and rather more informative on farm and field names than many of the earlier tithe accounts.[203] Fiddes died at Carlisle in September, 1734.

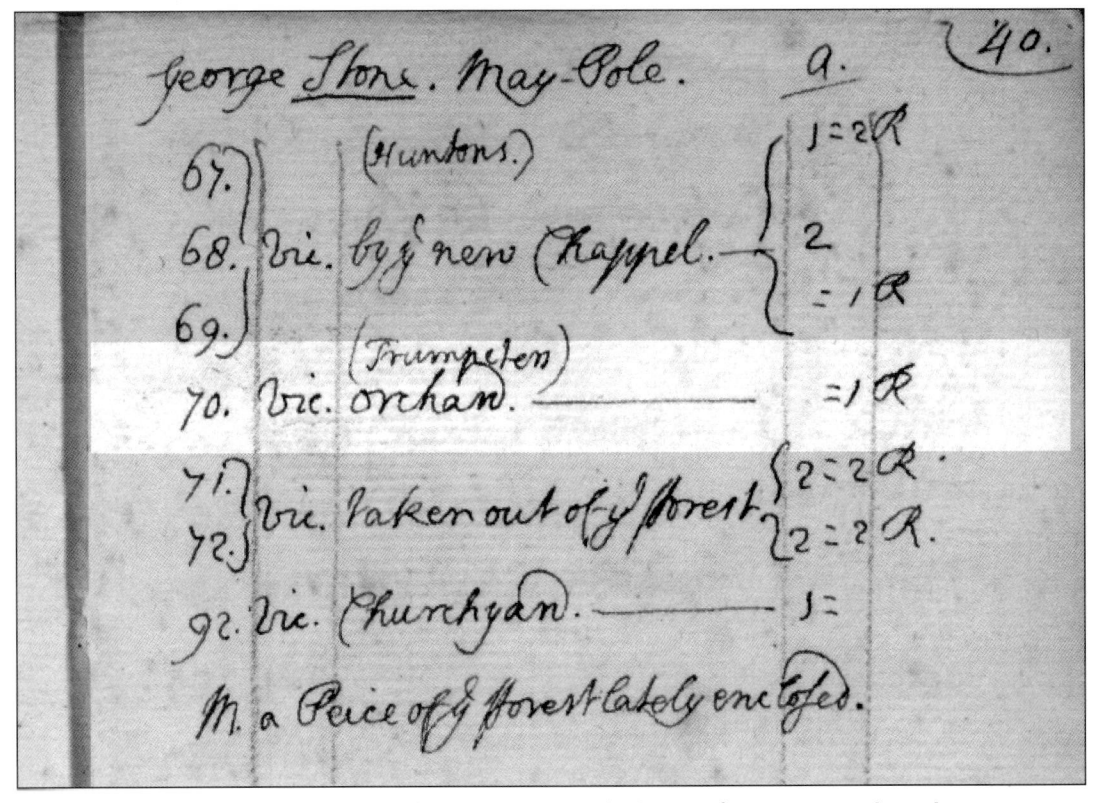

Fig. 11. Barking Tithe Book, c. 1750, p.40 (ERO D/P81/3/15). The entry for George Stone shows the connection between the enclosure called Trumpeters, the house called Hunts Hall (Hunters) and the Maypole Inn. The churchyard opposite was the site of the abandonned New Chapel. Note also the rateable values on the left hand side.

No new tithe survey was prepared by Fiddes' successor, the Reverend Leslie Owen (1734-1746) and no tithe accounts have survived for his incumbency. Following the death of Owen, Reverend William Stephens LL.D. was installed on 7 October 1746.[204] A fresh impetus was now given to the collection of tithe and by 1750 another tithe survey, the fourth completed in the series, had been put into use.[205] Again, this follows the pattern introduced by Cartwright in the previous century, but the dates recording annual payments during 1746-49 entered on the left-hand page opposite the holding seem to have been added simultaneously in another hand. It may be that they represent the collection of arrears after the survey had been completed, or they may have been written up from temporary lists made earlier. It seems unlikely that the survey itself was completed earlier than 1750. A new feature is the systematic recording of the rateable value of each property on the left-hand page. A few payments in kind still occur: a pig (*porcell*), a goose (*anser*) and in one instance, honey (*meleagnis*); the occasional lapses into Latin were perhaps intended to impress. The schedules of properties are on the right-hand pages with the usual parcel numbers, abbreviations for the tithings and field names. Entries are arranged topographically, but tenants dwelling outside the parish are grouped together under "Landholders". The divisions, such as "Forest Side" (Barkingside), and order of treatment are parallel to those used in contemporary rate books. At the rear of the book is a list of "Woods tythable to the Vicar" with dates of felling, an alphabetical index of tenants and an index of parcel numbers.

The extant dissected copy of the parish tithe map of 1666 may also be contemporary.[206] Certainly the names of tenants written on some fields are the same as those in Dr Stephens' survey, yet they seem to be subsequent to the other writing. Moreover, several sheets have a watermark that shows the paper to have been made c.1690. There therefore remains the possibility that the copying of the map may have begun earlier. Little attempt was made to bring the map itself up-to-date. The diversion of Oaks Lane that was made in 1728 to accommodate Colonel Bladen's new mansion at Aldborough Hatch is not shown, and, more surprisingly, the original New Chapel enclosure at Barkingside is added only in pencil, and that in the wrong position south of Fullwell Hatch Gate.[207]

This map has been described as a crude or rough copy. Strictly speaking such a description should only be applied to sheet one (Claybury), which is certainly a replacement. The remaining 21 sheets, though the draughtsmanship and finish are of poor quality, seem to be fairly accurate copies, possibly tracings, of the original. General structure and field-shapes are adequate enough to permit comparisons to be made with 19th century maps and the fields to be identified without difficulty. Most houses can be located with fair accuracy; some of the larger are shown in elevation – though the sketches are usually too rough to be convincing. The sheets are on thin white paper (perhaps to facilitate tracing) mounted on coarse linen stiffened with a blue, possibly cartridge, paper in between. Each sheet has been folded to pocket size.

Certainty is difficult because more than one sequence of sheet numbering has been employed, but there must have originally been at least 25 sheets: the missing three sheets would have probably covered Barking town, an area in Barkingside south of Gaysham and around Gearies and an area in Chadwell east of Barley Lane. The Barking town sheet can be largely reconstructed by using the equivalent extract by Luff (1861) from the manorial map of 1652-3 and identifying parcel numbers from the companion of 1666.[208] Other extracts from the manorial map permit partial reconstruction of the areas in Barkingside around Gearies and in Chadwell east of Barley Lane, but doubts must remain concerning portions between Beehive Lane and the Cranbrook Road, north-east of Mossford Green and along the forest fence between Little Heath and Padnall Corner.

Many features mentioned above support the hypothesis that this dissected copy of the parish tithe map was designed to be carried around by the tithe-collector. The original map of 1666 was certainly not portable. Daniel Lysons, seeking material for his *Environs of London*, saw it in 1796, probably hanging on the wall of the vestry, when he visited Barking "to make my first queries". Writing to the vicar afterwards he refers to it as "your great map". Probably almost eight feet high and with tithings distinguished by some 13 colours, it obviously impressed the historian and he asks pertinently, "is there no field book belonging?"[209]

There are a few additions in darker ink to Dr Stephens' survey, including one relating to woods dated 1752, but no tithe accounts are extant for the period 1751 to 1762, the incumbency of Stephens' successor, Dr Savage Tyndall. One gets the impression that tithe collecting was again neglected. This was no longer the case after the installation of Tyndall's successor, the Reverend Christopher Musgrave D.D., in December 1762. Musgrave came from a family of influential Cumbrian gentry, although his father, Sir Christopher Musgrave, being clerk to the Privy Council, resided in Middlesex.[210] Another fellow of All Souls, he is said to have begun his ministry as a curate under Tyndall. The late Dr Oxley in his study of Barking Vestry minutes observed that Musgrave and his parishioners "seem to have lived at loggerheads".[211] Tithe accounts (1763-1778) covering most years of his incumbency, together with surviving memoranda and letters, tell the same story as the Vestry minutes concerning his predilection for litigation. He produced no further tithe surveys himself, but he studied those made by his predecessors, and everything else that he could discover about the history of Barking tithes. Inevitably he concluded that he was not receiving all to which he was legally entitled.

In a letter dated 24 August 1763, he begins with the tithes of Ilford Hospital and writes, "When Sir Crisp Gascoigne got them in his possession he used all means to encroach upon his neighbours, as you may see in Dr Stephen's account… I shall speak to Mr Gascoigne at the first opportunity for his grant but do not think I shall have one sou."[212] Here, without doubt, the vicar is referring to Sir Crisp's son, the first Bamber Gascoyne (1725-91).[213] He goes on to show that he understands the historic process by which Henry VIII, after the Dissolution, granted estates "for a perpetuity in the same manner as the Abbesses had leased them tythe free", subject only to a modus, and "with the addition of the same parcels of tythes that had gone with them before". He then proceeds with his attack on the impropriators, "Here I complain that the grantees and their successors either cover too much under their moduses or take up the Vicars tythes as their own; and that they do now so openly as to take up the small tythes which they had never any right to in their grants".

He continues, "likewise they took the tythes from the new enclosures in the forest which could never be in their grants at all". This last complaint has to be seen in the context of a sea change in the administration of royal forests, as a result of which it was becoming a great deal easier for private landowners with woods under the jurisdiction of the officers of the forest to destroy them by obtaining licences to stub and grub.[214] Such clearances inevitably reduced the acreage of woods tithable to the vicar without necessarily permitting him to claim tithe of the crops or herbage subsequently grown on these new enclosures.[215]

He threatens "to bring these people to settle matters by filing a bill in the Exchequer against them". And in an undated but probably contemporaneous memorandum he grumbles, "the intermixture of these tithes have caused great encroachments upon one or other wherein the Vicar has been the chief loser who fixes his claim upon an old Survey wherein all the different lands in the Parish are marked and numbered from No 1 to No 1569... the rentals have been adjusted by these numbers ever since 1666 from Dr Cartwright's time, except by Owens".[216] Another undated memorandum is entitled "Queries for bringing a bill into the Exchequer for tithes", with answers in a different hand, no doubt that of a legal adviser.[217] The author has not found evidence of many cases actually pursued through the Court of Exchequer by Dr Musgrave, except that previously mentioned concerning the tithes of Stonehall in 1767 and against a tenant farmer called Linton between 1769 and 1770.[218] Perhaps he thought twice about legal action against so wealthy and well-connected a parishioner as the elder Bamber Gascoyne, lawyer, Member of Parliament and Lord of Trade.

Moreover, the vicar was also heavily engaged on another front. At the back of his first tithe account of 1763 is a new and complete schedule of tithe charges.[219] What changes this tariff incorporated is not apparent, but it probably contained increases on garden and root crops. Beans and peas were charged at 5s. per acre, potatoes at 5s. 6d., main crop turnips at 4s. per acre, and 'etch' turnips at 2s. Walled gardens were charged at 7s. 6d., open at 5s. These impositions should be viewed in the light of the expansion of market garden crops and improved rotations mentioned above in chapters one and three. The cultivation of the potato in particular was increasing rapidly in this area in the 1760s.[220]

Eventually the Barking Vestry reacted. Between 1768 and 1775 we find Musgrave appealing repeatedly to Quarter Sessions against his poor rate assessments, of which the major item was the rate for his tithes. The decision of the Quarter Sessions in July 1769 was, "Whereas Christopher Musgrave D.D., is rated at £5 for his house and £55 for his great and small tithes. It plainly appearing to this Court that the said Christopher Musgrave is not over-rated, the said assessment is therefore confirmed and the said rate, and it is hereby ordered to be paid". Musgrave went on protesting and the Barking Vestry were forced into the embarrassing position of having to apply for distress warrants against their own vicar. In 1771 an attempt to reach an amicable agreement with him over poor and highway rates was rebuffed and the obstinate vicar persisted in unavailing appeals against his assessments. By the end of his incumbency the parish rates had to be increased to pay the heavy legal costs involved.[221]

Musgrave may not always have been the aggressor. The author has a manuscript in his private possession, an autobiographical 'Memoir of Thomas Tyser 1770 – 1832' which presents Musgrave in a somewhat different light. The Tyser family were Barking builders and, as a child, Thomas explains "I had frequent opportunity to exercise and improvement from the private instructions I receiv'd from my late pious and venerable friend, Dr Musgrave, then Vicar of Barking and the brother of a Cumberland Baronet of that name… He lived opposite my Grandfather, and [at] this time [was] *violently persecuted by a Party in the Parish under the auspices of a great man at that time, tho' not over scrupulous in his conduct*, and in this conflict my Grandfather was a staunch stickler for the Doctor…" [author's punctuation and italics]. It seems highly probable that the "great man" was the first Bamber Gascoyne. Small in stature, he has elsewhere been described as "an active, bustling man … self-righteous and constantly engaged in litigation [with a] capacity to make enemies".[222]

Whatever the truth of the matter, the parishioners with whom Musgrave quarrelled were by no means indifferent towards their parish church. A legacy of £300 for a new organ was followed in July 1770 by the appointment by the Barking Vestry of a committee for the "repairing, ornamenting and beautifying the parish church of Barking", of which Bamber Gascoyne was a prominent member.[223] In the course of the next 14 months they carried out a considerable programme of restoration and improvement, including a ceiling of lath and painted plaster and the encasing of pillars in the same material. The scheme was devised by Gascoyne's own surveyor, William Hillyer, who had designed his house, Bifrons, in Barking.[224]

Musgrave died on 7 November 1780. His immediate successor, the Reverend Edmund Isham died within a few months and the Reverend Peter Rashleigh became vicar in 1781 and remained so until his own death in 1836. After 1788 he was also Rector of Southfleet near Gravesend where he preferred to live; so Barking once again had to deal with a non-resident vicar. Rashleigh was a more amiable character than Musgrave and anxious to restore and maintain better relations with the Barking Vestry. Although he paid periodical visits, his non-residence was criticised by Barking parishioners who provided over two-thirds of his, not inconsiderable, income, and by his bishop, concerned at reports that Methodists "daily gained ground in the Parish". Even the building of a fine new vicarage on the east of Barking in 1794, the gift of a former Fellow of All Souls, failed to tempt him to leave Southfleet. From 1809 it provided the Reverend Oliver Lodge, his new curate-in-charge, with a residence for his large family and room to board the paying scholars who helped to supplement his meagre stipend. In the dawn of the 'age of reform' this able, conscientious and popular clergyman kept the heat off Rashleigh until the growing demand from Ilford for the division of the large parish at length proved irresistible.[225]

At the outset of his incumbency, as the Barking Vestry minutes of May 1783 record, Rashleigh had accepted that he was rateable for all his tithes, and had "thrown himself upon the affection of his Parishioners". They, "being very desirous of living in harmony and good esteem with the said Peter Rashleigh their Vicar", unanimously assessed him at £100, for which he returned his thanks.[226] A decade later, in a letter dated 14 August 1794, Rashleigh upbraids the Barking Vestry for having discussed the rate for his tithes when he was unable to be present, and continues:

> *When I first came into the parish I was given to understand that my Predecessor and his parishioners had been involved in unfortunate disputes and that very expensive litigation had been doing great injury to both… before Dr Musgrave's death his rates were very much advanced and his disposition for litigation was given as a reason…[I] have the satisfaction of reflecting that I have been since the year 82 Vicar of Barking without any litigation or dispute with my parishioners and I have sacrificed during that time a very considerable portion of my property to that end as will appear when you compare the composition I took for my tithes with their value or with other compositions for the same in all adjoining parishes – this is well known to you all…*

He goes on to make comparisons with Stepney and East Ham where, in the latter parish, 7s per acre is demanded for potatoes against his own composition of 5s [Musgrave had asked 5s. 6d.]. He concludes by hoping that they will leave his rate at £100 without further discussion.[227]

Rashleigh's first tithe accounts (dated 1781) are extant.[228] They open with a schedule of "Compositions for Tithes at Barking" which shows that Rashleigh did indeed ask less per acre than Musgrave for peas, potatoes and turnips (though otherwise there was little change). In addition to occupiers and compositions paid, these accounts list fields and crops on many farms, understandable in view of the lapse of more than 50 years since the last tithe survey. On opposite pages of the notebook particulars from the Musgrave years are often entered in pencil for comparison. A list of "Disbursements" at the end of the book reveals that Mr Allis was paid £20 for collecting the vicar's tithes – no more than Thomas Cartwright paid to Taylor a century before!

Part II: Isaac Johnson's tithe survey and commutation

On the evidence currently available it is not certain whether the new vicar, Peter Rashleigh, or the new Master of the Ilford Hospital, the second Bamber Gascoyne (1758-1824), took the initiative which led ultimately to the joint commissioning of an entirely new tithe survey; the last Barking survey before the Tithe Commutation Act. On balance it would seem probable that Gascoyne was the prime mover.

Whilst temperament and situation counselled the absentee Rashleigh to keep on good terms with his Barking parishioners, there is no reason to suppose that he was any less interested than Musgrave in maintaining his income from tithe. Those pencil notes on the opposite pages of the tithe accounts surviving from Rashleigh's incumbency – particularly the last, dated 1793 – show an interest in detailed investigations using the 1666 map. Although the Vicar of Barking now had access to a more complete set of records than most contemporary incumbents, his basic information on the bounds and extent of the multiplex tithings in Barking parish was at least a 120 years old. Furthermore, during this time changes had taken place in field and farm boundaries unrecorded on the parish tithe map. In addition to the enclosure of woodlands that had so exercised Musgrave, a massive rearrangement of estates in the Ilford area took place during the incumbencies of Musgrave and Rashleigh involving Cranbrook, Highlands, Valentines and Wyfields between the 1760s and 1790s.[229]

As a result the ancient manor of Wyfields vanished, its lands absorbed into neighbouring estates. This was of especial concern to the impropriator of the Ilford Hospital tithing because the tithes of Wyfields had belonged to the hospital since 1219, whilst the surrounding lands belonged to the Gaysham tithe circuit. The first Bamber Gascoyne had acquired the mastership of the Ilford Hospital from his father, Sir Crisp Gascoyne, and had renovated the ancient chapel of the hospital in 1781-82. His son, the second Bamber Gascoyne, inherited in 1791 and immediately ran into problems collecting his tithes. Moreover his dispute with the Barking Vestry concerning the assessment of the hospital estates to the poor rate that came to a head in 1793-4 probably turned upon the value of these tithes.[230]

As shown below in chapter six, the records of the hospital included several early 'surveys' of the hospital tithing but, in the event of a dispute, they were not easy to elucidate without field maps.[231] So he turned to Rashleigh for help. The archives at Hatfield House include a 'copy of a paper received 26 Nov. 1792 from Rev'd Mr Rashleigh' containing lists of lands tithing to the Ilford Hospital identified by their numbers on the vicar's tithe map. It must also have been around this time that Gascoyne obtained a series of '12 sketches from the Vicar of Barking's Map', and probably his copy of the companion to the vicar's map (see chapter four). There are also various notes on disputed tithes in the same hand in this collection.[232] Correspondence preserved in the parish records also bears witness to the better relations developing between vicar and master; for example, in a letter dated 27 April 1799 Gascoyne looks forward to their next meeting.

On 26 June 1805, following a disagreement with Robert Raikes of Cranbrook over the "Tithe of Forty four Acres, as appears by your Map", he writes to Rashleigh at Southfleet, "I am in possession of no Documents upon which I would place greater reliance than I would do upon the Parish Map" and appeals urgently for the vicar's opinion.[233] This letter may indeed have been a catalyst because, before the end of 1805, these two major tithe owners had agreed to share the cost of a new tithe survey comprising map and terrier.

The professional surveyor they engaged for the task was Isaac Johnson of Woodbridge, Suffolk (1734-1835). He was an experienced member of a family of artists and surveyors who had undertaken a number of assignments in Suffolk and Essex, many involving large acreages; the previous year he had produced a parish map of Gestingthorpe.[234] The comparatively low charge of 3d. per acre and the title of 'The adjusted survey of Barking' suggests that Johnson did not re-survey completely but, working from the 1666 map, walked the parish inserting new boundaries and estimating areas where required. This suggestion is also supported by an item on Johnson's bill for "paper used in rough plans" and by many identical acreages, where the fields can be identified. These cannot always be recognised with certainty: firstly, because the original 1805-6 map has disappeared and only a single extract is extant and secondly, because Johnson adopted an entirely different system of field numbering. Johnson's final bill came to £155.16s.9d.[235]

The accompanying field-book has survived and takes a form distinct from the previous Barking surveys. It is, however, similar to that employed in many contemporary tithe surveys and in some respects foreshadows the system used for the tithe award. Each entry is headed with name of occupier and property. This is followed by a schedule in tabular form of fields or other parcels giving number, name, acreage and quality. A peculiar feature is that the acreage of each field is entered into a separate column according to the tithing in which it fell, i.e. according to the recipient of the tithe. Most properties required two or three such columns, some as many as six. This tabular arrangement facilitated calculation of the total acreage belonging to each tithing within a property, and the grand totals for the whole parish are listed at the front of the survey, together with the colours by which the 14 tithings are indicated on the map. The colour code, incidentally, seems to have been modelled as far as possible on that used in 1666.

Unusually, no tithe compositions are shown, let alone apportionments for the individual fields; actual payments are never mentioned. Documents reveal that another surveyor, John Skinner of Lawford, was engaged to value the tithes belonging to the vicar and the hospital. The original valuation may be no longer extant, although a 'List of Barking Tithe Holders 1807 from Skinner's Valuation' survives in the parish records. There are totals for the vicar and Gascoyne in the account sent by Skinner. He charged at five per cent of value plus £20.15s. expenses, a total of £147.5s., of which Bamber Gascoyne (by far the wealthier man) had still failed to pay his share of £47.5s. by 1812.[236]

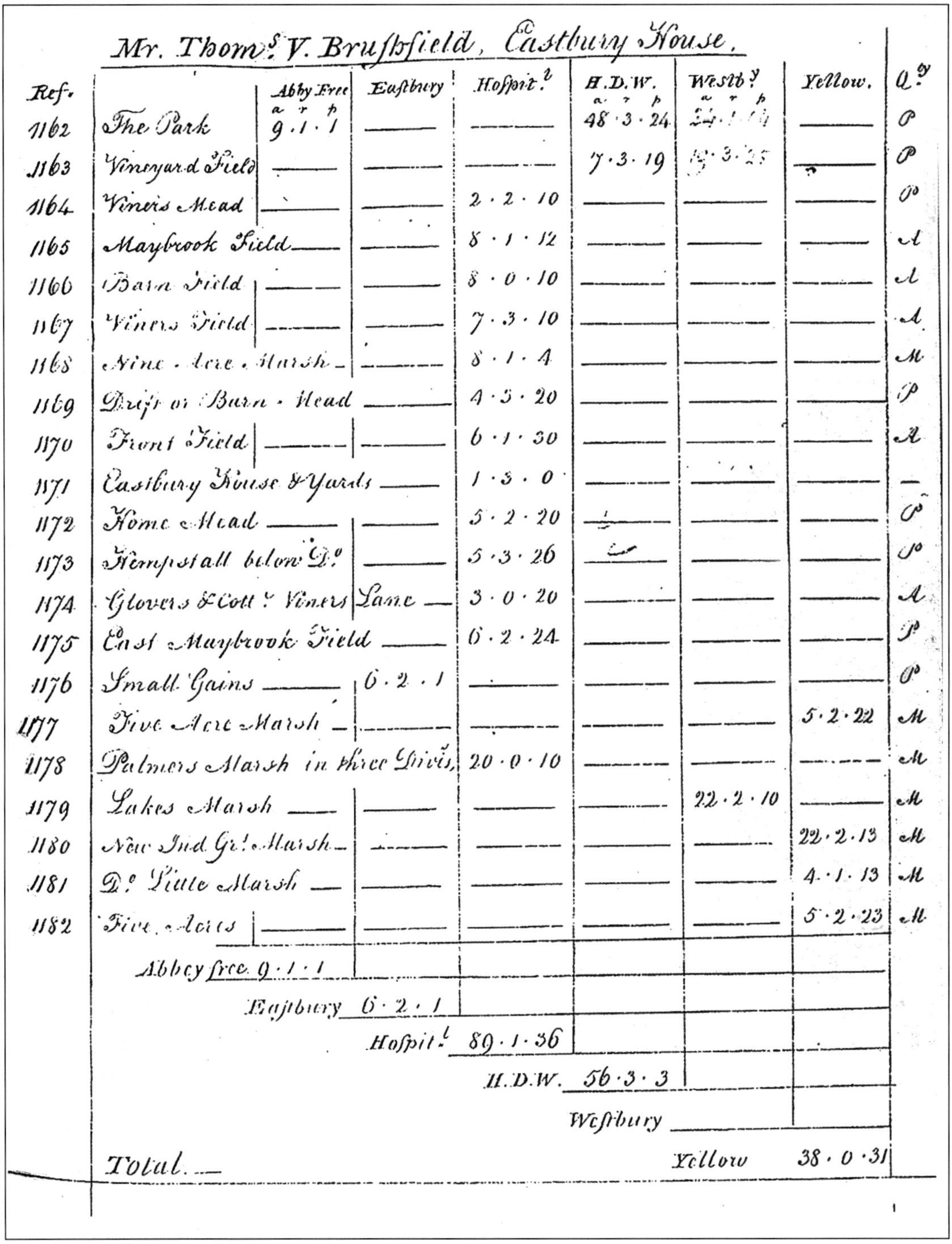

Mr. Thoms V. Brushfield, Eastbury House.

Ref.		Abby Free	Eastbury	Hospit.l	H.D.W.	Westb.y	Yellow.	Q.y
1162	The Park	9.1.1	—	—	48.3.24	24.1.4	—	P
1163	Vineyard Field	—	—	—	7.3.19	13.3.25	—	P
1164	Viners Mead	—	—	2.2.10	—	—	—	P
1165	Maybrook Field	—	—	8.1.12	—	—	—	A
1166	Barn Field	—	—	8.0.10	—	—	—	A
1167	Viners Field	—	—	7.3.10	—	—	—	A
1168	Nine Acre Marsh	—	—	8.1.4	—	—	—	M
1169	Drift or Barn Head	—	—	4.3.20	—	—	—	P
1170	Front Field	—	—	6.1.30	—	—	—	A
1171	Eastbury House & Yards	—	—	1.3.0	—	—	—	—
1172	Home Mead	—	—	5.2.20	—	—	—	O
1173	Hempstall below Do.	—	—	5.3.26	—	—	—	P
1174	Glovers & Cott.s Viners Lane	—	—	3.0.20	—	—	—	A
1175	East Maybrook Field	—	—	6.2.24	—	—	—	P
1176	Small Gains	—	6.2.1	—	—	—	—	O
1177	Five Acre Marsh	—	—	—	—	—	5.2.22	M
1178	Palmers Marsh in three Divis.	—	—	20.0.10	—	—	—	M
1179	Lakes Marsh	—	—	—	—	22.2.10	—	M
1180	New Ind Gr.t Marsh	—	—	—	—	—	22.2.13	M
1181	Do. Little Marsh	—	—	—	—	—	4.1.13	M
1182	Five Acres	—	—	—	—	—	5.2.23	M

Abbey free 9.1.1
Eastbury 6.2.1
Hospit.l 89.1.36
H.D.W. 56.3.3
Westbury
Total. — Yellow 38.0.31

Fig. 12. Barking Tithe Survey, 1805-6, p.51 (Valance House Local History Collection, Barking & Dagenham). The entry for Thomas Brushfield, farmer at Eastbury, who leased property in six tithings. This extract shows how the surveyor, Isaac Johnson, recorded such complications.

One feature of Johnson's survey of particular interest to historians (though probably not to contemporaries) is the attention given to the recording of field-names. Earlier surveys simply repeated those recorded in 1666-69. The 1806 survey not only gives later forms of some of these, but also contains other names, including some of apparently early origin. In this respect it is considerably superior to the later tithe award apportionment that, in the case of Barking, pays scant attention to the recording of field names.

The new survey and valuation was rapidly put to practical use. In June 1807 the vicar sent out printed demands for tithe which began, "Having lately employed a very eminent Surveyor to make a Valuation of the Tythes belonging to me… and who has accordingly accurately measured the lands occupied by each individual".[237] But even before this, in December 1806, the Barking Vestry had decided on a new survey of all rateable property in the parish and approached the vicar for permission to use his recently made map. The new rate survey was carried out in 1807 by Skinner and Lugar.[238]

The 1807 rate survey does not appear to have survived, but a further two volume rate survey and valuation made in 1829 by Twyford (which also uses Johnson's numerical reference system of 1806) is preserved in Valence House. At the rear of the valuation volume an attempt was made to assess each tithe-owner's liability to rates by valuing the tithes he should receive from the principal occupiers in his tithing. These entries were subsequently deleted (though in a manner designed to retain legibility), perhaps because the amounts or the layout were later challenged by some of the parties named.

Or was it a result of the division of the *ecclesiastical* parish of Barking which came about in the following year, and which meant that the tithes were split between two incumbents, although the rating authority (the *civil* parish) was not divided up until 1888? Predictably, there were objections from Vicar Rashleigh. In a draft letter dated 6 August 1829 to the Commissioners for Building New Churches he writes, "I strongly object to the proposed division of the living." He goes on to claim (echoing Musgrave) that the value of the living has been exaggerated, "one thousand acres (at the least) having been represented from the map as Great Tithes rec'd by the Vicar, all of which have been claimed by the owners of ancient grants… the above having been formerly woodland and having become arable." However the patrons, All Souls, had apparently already accepted the inevitability of reform gathering momentum in church and state.[239]

The division of resources finally decided upon was four ninths of tithe to the new ecclesiastical parish of Ilford, leaving five ninths to Barking. To achieve this it was considered necessary to deviate from the simple plan originally considered of combining the two wards of Great Ilford and Chadwell to form the new parish of St. Mary's, Ilford, leaving Barking Town and Ripple to constitute St. Margaret's parish, Barking. Instead, the portion of Chadwell ward south of the Green Lane and east of Goodmayes Lane was designated an ecclesiastical district still attached to St. Margaret's.[240]

Under the Poor Law Amendment Act of 1834, Barking civil parish became part of the Romford Union. At the end of 1838 the parish asked the Romford guardians to sanction another survey and valuation. The following year, in the face of keen competition, the contract was awarded to Frederick Drayson of Faversham who asked 8d per acre. It was stipulated that the plan should be divided into two parts according to the ecclesiastical divisions of the parish (Barking and Ilford) and it is highly probable that there was an unwritten intention that it should also be suitable for a tithe map under the Tithe Commutation Act 1836. It has been shown that this had already become a normal expectation amongst many Essex guardians when commissioning parish maps.[241] Certainly Drayson delivered his plan to the guardians by mid-1840 and the surviving copy 'No.2 Plan of the Ecclesiastical Parish of St Margaret's Barking', now in the archive of Valence House Museum, is marked "received Tithe Commission March 13 1841". Yet it was not until September 1842 that the Committee of Landowners of Barking finally agreed to pay the Romford guardians the £120 which they eventually asked for permission to copy it as a tithe map.[242]

There is reason to believe that a rival surveyor, Henry Crawter of Cobham, played a significant part in the negotiations. Crawter, with a London office, operated on a larger scale than Drayson, but had failed to obtain the original contract from the guardians. However, he secured a voice in the deliberations of the Committee of Landowners of Barking by acting as agent for the new vicar, Robert Liddell. In August 1842 Crawter offered to provide a cut-price alternative to the Drayson plan by revising Johnson's 1806 survey, "I have carefully examined the old map and have proved and tested the quantities by scaling several of the fields and I have found it correct… The cost of Making this Map shall be £75 – and the only extras… should be the Labourers to point out the occupancy of the Land. The Copies for the Tithe office should be made at the usual price of 2d per acre each."[243]

Only after protracted discussion with James Paulin, vice-chairman of the guardians and an influential member of the Barking Vestry, and the diplomatic intervention of the Assistant Tithe Commissioner, did the Committee of Landowners and the Board of Guardians agree upon a compromise price for Drayson's 1840 survey. Even so, it was Crawter who secured the contract for making the three official copies and he made certain that they bore his signature, not that of Drayson! In fact it would appear that the copies differed from the original only in the omission of detail; even the parcel numbers are the same as those introduced by Drayson. However, Drayson's map has his construction lines which are absent from Crawter's copies. The valuation was awarded to a Mr Boards of Edmonton, the same man who had completed the rate evaluation.[244]

It is curious to reflect how near the 1846 tithe commutation map of Barking came to being based upon a mid-17th century survey! As it stands this map does have one unusual feature which still links it to that early survey; in a number of instances fields are divided by broken lines which represent former field boundaries, usually those which continued to be the conjectural boundaries of tithings even though the original hedges or fences had been removed. A striking example of this is the broken line crossing Valentines Park dividing the southern portion of the park, which tithed to Ilford Hospital because it had once been parcel of Wyfields, from the northern portion which belonged to the Gaysham tithe circuit.[245] Since Johnson's map has not survived we cannot be certain whether this or the 1666 map (clearly still in existence at the time) was the immediate source for these conjectural lines.

It is to be remembered that the holdings in the 1847 schedule are listed primarily under the names of the landowners arranged in alphabetical order; the tenants of each holding are then listed under "Occupiers". This can be inconvenient to a modern researcher seeking particular tenants in the large volume without knowing the name of their landlord. The problem is even greater for those who seek a particular parcel of land whose number they have located on the map.

The penultimate column of the Barking tithe award schedule is headed "Names of Impropriators". The traditional names given to their respective tithings in previous surveys can only be discovered from the preceding text of the award; for convenience the names of tithings in 1847 with their corresponding owners are set out in table 2.[246]

The basic structure finally agreed is similar to that indicated by previous surveys, although there are some notable changes in the areas of tithings. Without detailed analysis it is impossible to say how far these were the result of the new survey or of the adjudication of conflicting claims. Moreover, surviving files of the Tithe Commission seldom record the arguments which were employed for and against such claims. But a cursory examination would suggest that the vicars of Barking and Ilford, now sharing the endowment, had lost some great tithe to lay impropriators and crown exemptions. Former Barking vicars, as we have seen, had anticipated this. The Master of Ilford Hospital seems also to have been a loser, and it is not clear whether these losses can be related to increases in the Eastbury and Westbury Circuits.

The claim by James Sharp, owner of Barking Mill, to the great and small tithes of nearly 13 acres of the mill's meadows probably derives from a sale by Gascoyne in 1795 of Mill Mead which included a quit-claim (release) of the great and small tithe due to Ilford Hospital out of this land.[247]

The award of the great and small tithes to a Joseph Perkins of Deptford arising from a small estate in Ilford parish, of which he himself was the landowner, demands more explanation. The bulk of this (22¾ acres, nos.1820-1822) was a smallholding south of Aldborough Hatch anciently called 'Whites', or 'Whitings', the tithes of which were formerly claimed by the Aldborough estate.[248] Presumably Perkins had acquired the title not only to Whites Farm but also to Whitings' tithes (in earlier times the vicar had taken the small tithe here, claiming that it was not covered by the composition/modus paid for the Aldborough estate). Perkin's further 4¾ acres (nos.1640-41) which lay in Seven Kings had been crown land and so exempt from tithe until sold off in 1817.[249] Or had Perkins, or a predecessor, actually purchased both of these small estates from the crown?[250]

This enquiry illustrates the importance of linking other types of document with the tithe material; a matter which will be considered further in subsequent chapters.

Table 2: Barking tithings and their owners in 1847

Tithing	Owner	Tithe type	Area
Vicar of Barking		Great and Small	747 acres
		Small	2,346 acres
Vicar of Ilford		Great and Small	786 acres
		Small	3,746 acres
Ilford Hospital	Marquis of Salisbury		
		Great and Small	1,467 acres
		Great	16 acres
		Small	124 acres
Demesne of Newbury	R. Benyon de Beauvoir		
		Great and Small (merged)	265 acres
Newbury Circuit		Great	1,291 acres
Demesne of Gaysham	John Wight		
		Great and Small	310 acres
Gaysham Circuit		Great	2,375 acres
Stonehall	Viscount Wellesley		
		Great	143 acres
Westbury Circuit	Wm. Murray (executor to James Cuff)		
		Great	1,052 acres
Eastbury Circuit	Fr., Hy & Hester Sterry		
		Great	1,614 acres
Wangey	(Lands owned by Samuel Pedley)		
		Exempt	c.68 acres
Uphall	(Lands owned by Richard Nixon)		
		Exempt	c.107 acres
Aldborough			
Aldborough Hatch & Bunting Bridge Estates	Fr., & Sam'l Stevens		
		Great and Small (merged)	194 acres
Perrymans & Shonks	Fr., & Sam'l Stevens		
		Great and Small	34 acres
Crown [mainly Aldborough House Estate][251]			
		Exempt	289 acres
Land parcel of former Abbey demesne inc. Abbey precincts & some marshes	(J.S.Thompson)		
		Exempt	133 acres
Nos.1820, 1821, 1822, 1640, 1641	J. Perkins		
		Great and Small	27a 2r 34p
Nos. 352, 353, 315 (Great & Little Mill Meadows, Saltings)	James Sharp		
		Great and Small	12a 3r 16p

Chapter six: Other Barking tithe related documents

Although the archives of institutions are more likely to survive than those of individual impropriators, the records of Ilford Hospital are less systematic and complete than those of the parish. However, amongst these are tithe surveys and other records much earlier than those remaining to the Vicar of Barking. The 'Tithe-list and Rental of the Hospital of St. Mary and St Thomas the Martyr of Great Ilford' has the double dating (in regnal years) of 1384-5 and 1401. Probably the earliest copy is that in the 'vellum book' at Hatfield House.[252] Another appears in the Valence House manuscript of Fisher v. Wite where the parchment was described as "copied out of a more ancient writing which was somewhat defaced". It was alleged by their opponents that the Fanshawes had pretended to have found it "in a cranye or crevis of a walle in the said Exchequer" (Thomas Fanshawe had been Queen's Remembrancer and his brother Godfrey a clerk of the Exchequer).[253] Little doubt now remains that the "ancient writing" in question was actually a lost cartulary of the Abbey of Barking, copied on the instruction of John Vaughan, former Master of Ilford Hospital, for the benefit of the Fanshawes.[254]

Fig. 13. Ilford Chapel and Almshouses, 1816. Founded c.1145 by Abbess Adelicia of Barking and well endowed with parish tithe. The chapel, enlarged in the 19th century, still exists today.

It is possible that the earliest tithe list was connected with the medieval dispute which cropped up again in 1450 between the hospital and Gaysham over certain tithes belonging to the former demesne manor of Emelingbury that had been absorbed by Gaysham in the 1390s.[255] It is only a list of lands by name, sometimes providing the acreage in round figures and, very occasionally, naming the tenant. Yet – as Bamber Gascoyne realised in the 18th century – many of these lands can ultimately be identified by correlation with the later hospital lists and then with the vicar's tithe books and map.

Another tithe list dated 1503 was also exhibited in the case of Fisher v. Wite. The schedule describes it as a rental "which maketh mention of divers farms & lands meadows & grounds and other tithes appertaining to the spitall of Ilforde." This is on similar lines, but also names tenants. Since no sums of money are indicated, it would appear that all tithe was then taken in kind.[256]

The transfer of the hospital to lay ownership following the Dissolution presaged fresh enquiries and disputes during the later 16th century. Even in the preceding centuries there is no evidence that Barking Abbey had used the endowments of the hospital to maintain the two priests and 13 poor or leprous brethren required by the agreement of 1219 and reiterated by the statutes of Bishop Stratford in 1346. An inquisition of 1397 had found but one chaplain and one poor man, and the chantry certificates reveal that there were still only two poor men and one priest in residence immediately following the Dissolution.[257] Indeed, it would appear there was only accommodation provided for two almsmen until several years after the crown grant of patronage of the hospital to Thomas Fanshawe in 1572. Then Thomas's brother Godfrey, whom he had appointed master, had four more houses built to increase the establishment to six as required by the terms of the royal grant.[258]

The failure of proprietors of the hospital to employ all the endowments in the maintenance of the poor was routinely criticised by opponents in tithe disputes. It may be suspected that much public criticism in Ilford was muted by the convenient provision of a minister and place of worship nearer than the parish church in Barking town. In effect, the chapel of the Ilford Hospital had become a chapel-of-ease, though it was never officially so designated.[259] During the Commonwealth it nearly became a parish church in the proposed threefold division of Barking parish.[260]

There is room for further research into the administration of the hospital during the Tudor period and subsequently; but throughout it was certainly the practice of masters to farm out the collection of tithes. Even after 1572, the profits seem to have been sufficient to warrant a patron, a master and a tithe-farmer. These profits are difficult to quantify; according to his will Henry Fanshawe paid £60 for a lease of the tithes about 1560, but when the hospital was sequestrated in the 1650s, the tithes were leased at £90 yearly and a bid of £120 was made in 1654.[261]

The Fanshawe interest had begun around 1560 when Henry Fanshawe purchased a lease of the hospital from Master Vaughan but retained Thomas Hopkins, who had been collecting Vaughan's tithes, as under-farmer. This arrangement was doubtless connected with the fact that Henry's first wife, Thomasina, whom he had married in 1554, was a Hopkins – possibly sister to Thomas Hopkins. Also, a new survey of rents and tithes belonging to the hospital made in 1560 may have influenced Fanshawe's decision.

Henry was the first Fanshawe to be appointed Queen's Remembrancer of the Exchequer, a prestigious office which nearly became an hereditary possession of the family. The Fanshawes became adept at maintaining a securely low profile in national affairs whilst using their positions as powerful royal officials to advance their local interests. So Thomas Fanshawe, nephew and heir of Henry, secured the patronage of the Ilford Hospital by royal grant in 1572 and installed his less able brother Godfrey as master, followed by Dr William Fisher in 1589 after Godfrey's death.

The Fanshawes tightening up on the collection of tithes provoked a series of disputes hard fought through ecclesiastical and royal courts, commencing in 1570 with a case concerning the tithes of Eastbury. In 1580 the Fanshawes used their influence to obtain a commission out of the Exchequer for an inquisition into the possessions of Ilford Hospital.[262] The 15 jurors empanelled and sworn seem to have had a fund of local knowledge. One of them, John Allen, "a man well experienced in learninge" had formerly farmed the hospital tithes and then become a tithe collector for the Vicar of Barking (copies of an undated 'Rentall of the Hospital of Ilford gathered by John Allen' survive in the Hatfield archive.)[263] Another juror, Thomas Stoddard, was married to the widow of Thomas Hopkins, Allen's predecessor. Several others were called as witnesses in tithe disputes. It is probable that they were selected as men likely to favour the Fanshawe cause, but they were not just tools. Godfrey Fanshawe was alleged to have got into such a violent argument with Allen about some item in the report that he threatened to draw his sword.[264] The allegations of disadvantaged opponents in subsequent legal disputes became increasingly desperate, characterising Fanshawe as a "frowarde, injuryous and mightye adversarye", claiming that the master and almsmen ought to be lepers, and purporting to show that the commission itself, as well as all previous surveys, was fraudulent and illegal.

The 1580 inquisition begins with a rental and continues with a tithe survey more comprehensive than any previous hospital tithe list. It not only names the tithable properties and tenants (sometimes also including previous tenants) but often endeavours to locate the property more accurately by giving abutments to neighbouring lands. In this respect it resembles contemporary manorial surveys rather than the 17th and 18th century tithe surveys described in previous chapters. For, although acreages are given in round figures for many properties, this is not a measured survey and there is no map or plan for reference. It must be admitted that a measured survey keyed to a map would have been a rarity at so early a date. Yet, curiously, one of the commissioners responsible for the 1580 inquisition was Israel Amyce, a pioneer of the cartographic survey.[265] Nor are valuations indicated for the tithes, although we know from the evidence given in these late Tudor disputes that the collectors sometimes arranged compositions.

There are some additions to the vellum book for the years before the Civil War and judgements in a couple of further Essex tithe disputes in the Court of Chancery (re. tithes of Warley in 1609 and of Claybury in 1621) are on record.[266] Otherwise little separate documentary material remains for the 17th century beyond deeds and lengthy abstracts of title. Although the Fanshawes had recovered possession of the hospital by 1656, following sequestration during the Civil War, financial constraints led them in 1669 to grant a lease for 1,000 years at a peppercorn rent as part of a mortgage deal.[267] Thus they lost effective control over future masters and there is no subsequent continuity of documentation. According to the Barking Vestry minutes an agreement was made with the master in 1681 to enable the parish to nominate when vacancies occurred in the almshouses (in return for exemption from parish rates), and it is said that the almshouses were rebuilt in 1719.[268]

However, in the first decade of the 18th century a major effort to recover tithes by legal action was made by Stephen Skinner who had become Master of Ilford Hospital in 1703. He began an action in the Court of Chancery in 1709 against nine tenants, including those of Claybury, Eastbury, Jenkins and Wyfields, and also against the vicar. A favourable judgement was obtained by 1711, but the legal costs must have been considerable.[269] The archives at Hatfield House include a number of documents of evidence in this case which could be of particular interest to the agricultural historian. The one concerning Wyfields details the cropping of every field from 1703 to 1708/9.[270]

This shows, for example, that on the acre of Upper Hoppet in 1706 turnips were grown upon which sheep were directly grazed, so fattening the sheep and at the same time fertilising the land to permit wheat in 1707. A similar novel practice of "some in Essex" was described in Houghton's *Collections on Husbandry and Trade* in 1694; the same small field was cropped with peas both in 1705 and 1708.[271]

Although the Gascoyne ownership of Ilford Hospital was not indisputably established until 1739, the executors of the above Stephen Skinner had assigned the mastership to Joseph Gascoyne, younger brother to Sir Crisp Gascoyne, in 1730. The new master was involved in another dispute in 1732 concerning tithe from Eastbury, Westbury and Loxford which appears to have turned upon methods of collection.[272]

Much of the early documentation of the hospital tithes was to prove of more interest to future historians than it was of immediate practical value to the new owners. The circumstances which, despite his inheritance of the foregoing archive, led the second Bamber Gascoyne at the end of the century to form an alliance with the vicar, Peter Rashleigh, were considered at length in the previous chapter.[273] The first fruits of this would seem to have been the 12 sketches, c.1790 and probably the copy of the companion to the vicar's map preserved in the Hatfield House archives. The ultimate result was the shared enterprise of the new tithe survey of 1805. This was no doubt to the direct benefit of the hospital and the church when compulsory commutation eventually took place. As far as we know only one other impropriator, the owner of Eastbury, had made even remotely comparable preparations.

Sufficient has been said in chapter three and elsewhere concerning the medieval origins of the Eastbury demesne tithing and the Eastbury tithe circuit and the many disputes to which these gave rise from the 16th to the 18th centuries. The survival in the Essex Record Office of some later documentation was partly due to the Commissioners of Sewers, responsible for the walls and drainage of the Thames-side marshes (Eastbury has sometimes been called 'the manor of the marshes'), and partly to the Sterry family, Romford solicitors, who owned the property for several decades prior to tithe commutation.

Three maps of Eastbury tithing, made for Mary Weldale when owner, are now preserved with those of the Commissioners of Sewers. The earliest of them shows Eastbury upland tithing (that part of the Eastbury tithe circuit lying to the north of the Ripple Road and stretching up to Green Lane, Goodmayes) by William Wyeth in 1735.[274] The second, by Nathaniel Hill in 1742, is virtually a copy of the first.[275] The third, also by Hill and dated 1742, covers the Eastbury marshland tithing in the south of Ripple.[276] All three are apparently based on the vicar's tithe map of 1666 (although the draughtsmanship is inferior) and the fields are numbered accordingly in black, with a red figure also which refers to "the Table", a terrier now missing. The names of tenants are on the map and ownership indicated by colour, but no farm or field names and no acreages are shown. However, the Sterry collection contains a schedule dated 1775 employing these red parcel numbers, listing the names on the maps as "Late owners and Tenants" alongside "Present Owners and Tenants" and supplying acreages and "Names of Closes".[277] It is evident from the preparations for a tithe dispute in 1752 that Mary Weldale was already placing the same reliance on the "authentick evidence" of the vicar's tithe map and tithe books as Bamber Gascoyne did in the 1790s.[278]

A fourth map is dated 1831 and covers the whole tithing of Eastbury, as well as the house and estate. It was made for Wasey Sterry and Henry Sterry by H. Walter.[279] It is a well executed map on a scale of 10" to the mile, but the parcel numbers refer to a schedule no longer extant and there is no means of ascertaining whether the map owes anything to Johnson's missing map survey of 1805-6. Nor does the map give field names or acreages. However, it does give the names of tenants and clearly indicates the boundaries of their holdings; major farm-houses are also named. Land use is indicated by colouring and tree symbols. The strips are carefully delineated in the open or common fields of Ripple and their occupants clearly named.

No other impropriators have left separate tithe surveys, accounts or even lists so far as is known at present. However the tithe circuit of Westbury in 1596 is described by an interrogatory on behalf of Thomas Fanshawe in a tithe dispute in his Court of Exchequer versus Vicar Wignall, All Souls College and the farmer of Westbury.[280] In form this resembles the hospital tithe lists of that period – useful if employed in conjunction with other documents.

This chapter seems the appropriate place to deal with that interesting survey of 1617, mentioned above in chapter four, since it reaches us as an interpolation in Cartwright's tithe book. Whilst it is not itself a tithe document, it was considered worthwhile to insert a complete copy after the tithe surveys of 1669-81 and then to meticulously cross reference it to these by adding the corresponding parcel numbers used on the vicar's tithe map of 1666.

This proves a valuable instrument to the historian since it creates a bridge between this comparatively early parish map and still earlier surveys and rentals (which will be considered in the following chapter). So useful is it in this respect that one wonders if the person responsible might have been motivated by antiquarian, as well as more practical, interests. It is undoubtedly the work of an educated man, and one who showed the detailed knowledge of local topography and tenures that might be expected of an experienced tithe or rate collector.

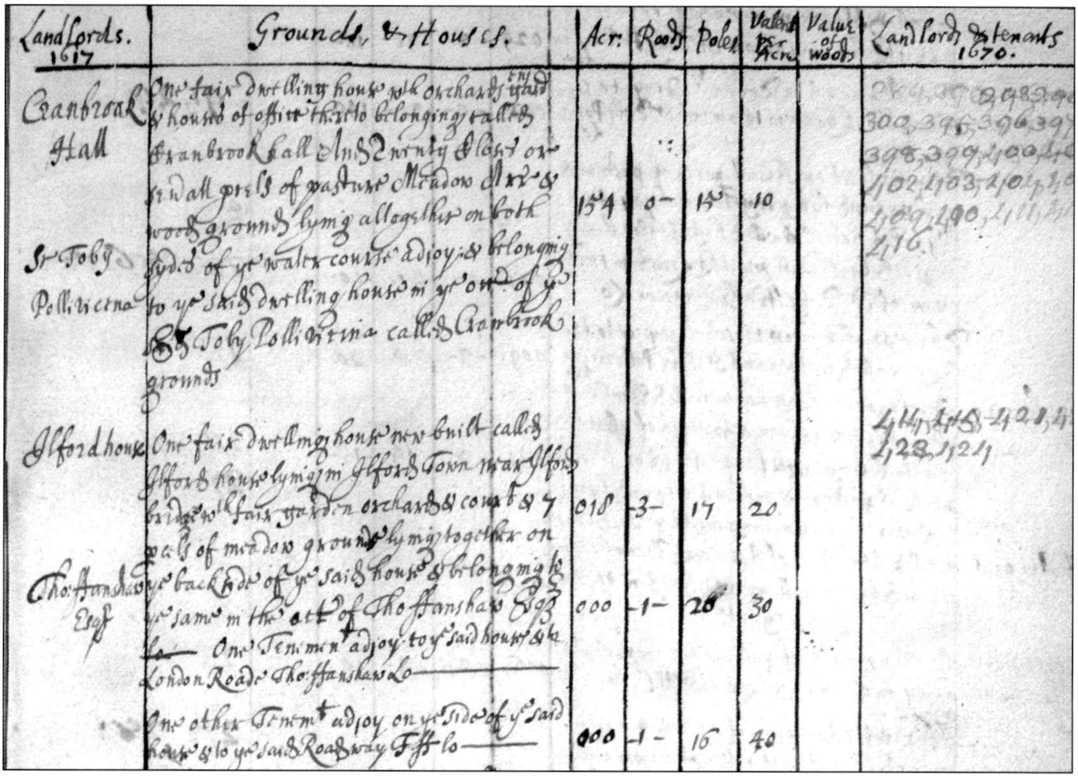

Landlords. 1617	Grounds, & Houses.	Acr:	Roods	Poles	Value p Acre	Value of woods	Landlords & tenants 1670.
Cranbrook Hall / Sr Toby Pallavicino	One fair dwelling house with orchards yard & houses of office thereto belonging called Cranbrook hall and [illegible] parcels of pasture Meadow [illegible] wood grounds lying allogether on both sides of ye water course adjoyning & belonging to ye said dwelling house in ye occ. of ye Sr Toby Pallavicina called Cranbrook grounds	154	0-	15	10		[illegible] 300, 396, 396, 39[illegible] 398, 399, 400, 4[illegible] 402, 403, 404, 4[illegible] 409, 410, 411, 4[illegible] 416
Ilford house	One fair dwelling house new built called Ilford house lying in Ilford Town near Ilford bridge with fair garden orchards courts & 7 parcels of meadow ground lying together on	018	3-	17	20		414, 415, 421, 4[illegible] 428, 424
Tho: Fanshawe Esqr	ye backside of ye said house & belonging to ye same in the occ. of Tho: Fanshawe Esqr	000	1-	20	30		
	One Tenement adjoyning to ye said house & ye London Road Tho: Fanshawe Lo—						
	One other Tenement adjoy on ye side of ye said house & to ye said Roadway Ffs lo—	000	1 -	16	40		

Fig. 14. Survey of Barking Parish within the Forest, 1617, p.1 (copy c. 1670; ERO D/P81/3/110, rear). Entries for Cranbrook Hall Estate (Sir Toby Pallavicino) and Ilford Hall (Thomas Fanshawe Esq.). Note that the last column, although headed "Landlords and Tenants 1670", has been used for the addition of identifying parcel numbers from the 1666 parish tithe map (and so creating a backward linkage of great value to historians). In some cases, later tenants were faintly pencilled in, as in the case of "Tho. Beacon Gent", tenant of Ilford House from 1692.

The parcel numbers were added subsequently to the text; but it is not certain that they were added by the same person who made this copy.

Entitled "The Surveigh & Admeasurement of that part of the Parish of Barking w'ch lyeth in the Forrest of Waltham taken by Vertue of His Ma'tyes Commission under the great Seale of England directed to Otto Nicholson Esq. & others. Anno Dni. 1617', it covered those parts of Great Ilford and Chadwell wards of Barking (and of Chadwell Heath in Dagenham parish) which lay north of the Romford Road.[281] The author has argued elsewhere that it was originally part of an abortive scheme by the crown to raise revenue by fining landowners within the royal forest for supposed encroachments by themselves and their ancestors. The survey was probably prepared by Robert Tresswell as Surveyor General of Woods.[282] Although a measured survey, it appears to have assumed the older form of a verbal description (like a manorial survey) rather than the type of cartographic survey of which Tresswell's father had been a pioneer, a point considered further below.

In all probability, Cartwright had been able to borrow a copy, if not the original survey, from Thomas Fanshawe and he, or his helpers, had set it out in columns, adding one for "Landlords and Tenants 1670", which it was subsequently decided could be more usefully employed for identifying the properties by the new numerical references. Another copy, although found amongst the records of the manor, is unlikely to be the original because the last column is headed "Landlords and tenants 1730" and this time an attempt was made to use it for the purpose indicated.

The 1617 survey covers 22 closely written pages of foolscap and describes the area in considerable detail giving the landlord, description of "Grounds & Houses" (including some indications of land use), acreage, and "Value per Acre" of every holding. Even small tenements are included and the names of farms and lands are frequently given, yet this is not a detailed field-book and a number of adjoining closes on a single estate may be grouped together. Take one entry from the second page as an example –

> Beehive. One fayr dwelling house called Beehive w'th orchards & garden & houses of office therto belonging & four Closes or sev(er)all p(ar)cells of pasture & meadow grounds lying together adjoy' & belonging to ye said house called little Beagles being severed by severall prickt lines in the occ. of – Fuller gent.
>
> 33 Acres 3 Roods 14 Poles.Val. per Acre 15

Apparently the tenants named were landlords and not necessarily occupiers; "in the occ[upation] of" seems to be only a standard form. The reference in this particular example to the division of closes "by severall prickt lines" clearly implies the existence of an earlier map. Other evidence suggests that in all probability this map was one made by Robert Tresswell during the preceding year in connection with another survey of the area ordered by the crown "for discovering of divers lands wrongfully detained and concealed from us within the precinctes of that Mannor [of Barking]".[283] This does not seem to have been completed; but a "plotte" [map], was certainly "ruffe made" although no longer extant, and 'A Rentall made and taken [out of] the Booke of Survey of His Maj's Mannor of Bark[ing] in Essex agreeable to a Plott of two parts therof taken Ao 1616' has survived, albeit in an unfinished form, amongst the manorial records now in the Essex Record Office.[284]

Obviously, Cartwright could also have borrowed this 1616 rental from Fanshawe, and it is conceivable that Cartwright and associates could have used the "plotte" of 1616, if it had survived until then, to assist in referencing the 1617 survey to their map of 1666.

More significantly for the researcher of today, the 1616 rental, though skeletal in comparison, covers all the rest of the manor not covered by the 1617 survey. It takes the form of a detailed field-book, although in many instances the only information this contains about a field or house, apart from owner, is acreage and number on the lost "plotte"; paradoxically this rental did not progress as far as recording the rent. However, the numbers are in a topographical sequence (as are those of the 1666 map) and given time and patience it might be possible to reconstruct much of the map and import additional information from near-contemporary manorial records indicated in the next chapter. One curious fact is that where the 1616 rental and the 1617 survey do cover the same area, acreages fail to tally exactly, although apparently measured by the same surveyor.

The rental of 1616 has a full index of owners at the front with some attempt to indicate whether their lands were freehold, copyhold or both. Another useful feature at the end is 'A Rental of his ma[jes]ties Towne of Barking… taken out of the Plott of Survey there of 1617', with numbers from 1 to 163, each covering from one to three dwellings, stating the names of most of the tenants, although no rents or other information is included. This is perhaps a convenient point to mention that one limitation of the tithe records is their omission of most town houses; presumably because their gardens, when existent, produced little that was titheable.

Chapter seven: Some documents complementary to Barking tithe surveys

This chapter will consider a selection of other documents which may usefully be employed in conjunction with the tithe and tithe-related documents described above.

Maps

Users of tithe records will not need to be told that maps can be important historical documents. As explained in the opening chapters, following the Tithe Commutation Act of 1836 every parish not covered by a previous enclosure act required a tithe award map, and these are often the first large scale maps of a parish (as distinct from individual estates privately surveyed). Even in parishes like Barking where earlier field maps do exist, award maps provide a standard of reference for any further investigation, including a unique field number.[285] Experience from parishes like Barking suggests that, except where extensive enclosure has occurred, most field boundaries remain the same. Nineteenth century fields are often combinations or divisions of earlier fields, so, with appropriate modifications, these parcel numbers can still be used for identification in previous centuries.[286]

However tithe award maps for different parishes vary a great deal in scale and in the type and amount of detail which they show. The Barking tithe commutation map of 1846 is six chains to the inch, or 13.3 inches to the mile (1:4732).[287] It could be termed an outline field map, since hardly any names are shown on the map itself; all such detail has to be sought in the written schedule of apportionments under the parcel number. Even then the information may prove inadequate for the purpose; on occasion even the name of the farm is omitted. Comparison is required with the maps of general record published by the Ordnance Survey. Fortunately, the first large scale maps of the Ordnance Survey were produced not many years later. The county of Essex was completely surveyed at 25 inches to the mile between 1862 and 1876, and maps at that scale and at six inches to the mile were published. The sheets covering Barking parish were among the first. The only major change in the landscape which took place between 1846 and 1862 was the disafforestation in 1851.

The coloured versions of this first series of the 25 inch (1:2500) are superb maps (works of art, as well as of science) and the Valence Library is fortunate to possess a full set covering the whole of Barking, Ilford and Dagenham. The portrayal of detail, both natural and man-made, is remarkable. Individual trees are shown in their correct position; buildings are accurately depicted in plan and coloured red if made of stone or brick, grey or black if made of wood or iron; farms and other large or prominent buildings are named, as are roads and various natural features.

Field boundaries are shown with great accuracy and fields numbered (but not named). Books of reference, or parish area books, were published for each parish giving the area of each parcel and the land use (in general terms e.g. arable, pasture, etc.). These books of reference name neither farms nor fields, nor owners or occupiers, and Barking has a separate and non-sequential series of parcel numbers for each of the four wards (rendering them much less useful for general identification than the tithe apportionment numbers).[288]

The six inch to the mile (1:10,560) maps were a black and white photographic reduction from the 25 inch with names rewritten, field numbers omitted, and contours added (the 25 inch has only spot heights). So both maps can act as a check and a complement to the tithe maps. This is particularly important in respect of areas now extensively urbanised.

The six inch scale provides enough detail for most research purposes and photocopies from the first series Ordnance Survey six inch (1:10,560) map make convenient base maps for entering data from the 1847 tithe award and from earlier sources for purposes of comparison. In Barking the 1666 vicar's tithe map and subsequent surveys spring to mind. Furthermore, in areas now built-up, the base maps can be photocopied again to make transparent overlays for use with fairly recent editions of the six inch map. Although a different projection was employed on later Ordnance Survey six inch maps it will be found that, within the area of a single parish, only minor adjustments are required for effective superimposition.

A little more difficulty may be experienced with the very latest editions because in 1970 the Ordnance Survey began use metric scale of 1:10,000 which is closer to 6.3 inches to the mile. Nevertheless, David Hall in his book *Medieval Fields* recommended it for field sketching in rural parishes for subsequent comparison with historical data.[289]

The smallest scale map showing field boundaries ever published by the Ordnance Survey is the 2¼ inches to the mile (1:25,000), introduced in the 1940s. F.D. Hartley used an outline edition in the 1950s to record the land use data from the parish tithe apportionments over a wide area of the Cotswolds.[290] The author has experimented with base maps created by photographic reduction to this scale from Old Series six inch maps. The resultant clutter of fine detail was difficult to interpret. However, density can be reduced in copying and since large areas can be covered by a single sheet, overall patterns can be readily observed and areas such as farms shaded or coloured.

Types of written document

It is helpful to make a broad division between those types of record which, like tithe documents, deal primarily with occupiers, and those which, like manorial and estate documents, deal primarily with landlords or owners (though some tenants, being owner-occupiers, fall into both categories). Legally, occupancy could be more easily established than ownership – a term which, when unqualified, is legally imprecise. For example, for some purposes leaseholders or copyholders could be regarded as owners if tenants for life. However, we are familiar with tiers of 'ownership', and although many householders today own the freehold of their property, much agricultural land is still held on a two-tier system where the occupier is a tenant-farmer holding his land by lease from a landowner who owns the freehold. Subletting is also possible, so even the leaseholder is not necessarily the occupier.[291] Before radical changes were made in land law in the 19th and early 20th centuries the position could be even more complicated with forms of tenure surviving from feudal times.

Hearth tax lists and rate books, like tithe documents, were mainly concerned with occupiers who bore the legal liability to pay such forms of taxation. Manorial documents in the narrowest sense deal almost exclusively with freeholders and copyholders who owed dues and services to a lord of the manor; but estate documents also include leaseholders paying ordinary rents. It can be peculiarly useful to find records which, like some late 18th century land tax records, or mid-19th century tithe awards, link landlord and tenant, ownership and occupancy, in the same document; sadly, these are less common than might at first be imagined.

Taxation records: hearth tax and parish rates

Hearth tax lists survive for Barking for 1662, 1664 and 1665 and extensive correlation is possible between the 1669 tithe survey and the returns for the hearth tax of 1671.[292] The tax return is generally a test of residency but, if estimates of population are in question, a notional multiplier is required since only one resident paid tax per dwelling, just as only one occupier was liable for the tithe of each property. The tithe survey makes it possible to locate the actual residence of a great many hearth tax payers; the remainder being mainly landless town dwellers (professionals, shopkeepers and craftsmen) who do not figure in most tithe records because their profits were liable only to uncollectable personal tithe. With some exceptions, the number of hearths paying tax throws light on the relative size of houses and can be employed, like the rateable values considered below, in estimating the wealth structure of a community.

Poor rates and church rates were charged upon the occupiers of houses and lands, and also upon owners of tithe (appropriators and impropriators) in a parish, but not upon landlords as such. The keeping of rate books listing the names of those liable, together with their assessments, was a legal liability upon the churchwardens and overseers of the poor. An almost complete series of rate books survives for the parish of Barking from 1737 onwards. There are often two parallel sets because the overseers for each of the four wards made their own working copies in addition to the general rate books which covered the whole parish. The ward copies, usually soft-covered exercise books, have not survived like the well-bound master copies, but they are able to fill most of the few gaps in the series of the latter. They are also easier to handle than the hardback volumes, each of which covers several years.[293]

Nevertheless, consulting rate books can be a tedious process. Each time a new poor rate was decreed by the parish vestry, fresh lists of ratepayers had to be drawn up even though there might have been few changes to record. This could happen up to four times a year by the end of the 18th century. The historian seeking, for example, to date changes in tenancy may need to run through a number of years at a sitting. Moreover, on the face of it a single rate book provides no more information than the average tithe account book: the ratepayer's name, possibly (by no means invariably) the name of his house or farm and acreage in round figures, a valuation (assessment) and the rate charged. So it is often necessary to depend upon a set order of entries and to call upon other sources. Fortunately the order of entries (probably based originally upon the most convenient itinerary for a collector) seldom changes between successive rate books, and the valuation usually remains a constant.

Even more fortunately there are close links with tithe records. As already noted, the 1750 tithe survey parallels contemporary rate books in respect of the division of wards and even the order of entries. Furthermore, the rateable values of all properties are shown on the left-hand pages of that tithe survey. It should be acknowledged that the tenant-occupier of land was not invariably resident in the parish. In other words, someone living elsewhere could be liable for rates or tithe; such persons are grouped together in the rate books under the title of 'landholders'.

In the period between the opening of the 19th century and the tithe award, the links between rate and tithe records become even closer. The new tithe survey carried out by Johnson in 1805-6 was quickly followed by a new rate survey in 1807 made by Skinner and Lugar, who employed Johnson's map references. Although this has disappeared, yet another rate survey and valuation made in 1829 by Romford surveyor Twyford is extant in the Valence Museum local history collection. This comprises two substantial bound volumes, the first of which is a terrier and the other the valuation (somewhat confusingly called 'Valuation Terrier'). The first volume refers to Johnson's map and uses his numbers, field names and acreages; the latter further describes the situation of each property. Used together and in combination with the volume of Johnson's 1805-6 tithe survey (also in the Valence collection), these present the investigator with a valuable research tool despite the loss of Johnson's map. Furthermore, if copies of the earlier 1750 tithe survey and the later tithe award can be consulted simultaneously, it is possible to identify most properties and many constituent fields on the 1846 commutation map. If an investigation justifies a thorough search of rate books and tithe accounts, the 1829 rate survey is a good point from which to work backwards.

The 1829 terrier has an index of occupiers and this first comprehensive rate survey to survive includes small town houses not included in the early tithe surveys, and small cottage properties usually omitted from earlier rate books. Reasons for the former omission have already been mentioned; the latter requires more explanation. It would appear that in general no attempt had been made to collect rates from poor cottagers who were tenants-at-will paying their landlords only a small weekly rent. But in 1819 the Barking Vestry decided to adopt the new Sturges

Bourne Act which permitted them to levy a rate on the landlord based upon the estimated annual value of such cottage property. Accordingly, the 1821 rate book includes lists of cottages showing both "Owners or Lessors" and "Occupiers". But over the next 15 years there was periodical defiance from owners of cottage property and a number of court cases resulted until the Barking Vestry secured the private Act for the Better Assessing and Collecting the Poor and Other Rates of the Parish of Barking.[294]

'Other rates' included the church rates which were only levied when St Margaret's was in need of repairs. Normally a church rate book holds no more information than a contemporary poor rate book. The church rate book for Barking parish in 1843 is exceptional because the parcel number from the later tithe award map was added to many entries.[295]

At this point it must be observed that, unlike some earlier 19th century sources indicated above (particularly the 1829 rate survey), the tithe award of 1847 frequently omits the names of small occupiers, grouping them together under "sundry". In such cases the only resort for an investigator may be to consult the census returns for 1841 and 1851 in the hope that the particular properties can be located and that their occupiers remained resident for several years.

Some local and family historians already familiar with the cognate process of linking households enumerated in these early censuses with actual buildings on the tithe map will readily agree with Adrian Henstock of the Nottinghamshire Record Office, "depending on circumstances it may be found that no more than one in four or even six households can be placed with certainty at first, but, having once established these 'hooks', the remainder can be pinned up in between".[296] Such 'hooks' may include farms and public houses; but complementary evidence like the annotated 1843 church rate book for Barking is nothing short of a gift to the researcher.

Taxation records: subsidies and land tax

Besides hearth taxes, some other forms of direct taxation resulted in local assessment lists that may interlock with rate and tithe books. 1798 land tax lists survive for all areas in the Public Record Office and local collections. In contrast, the survival of earlier tax lists (like tithe books) depends on luck. A miscellany of late 17th century assessments for parishes in Becontree and Chafford Hundreds has survived amidst the papers of the Harvey-Mildmay family and of William Holcroft in the Essex Record Office.[297] One is for the first land tax in the Ilford ward of Barking in 1698 containing around 60 names. Legal liability to pay land tax was more complicated than poor rates; in practice the tenant-occupier paid this tax also, but a leaseholder could deduct it from his rent to a landlord liable as 'proprietor'.

Earlier tax lists are extant for Barking Town (c.100 names), Ilford (c.120 names) and Chadwell (c.80 names) for the 'royal aid' or subsidy of 1664-5; and also for Ilford (c.100 names) and Ripple (c.33 names) for subsidies in 1655-58 during the Commonwealth. Holcroft has short lists of those paying on 'land' and 'goods' for all Barking wards in 1663-4.[298] Many servants and even some labourers were assessed on 'goods' for the subsidy collected between 1522 and 25.[299] There are around 256 names for Barking Town and Abbey, 81 for Ilford, 48 for Chadwell and 34 for Ripple. Though this last cannot link with tithe lists, it is fairly close in time to the 1540 minister's accounts noted below. A subsidy list of 1327 is mentioned below in connection with pre-Restoration manorial records.

Parish registers, vestry minutes and wills

The parish registers of St Margaret's, Barking are complete from 1558 except for the usual gap during the Commonwealth.[300] The Barking Vestry minutes are virtually complete from 1666 to 1926.[301] Most readers will be familiar with parish registers, so there is no need here to describe form or content. They are akin to taxation records insofar as most of those named in them are, or were, resident in the parish and it is often possible to distinguish those who are not from within the record itself. Tithe records may then supply the place of residence of the family.[302]

With even greater probability, those listed in vestry minutes as attending meetings or serving as parish officers can be identified as householders normally resident in the parish and possible tithe payers. In chapter four it may be recollected that attendance at the Barking Vestry was used to establish periods of residence of Richard Taylor and Curate John Chisenhall. Periodic lists of parishioners on poor relief are another useful feature of the earlier Barking Vestry minutes.

As with parish registers, many readers will have some familiarity with wills and realise that they state the parish in which the testator is resident. Their links with the registers are obvious and sometimes where matters of inheritance are concerned there are also links with manorial court rolls. Since even small landholders usually made wills, their names are frequently to be found in contemporary tithe records together with other parishioners named as legatees and executors, whilst witnesses may be close neighbours. Where available, probate inventories add valuable socio-economic detail, but Barking is deficient in this class of record.

Broadly speaking, the wills are very well indexed. The bulk of Barking wills from the Archdeaconry of Essex now at the Essex Record Office are included in Dr Emmison's three volume index *Wills at Chelmsford* which runs from 1401 to 1858, and he published the Essex wills themselves for the Elizabethan period in another nine volumes. The many volumes of the British Record Society's Index Library, now in the Public Record Office, cover those involving property in more than one diocese under the jurisdiction of Canterbury.

There is also a group of 15th and 16th century Barking wills in the archives of the Guildhall Library to which even the usual guide, Anthony Camp's *Wills and Their Whereabouts*, fails for once to point clearly. This group, which also includes some wills for Dagenham, East and West Ham and Chigwell, were those registered by the Commissary Court of the Bishop of London (London

Division). The British Record Society has published an index to these under the editorship of Marc Fitch.

Post-Restoration manorial and estate records[304]

The manor of Barking, though larger than most, was a 'text-book' manor in respect of its administration and compact geographical structure. Its area corresponded conveniently with that of the two parishes of Barking and Dagenham (apart from two small discrepancies, one on the eastern boundary of Dagenham and a second, still smaller one, on the south-west of Barking).[305]

The manorial map of Barking 1652-3, mentioned above as the parent of the vicar's tithe map, survived in the Hulse family archives into the 19th century, although it was most probably in a poor state of repair when existing extracts were made.[306] These few extracts are, however, sufficient to plug most gaps of the in the surviving 18th century copy of the derivative parish tithe map. A 1663 manorial rental, which survived into the 19th century when Sage was able to copy some extracts now in the Essex Record Office, is also missing.[307] From 1679 onwards the

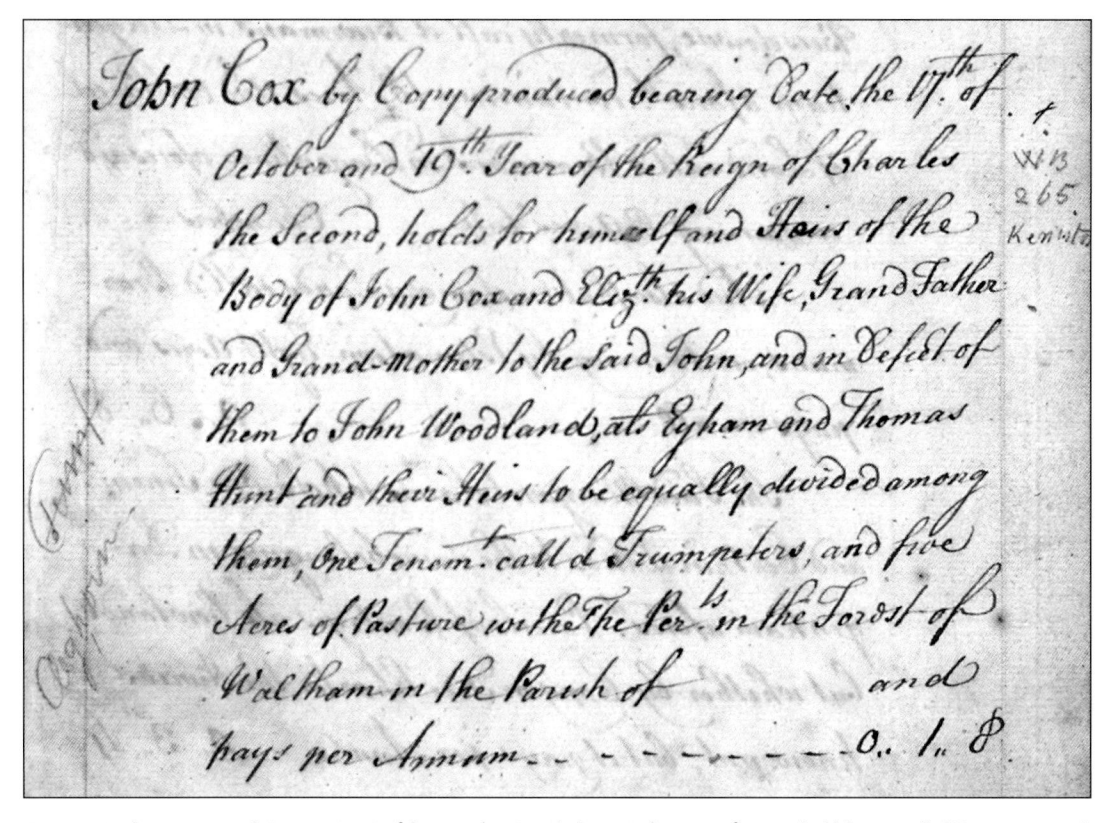

Fig. 15. Barking Manorial Survey, 1679, folio 67 (ERO D/Dhs M31). Entry for copyhold house called Trumpeters and five acres enclosed from the forest. Note that former tenants are named in the 'copy'.

Barking manorial records in the Essex Record Office are virtually complete. A manorial survey of 1679 and a rental of 1726, themselves linked by cross-references, are almost contemporaneous with tithe surveys.

The 1679 survey of the manor of Barking has come down in the form of a transcript from the original Latin made towards the middle of the 18th century, to which marginal cross-references to the 1726 rental were added in pencil.[308] The original Court of Survey was held in September 1679 by Edward Northey, Steward of the Manor to Sir Thomas Fanshawe, at the time when Thomas Cartwright was planning the second tithe survey which finally appeared in 1681.[309] This opens up the distinct possibility of identifying an estate in both tithe and manorial surveys, but whereas every Barking estate detailed in the manorial survey must appear somewhere in the tithe survey and on the tithe map, the reverse might not be true since, by the late 17th century, not all lands within the geographical boundaries of the parish necessarily came within the purview of the Manor Court. Each entry gives the name of the tenant and the class of tenure; "by Free Charter" (freehold), or "by Copy of Court Roll" (copyhold). This is followed by a fairly detailed description of the property and finally the quit-rent owed. There is an index "alphabetically digested" of around 283 tenants.

In the case of a copyhold the description is (by definition) that entered in the rolls of the Manor Court whenever an 'admission' or 'surrender' took place. It followed a formula which included the name of the property, with various other details such as location, area and abuttals, and even the names of some previous tenants with the date of admission of the last. On every occasion the previous entry was carefully copied, usually altering only the name of the last tenant and date of admission. Thus a copyhold title can include information, even names of 'sometime' tenants, preserved for centuries.

A Barking copyhold typically comprised a 'yardland' (a 'virgate'), the customary area of which was 16 acres.[310] The customary local virgate frequently varied from the 30 acres quoted as standard in textbooks. The warning that a virgate is a "quantity of land differing according to the place or county; as at Wimbledon… it is but 15 acres, in other counties it is 20, in some 24, in others 30 or 40" has been attributed to the 13th century lawyer, Bracton.[311] It could differ even in adjacent localities; Havering, for example, had an extraordinarily large virgate of 120 acres.[312]

The description of a freehold was generally taken from the owner's title deeds (the charter was usually a legal fiction) and the amount of information given varied widely, it could sometimes be more meagre than for copyholds. In both, the quit-rents may appear remarkably small in relation to the acreage of the property, but, as in the parallel case of the tithe modus, these amounts had been fixed long before the inflation of the 16th and 17th centuries and the lord of a manor had no legal powers to increase them in line with real market value. It should be noted that Barking copyholds were hereditary, as was probably the case in most Essex manors.

Sometimes the tenant named is also the occupier, and in some other instances the occupier is actually named. In these cases it should not be too difficult to identify the lands in the tithe survey. In other cases the name, and even details such as area, may assist recognition.

The cross-references in the margin of this manorial survey to pages in the 1726 rental are all prefixed with the letters 'W.B.'[313] It is to be supposed that this stood for 'William's Book', properly described as a 'Rental of the estate of the Hon. Sir William Humfreys, 1726'.[314] Sir Thomas Fanshawe's grand-daughter, Susan Noel, had sold the lordship and estates in Barking and Dagenham to Sir William Humfreys in 1717.[315] The rental is more structured than the survey, being divided into sections in each of which the tenants are entered alphabetically.

One section lists "Quitrents" with each property briefly described. The same tenants reappear in the sections headed "Copyholders" and "Freeholders" where there are fuller descriptions of the properties. A cross-reference is given to the tenant in 1679 by name and page; although since the page indicated is not that in the transcript, it must refer to the original survey, presumably still available in 1726. These sections also contain a few properties in the manors of Jenkins and

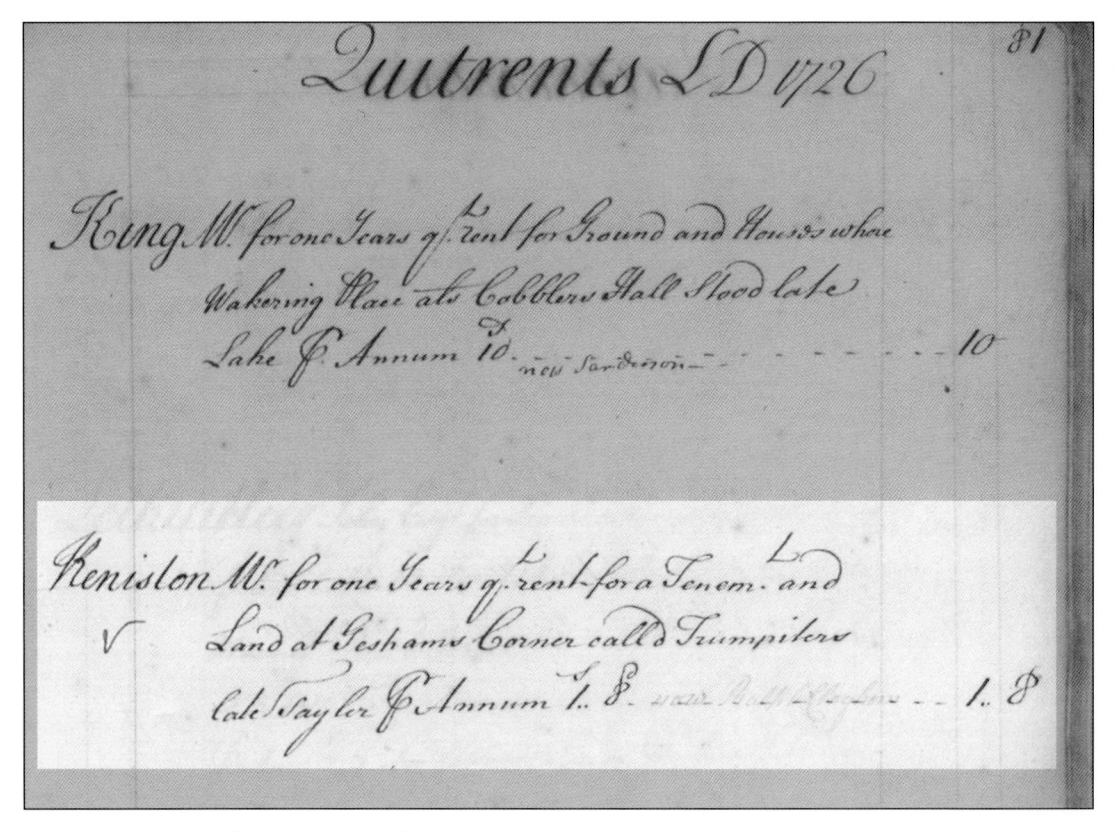

Fig. 16. Estate Rental of Sir William Humfreys, 1726, p. 81 (ERO D/DHs E2). The name Trumpeters and the quit-rent of 1s.8d shows Keniston holds property held by Cox in 1679. Geashams Corner was a loop in the forest fence north of Fulwell Hatch and Trumpeters, site of the Maypole Hotel.

Fulks which are not listed in 1679. Of greater importance are two other sections which list leasehold properties, and which are entitled "Farm Rents" and "Reserved Rents".

Farm rents were for those parts of the demesne leased out, often as substantial farms. These included former copyholds which had fallen into the hands of the lord, merged into the demesne and then been re-let as leaseholds at new rents approximating to market value.[316] There is an interesting appendix of some dozen pages at the rear of the rental giving a more detailed breakdown of some of these leasehold farms, with annual values and the acreage of individual fields. The names of occupiers are also shown where subletting was taking place. Some subsequent purchasers are noted down to 1784. Reserved rents were those received mainly for cottages with small parcels of land enclosed from roadside waste. The normal lease for such cottages was 21 years at a rent of five shillings per annum. These small enclosures may be subsequent and additional to those shown on the 1666 tithe map. In some cases changes of tenancy are indicated. This 1726 rental is almost contemporary with the tithe survey of 1727-28 and the amount of information concerning tenant-occupiers facilitates correlation with the tithe records.

There are no further manorial surveys or rentals as comprehensive as this after 1726. Yet the account of fines 1705-1741 is a peculiarly useful volume (despite the absence of an index) because it extracts all the admissions to copyholds from successive court rolls during these years. The customary descriptions of the properties are given, former and new tenants named, with the quit-rent and fine on admission.[317] Changes in tenancy can be followed and sometimes wills and other family events affecting inheritance can be dated.

Thereafter, manorial record coverage is patchy for a period – perhaps because the lordship was divided between the daughters of Sir Orlando Humfreys and their husbands. In 1754 Smart Lethieullier (a distinguished antiquarian of Huguenot descent, who already owned several estates in Barking) bought the manor and there are rentals extant for 1755, 1757 and 1760. These list alphabetically all copyhold tenants with their quit-rents and some with brief details to identify their properties. Also over 70 cottage tenants are named at the rear under reserved rents with dates of leases; and the 1760 rental has a brief note of the location of each cottage. So, although there is also a gap in the tithe records after 1733, the survey of 1750 ensures that tithe and manorial records can still complement each other around the mid-18th century. From 1788, after the Hulse family had taken over, annual rentals survive.[318]

The court rolls themselves are available for every year from 1679, but present a more formidable problem to the researcher, comparable in a way to consulting the rate books, with the additional difficulty that they are in Latin until 1733. Yet they do contain information beyond the routine surrenders and admissions to copyholds, sometimes including details of family relationships and even contents of wills. The task of consulting the court and minute books (the actual form taken by the rolls) is made easier after 1764 by an index volume covering the years 1764 to

1856 (in which the 1838-56 volume is lettered 'A' and so on back to 1764-82 which is lettered 'F').[319]

The Essex Record Office holds the Hulse family archives which include many more useful Barking documents than can be detailed here. The D/DHs T series at the Record Office contains deeds of estates in Barking, Dagenham and neighbourhood, from large farms to small properties, copyhold and leasehold, some with field names and plans dating from the 17th to the 19th centuries. The Essex Record Office catalogue (Seax) gives particulars. The D/DHs E series contains over 160 leases mainly from the 18th and early 19th centuries, some of large farms such as Loxford, Longbridge and Wangey Hall with field names, and many of cottages on roadside waste. Generally these reserved rents are also listed in a schedule and abstract of leases of wasteland and cottages 1773-1811, which also contains a list of tenants in 1834. Such small properties may also be sought in the tithe survey of 1805-6, the 1821 rate book and the 1829 rate survey.

Pre-Restoration manorial and estate records

Many places are better served than Barking in respect of early court rolls and cognate documents. The royal manor of Havering for example has a detailed extent for 1250, another for 1352/3, court rolls for the latter date and then in a fairly continuous series from 1380; all of which have been put to good use in the works of Professor Marjorie McIntosh.[320] It is interesting to note that the Havering extent of 1352/3 includes even subtenants of subtenants, so that unlike the usual manorial survey, it probably includes most occupiers in the manor.[321]

Apart from extracts concerning the appointment of tithe collectors in the Middle Ages mentioned in chapter three, a Barking court roll for 1440-41 is the only one to survive from the whole of this period; the only surviving Barking rental of 1456 is dealt with below.[322] Also mentioned below is the earliest manorial document of substance connected with Barking which is the reeve's account for the demesne farms of Westbury and Dagenham for 1321-22.[323]

Many Barking Abbey documents were dispersed following the Dissolution and the take-over of the manor of Barking by the crown and, although rentals of the 1550s and yet earlier court rolls were still preserved in the record loft of the Court House at the beginning of the 17th century, they do not appear to have survived to the end of that century.[324] One court roll was certainly destroyed by fire between 1656 and 1680, and possibly the destruction on that occasion was widespread.[325] It is doubly unfortunate that a gap in manorial records coincides with the usual gap in the parish registers during the Commonwealth period. However, the two cartographically based surveys of 1616 and 1617 already described (the latter of which has been linked so fortuitously with the parish tithe map) are not the only ones to survive from the early 17th century. A manorial survey had been conducted only a few years earlier, and described as "a most voluminous and minute survey." (Barking manor was retained by the crown until 1628.)

Fig. 17. Barking Court House, c.1800 by Edward Sage. Also known as Market House and Old Town Hall.

This 1609 survey of the manor is a descriptive survey of the classical type conducted by local jurors at a specially summoned Court of Survey where previous court rolls were examined and tenants exhibited their title-deeds.[326] This jury did not content themselves with repeating the customary descriptions of properties; where doubts existed they added their own particulars complete with abuttals and further information. Most of their descriptions are so explicit that, even in the absence of exact measurements or an accompanying map, there is seldom difficulty in identifying the property on the later parish tithe map, especially within those northern parts of Barking parish where the annotated 1617 survey serves as a bridge.

Freehold properties are dealt with in the first part, copyhold in the second part of the 1609 survey. Some 23 tenants failed to appear, including holders of six or seven substantial estates. More to the point, there is no record here of demesne leased out by the crown who still held the lordship. The extensive survey is written in Latin in a small, but neat, secretary hand (less difficult to read than it first appears). A very useful manuscript English translation with an index of persons and places was made by J.G. O'Leary and Cyril Hart in 1949, although where an entry is critical, details should be checked with the original of which Valence Library has a bound photocopy.[327] From the vantage point of 1609 it is possible for many purposes to continue to explore retrospectively using two earlier manorial 'surveys': the ministers accounts of 1540 and the Abbey rental of 1456.

The 'Ministers' Accounts of Lands and Possessions lately belonging to the dissolved Monastery of Barking' was not the work of a Court of Survey (although one may have been held by the Abbey's last steward William Pownsett, as late as 1531).[328] Instead it is one of a series of government reports on monastic spoils; a special rental compiled from the separate accounts and lists of the collectors who had previously served the Abbey but who now rendered account to the crown. It is therefore divided into sections corresponding to the 'offices' or administrative departments of the former abbey: "cellaress", "shrene rent", "coteland rent", "bedell's rents for the north and south parts", "collector of the pensions" and "sacristan". Each section is then sub-divided into the "rents of assize" (the fixed quit-rents) of the freeholds and copyholds and the "farm rents" (the leaseholds). In conclusion the leases for the demesne manors are set out separately (only Fulkes having been granted away by the King at this date). Incidentally, tithes are mentioned only in connection with Dagenham and Gaysham Hall, and the lease of the latter is specifically said to include the tithes of grain and hay *ab antiquo* (from ancient times).

This survey of 1540 is therefore the only one which covers (in intention at least) all lands and houses within the geographical boundaries of the manor of Barking. The original is in Latin, written throughout in a bold office hand. Once again Valence Library has a bound photocopy and a manuscript translation with an index made in 1950 by the late John O'Leary. Admittedly there are some difficulties attending its employment. Though a valuable finding-aid, this translation was written under pressure, and both the text and the transcription of names must be checked from the original ('Nicholas Hennynges', for example turns out to be 'Nicholas Gennynges' when investigated).[329] There is also reason to suspect that the 16th century compiler may himself have misspelled a few place names and even transposed one or two abuttals. Moreover some of the descriptions, unlike those of 1609, are brief to the point of obscurity.

Yet, much can be elucidated with the aid of the 1609 survey and other later documents, and the wide coverage and the inclusion of so large a number of minor place and personal names justifies the labour. Some correlation is also possible with the personal names in the extensive subsidy roll of 1522-24. Furthermore, by far the largest section in 1540 is the beadle's rent roll and this has a medieval parallel in the Abbey rental of 1456, which was rediscovered in 1923, and a full translation, edited by J.E. Oxley, was printed in 1936-7.[330] This confirms the medieval origin and form of many names. Unfortunately, no rent rolls have survived from this early period from any of the other officers of the Abbey.[331] The boundary between the north and south parts of Barking into which it is divided seems to lie along East Street and Longbridge Road. This does not correspond to any later administrative division, but is probably connected with the earlier division of the parish between two vicarages.[332]

None of the hospital tithe lists considered in the previous chapter are close contemporaries with these surviving manorial surveys. The most comprehensive, the inquisition of 1580, falls nearly half-way between the 1540 ministers' account and the group of surveys in the opening decades of the 17th century. They are complementary sources of field names and sometimes of tenants;

and, as was suggested in chapter six, most of the lands on these hospital tithe lists can be identified and located from the later parish tithe surveys and map. Although exact correspondences with earlier or later manorial surveys may be difficult to work out, many pieces do fit together and portions of the 16th century landscape emerge from the jigsaw. At some points the first hospital tithe list can carry us back into the 14th century, further back than the 1456 rental or the solitary court roll of 1440-41.[333]

The reeve's account for Westbury and Dagenham of 1321-22 takes us back further still. The information it contains regarding medieval farming practices on the Abbey demesnes has been extensively used by Sister Sturman in her 1961 thesis and by *Victoria County History of Essex*.[334] The business of tithe collection is mentioned in the account. Furthermore it includes early forms of various field names, particularly in the south of the parish. Many surnames in the near contemporary lay subsidy list of 1327 (of which a printed transcript is available) contain elements of minor place names which occur in the area.

Forest documents

Finally it must not be forgotten that, until 1851, all that portion of the parish north of the High Road to Romford lay within the forest of Waltham which comprised Epping and Hainault. Even the wastes of Hainault forest beyond the forest fence were of considerably greater extent than the present woodland of that name which is but a remnant. In addition, much of Great Ilford and Chadwell wards, though south of the fence, were legally within the forest because they were subject to the laws of the forest. So most of Ilford was in West Hainault walk, and most of Chadwell and Chadwell Heath (Dagenham) in East (or, Chapel) Hainault walk.[336]

The survey of 1617 dealt with above was, strictly speaking, a forest document. A variety of documentation was engendered by the courts and officers of the forest – even though the higher courts of the forest met only very occasionally, and not at all after the 17th century. The records are to be found in both central and local repositories, but it is not possible here to do more than mention three or four later examples.

The Public Record Office contains the presentments of the regarders for 1630 naming some 48 offenders against forest law in Barking within the last 50 years, for 1634/5 naming 114 (including some with fines unpaid from the previous regard), and also for 1670 accusing 26.[337] Such offences included enclosure of waste (often roadside waste), the felling or grubbing-up of trees without licence (even when the offender owned the wood), the possession of dogs which disturbed the deer and so forth. The Essex Record Office has approximately 70 warrants to view woods for the purpose of granting licences to fell, etc. from the Mildmay family collection, and some from the Holcroft papers because Carew Mildmay of Marks Hall and William Holcroft of Walthamstow were both verderers.[338]

The rolls of the Court of Attachments, 1713-1848 (the lowest of the forest courts and the last to cease functioning) were printed by the Epping Forest Commission in 1873; there are copies in the Essex Record Office, Valence and Walthamstow Libraries. The Bodleian Library has a copy of the rolls of the Court of Swainmote from 1593 (the forest court immediately superior to the Court of Attachments) and the Essex Record Office has a transcript and translation of these. Most of the cases presented in the 16th century were offences against the 'venison' (illegal hunting) rather than against the 'vert' (destruction of woods). The proceedings of both courts include a number of local references.[339]

There was an obvious overlap of jurisdiction between the forest administration and the manor courts in regard to enclosures of roadside waste within the forest. So the erection of a house or cottage may be referred to in both types of documents; and other interconnections may be found in matters of wood and pasture rights. Similarly, tithe and forest documents interlock because, for reasons explained earlier, the areas of private woodland and dates of felling are carefully recorded in tithe surveys.[340]

Chapter eight: Research potential of the Barking documents

Preliminary considerations

When embarking upon this topic two important premises are to be drawn from the preceding chapters, both of which were touched upon in the introduction. The first is that any realistic programme of research is likely to employ a variety of other historic materials in conjunction with tithe documents. The second is that for most practical purposes it would be foolish to draw a line between pre-1836 material and the tithe commutation award which will be a necessary starting point for many studies. On the other hand, the projects considered below involve working backwards rather than forwards from 1847.

The reservoir of names

The huge reservoir of personal and place names provided by all the classes of documents listed above is an obvious point with diverse applications (field and other minor place names will be dealt with later). Incidentally, the close association between the origin of many family names and minor place names is well illustrated by the lay subsidy of 1327.[341] The stock of personal names is probably of most direct interest to the family historian. The size and accessibility of the reservoir of names for Essex as a whole was emphasised by Dr Emmison in his 1983 article in the *Genealogists' Magazine*, 'Essex Genealogical Indexes: A million references to personal names'.[342]

In Barking there are 236 names of tithe payers in the index to the 1669 tithe book alone and, as previously explained, nearly all of these were actually resident in the parish; the small number of occupiers residing elsewhere are identified mostly as London butchers leasing marsh pasture. Again, almost every entry contains further names under "Alterations", though most of these recur in the succeeding surveys and accounts.

Tithe documents can play a part – though only a part – in demographic studies and investigations of population mobility. Some of the relevant issues and interconnections were mentioned in chapter seven.

Landholding and patterns of settlement

Barking tithe records would appear to be fully adequate to support the construction of a series of parish maps to show the extent and structure of landholding at various points between the 17th and the 19th centuries. Over long periods it should be possible to record the sequence of tenants and any changes in the size and pattern of farms; for example, if consolidation or fragmentation occurred. Causes of change could be usefully investigated further with assistance from other records and comparisons with neighbouring areas.

Tithe records and farming conditions: a 17th century example

Sometimes even tithe accounts alone can offer valuable clues. For example, William Drury is shown in the 1669 tithe survey as holding 15 acres in "Goodmay streete" (Goodmayes Lane) including an orchard and a nursery, which was unusual at the time and could suggest that Drury was an early specialised gardener. The 1671 hearth tax shows him living there in a dwelling with one hearth. Between 1674 and 1680 Drury also took over a 54 acre farm (Kennites) further up the lane containing a larger house with three hearths (called Spratly Hall on the six inch Ordnance Survey map), so we may assume he had been thriving. Then the tithe accounts for 1684-5 show the good times are over. Drury owes three years' arrears of tithe on "his own farm" and two on his more recent acquisition and these are "all lost for he is run away".[343]

The same accounts show he was not an isolated figure. Henry Hutchinson similarly abandoned his farm at Aldborough Hatch, the tithes of Richard Clark were "all lost for reason of poverty" and another was in arrears for five years. There is reason to suspect that other places may have evidence of agricultural distress at this time; from external sources we know that from 1676 to 1691 was a period of almost continuously falling prices and that the winter of 1684 was one of the coldest on record. We can only guess at the human misery of the smallholders and their families which lies behind these bare facts.

Incidentally, Drury's first holding – probably a medieval virgate in origin – corresponds to nos. 495-8 in the tithe award and, virtually unchanged in shape and size, is now occupied by council allotments. Drury's wooden house was replaced during the 19th century by brick cottages (called Poole's Cottages, perhaps named after some later tenant) and then, around 30 years ago, by a block of modern flats (Poole's Court). Further north in no.504, Spratly Hall was demolished in the late 19th century and the site subsequently occupied by semi-detached housing.

Other potential areas for agricultural enquiry

Various other specialised lines of enquiry suggest themselves for Barking in conjunction with adjacent parishes. The material for studying the development of market gardening during the 17th century and of specialised potato culture during the 18th century has already been mentioned several times. Access to London's markets and manure might itself prove a theme.

In addition to a wealth of tithe records, the extensive Barking parish has the advantage to the student of agricultural history of stretching through several zones from riverside marsh in the south, through the gravel river terraces, to the clay on the north. Arthur Young in his *Survey of*

Essex (1807) selected Claybury on the London Clay, Aldborough Hatch on the upper terrace and Loxford on the lower (with brickearth as well as gravel), as typical examples of farms in the area.[344] An interesting practice not touched upon by Young was the holding by 'upland' farms of patches of marsh pasture. Even small farms did so: Robert Cawdle (Cordell), the tenant of Kennites before Drury (above), held five acres of marsh called Halfpenny, a couple of miles away, and we know that his livestock holding in 1671 consisted of two pigs, six cows, 40 sheep and 60 lambs.[345] On the evidence of Commission of Sewers documents, the *Victoria County History* has calculated that, in 1740, Eastbury, Westbury and Ripple levels contained 182 parcels of marsh totalling 1,601 acres divided amongst 48 owners "most of whom held land in the 'uplands' of Barking".[346] These arrangements, including the tenurial links and distances involved, would no doubt bear closer investigation. Farms north of the Romford Road, being within the forest, had an alternative of common pasture in the wastes of Hainault; some used both.

Marsh-edge settlement

In Ripple, where upland and marsh met, a more permanent relationship developed at some very early stage and produced an interesting local pattern of marsh-edge settlement. A string of small farms were spaced out along the southern edge of the lower gravel terrace. Their buildings overlooked the alluvial marsh where each held narrow parcels of pasture running down towards the river. On the north side of these settlements, the Ripple Road ran along the terrace linking them with Barking and Dagenham. Beyond this road lay a zone of open field (Rippledown) in which each farm held strips of ploughland. So, in effect, each little farm was a compact north-south ribbon embracing both types of land-use.[347]

This pattern is revealed most plainly by the map of Eastbury tithing in 1831 where the names of tenants appear on the plan. Faint lines indicate the boundaries between the smaller strips. The total area so divided, and named as common field, is less than 30 acres; but the overall east-west design including the enclosed fields on either side strongly suggests a larger zone of open field in which consolidation has already taken place. This is highly probable since the abundant feeding and hay available to each farmer on the southern section of his holding would reduce the need for depasturing on the arable and hence the need for regulation of the common (for which no evidence has come to light).[348]

Consider, for example, the lands tenanted by James Scratton in 1831 which adjoined the Dagenham boundary. His farm buildings stood on the southern side of Ripple Road at the head of three parcels of marsh which stretch south as far as an enclosure marked "Hospital Tithing" which is near the river bank (earlier tithe documents identify this last as "Priests Marsh" or "Priests Mead"). North of the road opposite his farmhouse he has one long north-south enclosure; and parallel to this on the west he holds a small strip in the midst of the common. In the tithe survey of 1750, a predecessor of James, the widow Pamphlin, similarly holds 22 acres of house-ground and marsh south of the road, with $31\frac{1}{2}$ acres to the north. The latter consists of seven and 17 acres in enclosed parcels and the rest in three smaller parcels, of which two are described as part common field.[349]

In earlier times, before it became known as Scrattons Farm, it was called by the medieval name of Oskinshaugh or Osekyns Hawe. That part of the vellum book at Hatfield House, which is believed to have been copied from the cartulary of Barking Abbey, contains a late 13th century conveyance by John Osekyn to his daughter Alice of a "messuage in Ripplestreete... extending from the meadow called Prestemede in the south to the King's street on the north"; together with "12 acres of arable land...of which six acres lies upon Rippledowne aforesaid" to the north of Ripple Road, "and six acres of marshland lies in Ripplemarshe". This is a farm identical in structure to Scrattons and it bears witness to the antiquity of the settlement pattern even more certainly than does the fact that the common field ignores, and presumably pre-dates, the boundary between the parishes of Barking and Dagenham. Interestingly, both the Scratton and Pamphlin families in their time held some other land in Dagenham.[350]

Much of the pattern persists in the tithe award of 1847 and even in the plans accompanying a sale catalogue of 1894 when a number of parcels of "Fertile Market Garden Ground" and "Rich Old Grass Marsh" were offered for sale, with the ominous hint that they were "ripe for development as building land". The Ripple open field finally vanished in the 20th century without the need for an enclosure act. This, and the lack of earlier regulation which facilitated the process, may help to explain why the only substantial example of open field in the manor of Barking received virtually no mention from historians prior to the appearance of the *Victoria County History of Essex*.[351] The subject has scope for further development than has been offered either there or here, including changing farming practices within the geographical constraints in response to market forces; from the milking of ewes for cheese to the fattening of cattle for market; from the production of rye to market gardening. At high water most of the levels were protected only by the embankments of the Thames and adaptation to the dangers and opportunities of intermittent flooding of the marshes is another topic that might be usefully examined.[352]

Flooding and drainage

A legacy of the extensive inundations of the late Middle Ages was a flood-lake just below the terrace edge in Ripple opposite the foot of Lodge Lane. Despite the former efforts of the Abbey to embank and reclaim marshes, the 'Rant', as it was called, was still 40 acres in extent and 24 feet deep in the late 16th century. Several of the more westerly farms, such as Mogges and Malmaynes of Ripple, thus lost land and direct access to their marshland further south. A horse and cart had to go into Dagenham parish to reach the New Ways to Thames-side.

In 1582, Thomas Fanshawe, who himself owned almost a quarter of the land under water, used

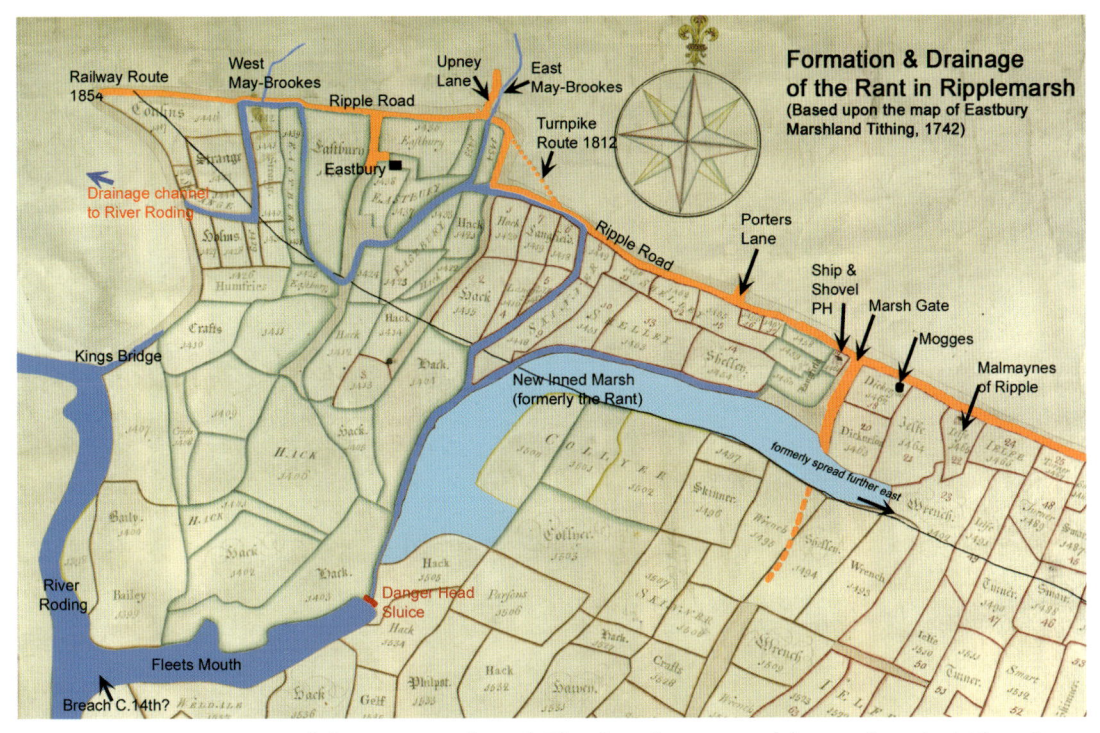

Fig. 18. *A Map Reconstruction of the Rant in Ripplemarsh.* This shows formation and drainage from the 16th to the 18th centuries. The map base is ERO D/SH 16 (1742).

his influence as Queen's Remembrancer and the leading expert on Exchequer procedure to obtain a royal commission from the Exchequer to enquire into draining the Rant. It is more than probable that he hoped to involve the Queen in providing further assistance, even though the crown owned only four acres of the ground in question. If so, he may well have been surprised and disappointed by the less than enthusiastic verdict from the select jury of 40 local people.

According to the evidence of Thomas Brewer of "Garlestreete" (Gale Street) local farmers had obviously adapted to the situation and discovered the advantages of multiplying their hay crops by 'floating' (irrigating) their marsh meadows. Apart from the possible cost of reclamation they feared the loss of sufficient water for "ye watteringe and rewateringe of ye said grounds and marshes so adjoyning". The advantages of "free watering by ye said Rant" outweighed even the "discomodities" of losing some land, of driving animals by circuitous ways, of maintaining the embankments and suffering the stench of stagnant waters near their houses. They had, of course, no way of connecting the endemic "tertian agues" with the malaria carrying mosquitoes which then bred in those same stagnant waters.[353]

The subsequent course of events wants elucidation, but there is no doubt that reclamation eventually went forward and the Rant became the 'New Inned Ground' (nos.737-9 plus). The work would have proceeded without pumps, but the mid-18th century copies of the 1666 tithe map indicate a contour drainage channel in a loop to the south of Eastbury House and across to

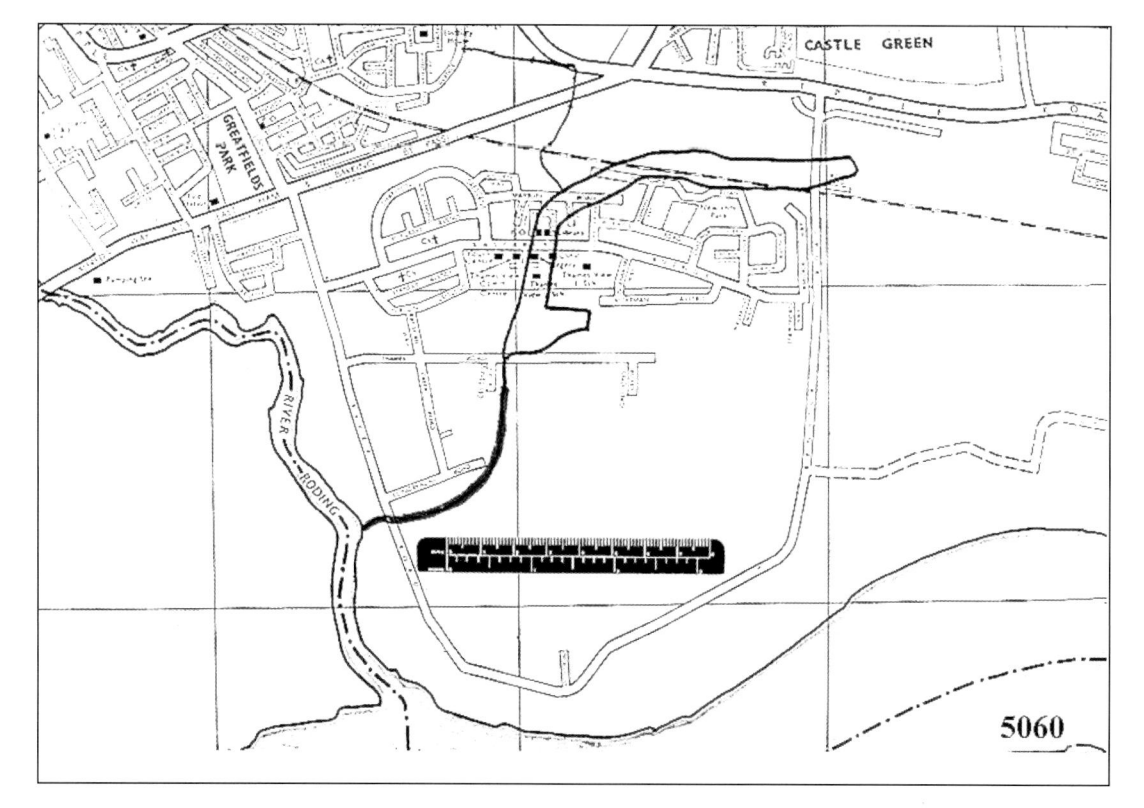

Fig. 19. A Conjectural Reconstruction of the Rant. The 16th century Rant is superimposed over a modern street map. In recent times the drainage position has been modified by the railway embankments and the Barking barrage.

the River Roding. This must have operated at low tide to drain the Rant and deflect fresh water from the two channels of the Mayes Brook. Sluice gates would have been employed to prevent water returning as the tide rose.[354] The 'Marsh Way' (otherwise 'Mogges Lane') which gave access to marsh pastures further south was restored; the keys of the New Inned Gate were eventually put in the custody of the landlord of the Ship and Shovel public house (no.784) erected in the 18th century at the corner of the lane which is now Renwick Road. There are suspicions that this route was then used by smugglers carting contraband landed at night from ships in the Thames.[355] There is matter here for further research, but the list of over 40 jurors and witnesses for the Inquisition of 1582 (mostly local inhabitants) is most useful in itself.

Forest enclosure

Turning to the northern part of the parish the clearance of woodland becomes a leading theme. Since most of this clearance took place between the 17th and the 19th centuries, the process is well covered by tithe records in conjunction with forest documents. The distribution of woodland in the early 17th century can be shown from the parish tithe map (since this is virtually a copy of the 1652 survey) with some assistance from the 1617 survey of lands within the forest.[356] Comparison with the distribution in the 1847 tithe award demonstrates the overall pattern of change during the period. There is plentiful material for examining the shorter term changes in land-use within this space of time and probably adequate material for exploring the interaction with local farming practices.

The reports of the verderers upon viewing private woodlands, the subject of applications to fell or to 'stub and grub', demonstrate changing attitudes towards clearance (although these also reflect changes in public and state policy). At one period the King's forests were regarded predominantly as game reserves for the royal chase, at another as a source of extraordinary royal revenue, at yet another as reservoirs of timber for the Royal Navy. Eventually the 'economic' view prevailed that they were a misuse of the capital resource of potential agricultural land, as well as an encouragement to poachers and idlers. Disafforestation followed in 1851 with widespread enclosure of the wastes of the forest and conversion of woodland to farmland.

Vestiges of earlier clearances in the medieval period also invite investigation, although information here is harder to come by. Field-names, such as those incorporating 'ridden' or 'reden', seem to offer the best clues at present. As early as 1935, Reaney pointed out that 'ryden' (meaning 'cleared land') was very common in Essex.[357] The tithe surveys and the hospital tithe lists are valuable for locating the many Barking examples. Sometimes the first element of the name is highly suggestive, as in 'Colleriddings' (nos. 2509, Furney Field, and 2510) where an adjacent tenant in 1456 was a Thomas Colyer, doubtless not the first collier (charcoal burner) to have his furnace there.[358]

It has been suggested that these reden names were created from the mid-13th century, but it would be most useful to know more precisely at what period they ceased to be coined. 'Baronesredene' (nos.1625-6) was certainly so named by the 1330s.[359] This was just west of 'Dunshall Ridden' (nos.1630-32) and 'Levesons Grove' (nos.1634-37 & 1640-42) which last was probably not cleared until the mid-18th century.[360] On the opposite (south) side of the High Road to Romford lay no.1266, described as 'Crekelwodreden' and as 'Krekelwod Ryden' in the surviving court roll of 1440-41.[361] Some 20 or so acres of 'Cricklewood' (now Cricklefields) adjoining to the east was still wood at the Dissolution and some of its trees provided timber for repairing the mill and bridge over the River Lea at Stratford.[362] Remarkably, woodland must have lined the High Road on much of its course through Ilford in the early Middle Ages – even Ilford Hospital, near the centre of the village, was built in 'Spittle Grove'.

Prior to 1851 grants of assarts (or enclosures) from the principal wastes of the royal forest were exceptional: several enclosures for the building and endowment of a New Chapel at Barkingside in the 1650s and '60s were described in chapter four; and a 12th century assart at Claybury, also, for 'religious' purposes, will be described in later.[363]

However, Queen Elizabeth discharged debts to two royal servants by making grants from the wastes of Hainault. The first of these was the nine acres adjoining Aldborough Hatch granted in 1583 to Andrew Tuggell, a royal armourer "old and decrepit". Although by the 19th century the three small closes of the 16th century enclosure had been absorbed into the farm to the south, it is still possible to recognise the area on the 1846 tithe map. There, for no obvious reason, a broken line crosses fields nos.1710 and 1711 distinguishing them from their southern parts 1710a and 1711a. This indicates the vanished boundary which followed the course of the pre-1583 forest fence. Until the 19th century tithe award, only the vicar had enjoyed the great tithe of this 'new' enclosure, but then the impropriator of the Newbury circuit established a claim. Tuggalls Hall itself had already duly metamorphosed into the Aldborough Hatch Smithy which stood just within the erstwhile Forest Gate up to the early years of the 20th century.[364]

Again, in 1602 the Queen granted an enclosure of five and a half acres north of Fullwell Hatch, Barkingside, to the widow of a royal forester to whom two years' wages were owing. The widow had remarried William Hunt, a Queen's Trumpeter, hence the close (nos.2090-91) was known for many years as Trumpeters and the house erected there as Hunt's Hall, which eventually became the Maypole Inn. This was enfranchised in 1859 as "a public house in the Manor of Barking known as the Maypole Inn, formerly the Trumpeteers."[365] Almost opposite the Maypole was 'Chapel Piece' (no. 2083) enclosed in the 1650s for the New Chapel (see above), whilst 'Chapel Field' (no. 2106) and 'Fencepiece Farm' further north were enclosed later as endowments for the New Chapel.[366]

Two larger and curiously named enclosures shown on the 1846 map raise wider issues. According to the tithe award both were approximately 25 acres in extent and belonged to the parish of Barking. One (no.1742) named 'Lower Canada', lay just south of Fullwell Hatch, whilst 'Upper Canada' (no.1180) was outside the Little Heath Gate. Barking Vestry minutes reveal that they were created in 1832 in pursuance of the 1831 Act which authorised the churchwardens and overseers of a parish to enclose up to 50 acres of any forest or waste belonging to the crown to provide allotments for the poor (provided that they obtained authority from the Treasury). By the end of 1839 there were 88 allotment tenants at Barkingside and 92 at Little Heath, with plots averaging a quarter of an acre for which they paid ten shillings a year. It had been necessary to adopt a liberal interpretation of 'the poor', namely "any industrious cottager of good character (being day labourer or journeyman – legally settled in the said parish and dwelling within or near its bounds)".[367]

Although the minutes do not explain the choice of name for the enclosures, newspaper reports of the time are able to throw some light on the matter. The leading local campaigner for the 1831 Act was Montague Burgoyne, an Essex country gentleman married to the daughter of Eliab Harvey of Claybury Hall. A radical Whig, he had been a verderer of Epping Forest from 1798 to 1819 and a strong advocate of an unsuccessful disafforestation bill of 1818 which he had declared "would provide employment and food for a super-abundant population, who were starving for want of work". He addressed a meeting of the overseers of parishes in support of the more limited measure of 1831. Observing "that it was a cruel thing to tell the inhabitants of this country that there was not employment for them and that they must seek it in Canada and other foreign countries, when there were 13,000,000 [?] acres of wasteland in Great Britain and Ireland", he invited his audience to compare and contrast the remedy now proposed (a form of home colonisation) with assisted emigration to the colonies – the method of disposing of surplus population then supported by Gibbon Wakefield and Lord Durham.[368]

The point made by the unknown wit who suggested naming the allotments, Upper and Lower Canada, would not have been lost upon the Barking Vestry; in 1833 the Barking directors of the poor paid for the passage of ten paupers to Canada. One wonders about parallels in other areas. In his work on English place names, Reaney mentions 'Canada Allotments' at Astley in Cambridgeshire and allotment gardens in Walthamstow "known as Canada, which by 1884 the local dialect had turned into Kennedy". This latter was a ten acre enclosure in Epping Forest made in 1834 for the poor of the parish of Walthamstow divided into quarter acre plots for the purpose of "spade husbandry". Even in the 20th century, when the Barkingside allotments were divided by the railway (they were eventually turned into playing fields), local inhabitants called them the 'Canadys' and some curious explanations were invented for the name.[369] Part of Upper Canada still provides allotments alongside Hainault Road, Little Heath.

Waste-edge settlement

The enclosures described above, together with some smaller enclosures not yet examined, can be considered as part of a larger socio-economic issue which offers ample opportunity for further research. This phenomenon presents itself clearly on looking at the Chapman and André map (1777) which at two inches to the mile is the first printed map to show the whole area in sufficient detail. Here the Barking side of the forest in the 1770s is seen to be a string of small properties running down the forest fence from Tomswood past the Maypole Inn and Fullwell Hatch to Tanners Gate. From there some further cottages cling to the fence as it continues eastward to Aldborough Hatch, there is then a short break around the former Tuggalls Hall and the pattern then reappears approaching Little Heath. It continues along the fence to Padnall Corner, turning up past Rose Lane and Marks Gate into Havering and so along the significantly named Collier Row, until it thins out along the southern bounds of the royal park. The cottages on roadside waste along the wide verges approaching gates such as Aldborough Hatch Green and around Little Heath can be seen as an extension of the pattern.

This has some parallels with the marsh-edge settlement in Ripple and Dagenham, such as the ready availability of pasture, but whereas areas of common marsh were small and exceptional, all the wastes of the forest were pastured in common except during the 'fence month' when the deer were breeding. All adjoining parishes with parts within the forest practised inter-commoning, where animals were not confined to a particular area but were instead distinguished by brand marks. According to the regulations any poor cottager with rights of common could graze two cows or a horse in the forest, and farmers could do the same for every £4 which they paid in rent.

Nor, so far as is known, could these rights of common be leased to outside graziers as could severally owned marsh pasture. The quality of wood pasture was not equivalent; a more progressive farmer might be reluctant to common his stock with other, possibly diseased, animals, and there was no alternative of hay production as on marsh meadow. However, firewood was easy to obtain because many owners of estates within the forest, and even some cottages, were entitled to generous biannual fuel assignments (estovers) and could also apply for fencing wood when required. The marsh-edge settlement mainly comprised small farms spaced at more or less regular intervals; the forest-edge chiefly comprised cottages with gardens, closely or irregularly spaced, held on manorial leases at low rents or even on weekly tenancies.[370]

Some of the forest side inhabitants worked regularly on neighbouring farms or in the forest as woodcutters, herdsmen or charcoal-burners. Others seem to have subsisted by casual labour at harvest time and potato picking, periodical tree felling and on occasions such as the annual Fairlop Fair. Some even had a horse and cart that enabled them to do any jobs which they could pick up. They maintained themselves and families in the meantime on the produce of their gardens and animals, supplemented by poached small game and occasionally by 'black mutton' (the local euphemism for stolen venison). Thus they lived in a state of poverty but relative independence, subject to frequent censure from their 'betters'. As the ex-verderer Burgoyne said in 1831 "the country at large is greatly injured by the encouragement and shelter given by the forest to idle and dishonest persons." Such an opinion was typical, and critics of his favourite scheme may have regarded the provision of allotments as just another such encouragement.[371]

If the disafforestation of 1851 removed the cause it still left, according to a magistrate in 1915 with over 30 years experience on the local bench, "a race that dwells on the edges of the old forests and heaths, who have been for countless generations deer-stealers and 'coney-catching rascals', but for lack of game, are now obliged to take to more recognised avocations – always, however, of a somewhat independent kind… They are an interesting and useful element in our population – even if sometimes they get onto the wrong side of the law."[372]

There must be a suspicion that not a few of this 'race' are hidden under the conveniently blanket classification of 'Ag. Labs.' in 19th century census returns. It may be significant that all of the 11 "Jobbers" listed in Kelly's *Essex Trades and Professional Directory* of 1906 came from Barkingside. They were defined narrowly as "dealers in market garden produce", so did not include the hay and straw dealer, the firewood dealer, the two general dealers and some of the seven florists and four greengrocers in the village who, having no retail shops, may have been itinerant and selling from carts. In another age these too might have been called jobbers or higglers. George Gott, an early chairman of the Ilford Urban District Council (who famously described the Barkingside of his childhood as "all sky and turnips"), was the son of James Gott, described in the 1851 census as a "Jobbing Labourer" but who eventually became a farmer and timber merchant.[373]

The evolution and survival of this quasi-peasantry who preferred to work for themselves in the waste-edge settlements would, therefore, seem to offer a promising line of research. It is fortunate that tithe records were virtually completed as a result of the Tithe Commutation Act before the disafforestation took place. This is an area of socio-economic history where co-operation between family and other historians might yield interesting results.

Trade and industry

In view of what has been said regarding the incidence of tithe one would not expect tithe documents to be much help in investigating local trade and industry, yet they can be of some use. For example; the *Victoria County History* has shown how Tanner Street on the north of Barking town was a centre for tanning through to the 16th century. The 17th century tithe books continue the story, for the 1669 tithe survey records two tanners, Joseph Dodson and Nicholas Mead, still operating on the north side of Tanner Street (where the Loxford Brook supplied water for the tan vats). In 1681 the second tannery was still in operation by John Chapman, and during the 18th century other sources reveal it was known as Tanners Farm.[374]

Although it is unlikely that tanning carried on at Tanners Farm or elsewhere in Tanner Street, tanneries are shown as operating close to the forest fence, where tanbark was available after felling. The earliest direct mention of the tanhouse at Barkingside is in the 1617 Survey. It lay opposite the southern end of Tanners Lane and near Tanners Gate – to both of which it gave a name. It was also known as Red Rose House or Farm (no.1750) and in the tithe surveys of 1669, 1681 and 1727/8 it was occupied by tanners called Thomas Nichols (possibly a father and son). Red Rose was still being called Tan Office Farm in the 1806 survey and Tanyard Farm in the 1840s. The tithe award gives the name Leather Hoppit to field no.1756 (running down towards the former pond no.1757, see below) on Buntons Brook which supplied the vats. Local historian Tasker produces no evidence in 1901 to support his implication in *Ilford Past and Present* that tanning was still being carried on there as late as the 1840s. However, 30 to 50 loads of oak-bark for tanning were being auctioned each summer at the Maypole Inn during the first decade of the 19th century by order of the Commissioners of Woods and Forests.[375] The tithe survey of 1727/8 also includes another tan yard, occupied by a Mr Bourne, along the forest fence between Little Heath and Padnall Corner; and a conveyance of 1683 suggests that a tanner called Christopher Spencer was operating this at an earlier date.[376]

Even today traces remain in the valley of Buntons Brook (the upper Cran Brook) of what might be termed, without too much exaggeration, a proto-industrial area of the Tudor and Stuart periods. Below the Barkingside tannery, an artificial channel by-passed fishponds and a series of dams created millponds to provide power for a water-mill where Chase Lane crossed the brook. On the eastern slope of the valley near the Aldborough Hatch end of Chase Lane there also stood a windmill (east corner of no.1804).

It is probable that all these were due to the enterprise of the Barnes family, wealthy London merchants who bought Aldborough Hatch at the Dissolution. Amongst the legacies in the will of Thomas Barnes [II] in 1596 are "my water-mill and my windmill with the 2½ acres occupied therewith". Both are mentioned in the 1616 rental, and the water-mill is noted in the 1617 Survey. The vicar's tithe map has a neat drawing of a post-mill in the appropriate field. According to the 1669 tithe survey the miller leasing the windmill was Henry Hutchinson. In 1681 John Jolley was the miller there, but the tithe account of 1684/5 stated he had departed and queried the name of a successor. The 'Lockey' map (c.1725) shows the ponds in detail, but does not indicate any buildings; perhaps had the mills been demolished. The Chapman and André map has a circular symbol which might represent a windmill, or it might indicate the mill mound alone. The areas of former ponds are outlined by broken lines on the early 19th century map of the Aldborough Hatch estate extracted from Johnson's 1805/6 survey. The mill-ponds tithed only to the vicar.[377]

Landlords: tenements and titles

One factor that might have been considered in the section on waste-edge settlement was the lack of influential resident landowners in the Barkingside area. Gaysham Hall was the largest of the local estates, but from the early 18th century until 1918 it was – like almost all the others – in the occupation of tenant farmers renting from absentee landlords. Yet it could be argued (e.g. from the early disappearance of labour tenure) that no part of Barking had remained highly manorialised even when Barking Abbey was still in control, and that this had continued to be the case despite the influence exercised by some powerful resident families like the Fanshawes. It could perhaps be maintained that even when owner-occupiers predominated these were London merchants and government officials, concerned more with the convenience of their houses than with farming their estates. If London's markets were within range of a farmer's cart, London's offices were not too long a journey on horseback or in a private coach. It is perhaps not surprising that many of London's lord mayors were resident in the Barking and adjacent areas over the centuries. Sage lists 18 between 1495 and 1760 in his manuscript 'History', although its popularity as a residential zone for wealthy citizens was waning well before suburbanisation.[378]

Prior to 1847 when the tithe award gives names of both landlord and tenant, tithe maps and surveys do not provide the same direct facility for mapping the extent of units of ownership (as distinct from occupation) at different periods and for identifying changes of ownership as in the case of farms and farmers. However, the demesne tithings show the original extents of many larger estates or manors. Moreover, close correspondences may be established between manorial and tithe records at several points in time, such as the surveys of 1679 and 1681.
On the face of it, the succession of owners of larger freeholds is adequately covered by the

descents of manors which have been part of the stock in trade of county and local historians from Morant and Lysons to the *Victoria County History*. Originally these were based upon abstracts of title obligingly supplied by owners or their lawyers. More recent research in the Public Record Office and other archives has not always been able to fill the gaps. It should also be remembered that lawyers in times past were more concerned with establishing the legal validity of a title than with substantiating what they termed the 'corporeal hereditaments' – the tangible lands and houses conveyed by the title. The inclusion of detailed plans and Ordnance Survey reference numbers are comparatively recent practices. But the historian often has – or should have – different priorities; (s)he wants to know exactly what property is in question.

The descent of the ancient manor of Porters in Ripple illustrates the scope for error so far as Barking is concerned. In 1966 the *Victoria County History of Essex* followed previous historians in identifying this medieval manor with an estate called 'Great Porters' in Gale Street (no.599 etc.) and providing an apparently continuous descent of title over the years. However, further analysis shows that these were two distinct, though neighbouring, estates.[379]

Lysons writing in 1796 was uneasy because, having traced the descent of the manor of Porters down to 1635 (when, according to Morant, it had come into the hands of the lord of the manor, Thomas Fanshawe), he had found himself, "unable to learn anything of its proprietors till 1701" – a gap of 66 years.[380]

For the descent from 1701, Lysons relied upon a Barking informant, Robert Newman, who had recently bought the Great Porters estate, which name may have led him to believe that he had acquired the ancient manor of Porters. The earliest tenant of which Newman was aware was a Godfrey Woodward in 1701. But the first tithe survey of 1669 shows that an earlier tenant of the farm in Gale Street was William Porter. Next, from the manorial surveys of 1663 and 1679 it becomes plain that members of the Porter family were then owner-occupiers of both freehold and copyhold properties in Barking and Dagenham. Finally, a series of wills show that William's grandfather, Stephen Porter, citizen and grocer of London, had acquired these properties in the late 16th century. The house in Gale Street, their family residence, is not named there, acquiring the name in retrospect after a century of association with the Porter family. The tithe account for 1697 appears to show that Godfrey Woodward Esq. took over in that year. The adjective 'great' was possibly added when a more pretentious house (castellated!) was built on the site later in the 18th century, perhaps by Robert Newman himself.[381]

Nevertheless could Stephen Porter by a further coincidence have actually acquired the old manor house of Porters? The tithe survey of 1669 once again proves otherwise because it shows that a "John Downer of *Porters*" was then the tenant of a farm comprising 99 acres of upland and 24 of marsh. The upland lay to the west of William Porter's farm and the house is in no.611-612, the site of Porters Lodge. John Downer was dead by 1697 and his widow paid tithe for the identical farm according to the tithe account for that year. Next, the manorial records include a lease of this same upland farm to Mr John Shelley dated 1728 under the new name 'Porters Lodge'; Shelley's lands are clearly marked on the Eastbury tithing map of 1742.[382]

The tale can now be untangled. Sometime between 1630 and 1635 Thomas Fanshawe, Lord of the Manor of Barking, acquired the freehold of the ancient manor of Porters, the lands of which were next to those of Jenkins (alias Dagenhams) where he dwelt. The title was absorbed into his demesne, the lands were leased out as a farm and the old house, presumably having been demolished, was replaced by a farmhouse known as Porters Lodge. Meanwhile the estate adjoining to the east, having for many years been owned by a family called Porter became known in course of time as Porters, promoted to Great Porters by new owners in the 18th century, all to the ultimate confusion of historians!

Once the tithe documents have supplied the essential clues, further supporting evidence can be recognised elsewhere. Unfortunately for previous historians, both Stephen Porter and Sir Thomas Lucas, then owner of the manor of Porters, were amongst the 23 tenants of Barking manor who failed to attend the Court of Survey in 1609. But the 'skeletal' rental of 1616 has an entry "Mr Thomas Lucas for Porters", and Mr Thomas was the son and heir of Sir Thomas Lucas. The entry includes "house and close called Porters" (not yet called Porters Lodge) and the adjoining 14 acre "close called Appletons" (the two 7 acre fields of that name north of the house in the 1669 tithe survey). The estate was larger than Downers farm in 1669 for it included a 61 acre "Parke" and a "Bowling Ground" (both items suggestive of status). Quite distinct are the two entries in the 1616 rental for "Mr Stephen Porter" who holds several unnamed estates; although one of them has parcel numbers almost in sequence with those of Lucas of Porters to which they must have been adjacent.

The park was probably the land held by Shelley in 1742 on the west of Porters (Lodge) Lane which continued to be called Porters Warren. When the Becontree Estate was built in the 1920s and '30s, much of this remained open as part of newly created Mayesbrook Park, whilst Porters Lodge Lane was straightened out to become Lodge Avenue, and the farmhouse was pulled down.[383]

Not all problems of a similar nature can be solved so neatly as that of Porters, even with the aid of tithe documents. Some require the assistance of estate documents which may lie still unrecognised in private, or even public, archives – or may have completely disappeared. In the case of Barking it often proves worthwhile to sift through the Essex Record Office's D/DHs catalogue (manorial and estate documents).

In difficult cases it may also be useful to remember that occasionally private acts of parliament were used to cut a way through the jungle of land law and inheritance surrounding large estates, particularly where minors and females were involved. The act of 1748 for the Sale of Certain Lands... of Sir Orlando Humfreys has already been mentioned. A similar act concerning the will of Dr John Bamber for the sale of entailed estates is considered below in reference to Wyfields, but perhaps the widest coverage in the Barking-Ilford area was afforded by the 1693 act for the sale of the estates of Francis Osbaldeston (Osbaston) of Aldersbrooke (died 1678) to raise £10,000 for his 16 year old daughter, Mary, and so fulfil the provisions of his will. These estates included Loxford, Clements, Valentines, Beehive, Wangey Hall, as well as a number of smaller properties. The terms of this act and of the subsequent conveyances – mainly to John Lethieullier, the father of Smart – include many details of lands and tenants and may provide the missing links in some descents.[384]

The study of field names

Amongst the first to recognise the great potential of tithe documents for the study of minor place-names was the assiduous Loughton antiquarian, William Chapman Waller. In the 1890s, long before the development of county record offices had simplified access, Waller obtained special permission from the Board of Agriculture to use the original post-1836 tithe awards to prepare lists of field-names for Essex parishes. These lists, printed in the *Transactions of the Essex Archaeological Society*, were unique at the time and Reaney later paid special tribute to their value in the preparation of his standard work, *The Place Names of Essex*.[385]

Yet, the fact that the names on Waller's lists were not linked in any manner to the accompanying tithe maps imposed a distinct limitation upon their further use. In order to speculate usefully upon the meaning or origin of a field-name, or to apply the information to other investigations, it is advantageous to know the exact location, shape and size of a field, as well as its name and parish. On the macro-scale Reaney moved a little further by including a county map showing all parish boundaries, whilst within the parish he acknowledged the value of the six inch Ordnance Survey map for locating minor place-names. In an introductory note the English Place Names Society, sponsors of the series, mentioned the co-ordinate reference system which the Ordnance Survey had recently introduced, but commented somewhat haughtily that such references "do not lend themselves to popular use". In fact, to provide each minor place name in the book with a map reference would have placed an intolerable burden upon the author.

Patricia Murphy in *The Essex Review* drew attention afresh to the potential of the tithe apportionment maps and surveys "now in the Essex Record Office at Chelmsford".[386] Most recently the Essex Society for Archaeology and History (the former Essex Archaeological Society) launched a bold initiative to co-ordinate individual research in an Essex Place Names Project. Working initially from the tithe awards, local volunteers extract place names which are then recorded with map references obtained from the Ordnance Survey National Grid (which, in the 1940s, replaced the co-ordinate reference system referred to above) on a central database. This scheme goes a long way to solving the logistical problem associated with research and recording on this scale.

At the same time the use of the Ordnance Survey National Grid provides a reference unique within the country, let alone within the county. There is a practical difficulty here because the individual researcher has to estimate the centre of a field on the mid-19th century tithe map and then refer to a post-1947 Ordnance Survey map of a convenient scale marked with the grid in order to estimate the co-ordinates.[387] However, the researcher is also asked to give the number of the field on the tithe map. This alone if preceded by code letters identifying the parish would provide a unique reference within the county to an actual field of particular shape and size, as well as to a position. This procedure could be of particular value in the parishes where subsequent development has rendered former field boundaries difficult to trace. Nor is it likely that these field numbers would have to be generally discarded when moving into earlier periods. Experience suggests that, except in parishes that have undergone extensive enclosure, field boundaries have considerable persistence and fields in the tithe award maps are either accumulations or divisions of earlier fields retaining an overall pattern.

Whilst it is inevitable that a countywide study of place-names should begin by extracting field names from the ubiquitous post-1836 tithe commutation maps and awards, it is the expressed intention of the Essex Place Names Project to progress to earlier sources. Indeed, Waller himself admitted a basic limitation of his material in some parishes, including Barking and Ilford, where the space in the schedules of tithe apportionments for field names was "very sparsely filled in". The inadequate recording of names in the Barking tithe award has since been amply exposed by the discovery of the extensive pre-1836 tithe documentation described above in chapters four and five. An amusing example from the Ilford area is that which Waller listed as 'Doyper Field' – the original entry proves to be parcel no.1757, Doypen Field. Earlier sources show that this field was actually called Dry Pond Field in 1800 and formerly Pond Field. It is easy to imagine evidence given in local dialect to a recorder little concerned with entering the right name.

Dr James Kemble rightly draws attention in his publicity for the Essex project to "the many useful lessons which can be learned from this sort of study". Various examples from Barking and Ilford have already been cited in this chapter, such as the significance of 'reden names', but it is instructive to examine a more complex case where earlier names "reveal early use of the field".

Two or three fields once bore the name 'conduit' in reference to the medieval water supplies of Barking Abbey. The 1669 tithe survey names a four acre meadow alongside the River Roding, south of Uphall, and corresponding to no.323 of the tithe award as "Conduit Mead". The name also occurs earlier in the 1540 ministers' accounts and it undoubtedly lay on the course of the Abbey's first water supply from springs at Cranbrook in Ilford. This conduit, parallel to the Roding, dated from the 13th century at least, but had to be abandoned in 1462 as the result of a dispute with John and Joan Rigby, the owners of Cranbrook.

But Conduit Field to the south of Green Lane was on the route of the Abbey's new conduit from Newbury. The course of these replacement pipes was carefully documented in 1463 (in English) by the Abbess Katherine de la Pole in her 'register', preserved by the 18th century antiquarian and lord of the manor, Smart Lethieullier. The summary in Lysons (who was subsequently given access to Lethieullier's notes) hardly does justice to this account of medieval water engineering, which is also a source of field names almost contemporary with the 1456 Abbey rental.[388]

To protect it from interference, the new "Course of the Conduit" was designed to run only through Abbey demesnes such as Newbury, Downshall and Loxford and copyholdings belonging to the Abbey. The lead pipe ran under the High Road, into the north-west corner of Cricklewood (the later Cricklefields, now a cemetery), and over the Cricklewood Ditch (cradled in a tree-trunk) into Cricklewood Reden to the west.

It continued south-west through Combecroft and over the Green Way (the Green Lane) into Serlis Croft, "and so over that croft into a land that longeth Loxford called Ravenynefield, and there is a vent in a house of brick, and so lieth forth by the south east corner of a field that is called Purpenfield".

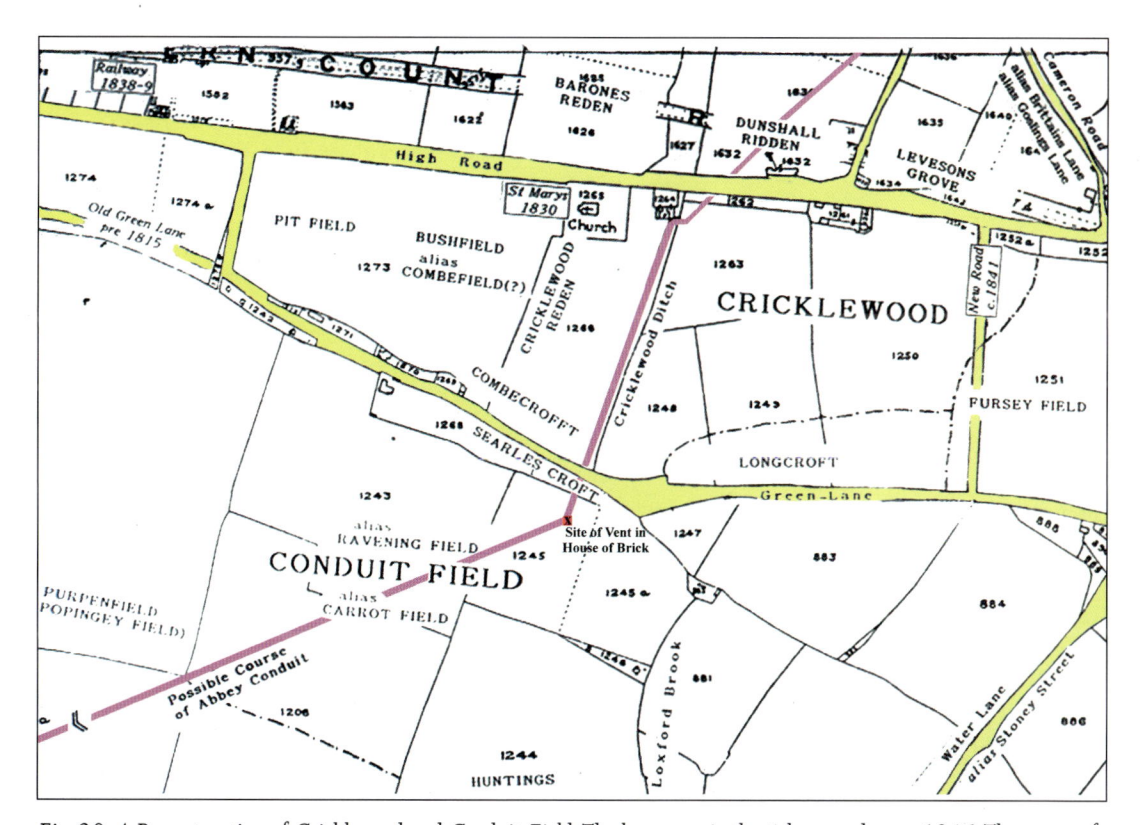

Fig. 20. A Reconstruction of Cricklewood and Conduit Field. The base map is the tithe award map, 1846. The course of the Barking Abbey conduit is shown. Note also the field names indicative of clearance of medieval woodland.

Searles Croft is recorded in the 1750 tithe survey and can thus be identified (via the early tithe map) as a roadside enclosure numbered 1267-8 on the tithe award map of 1846. It is described in the 1609 manorial survey (item 524) as two acres of arable held by copy "between Green streate and Ravenings fielde to the south". This older name of the field to the south (no.1243 with 1245) is thus confirmed; almost certainly it derives from a medieval tenant.[389] Note also that 'field', not 'fields' is used because no.1245 was part of 1243 on the early tithe map – the broken line between 1245 and 1245a is the old field boundary. In the same 1609 survey (Item 155) Henry Pownsett, the owner of Loxford, held 45 acres of arable land in four parcels called the Conduit Fields, described in abutments [Item 370] as Conduite Field alias the Ravening Field. This larger area included most of no.1208 which was still part of Loxford Farm at the time of the tithe award.

No name is given to these field(s) in the vicar's tithe books or on the 1666 map. But, curiously, this map shows a building in the east of the field no.1245 just south of Searles Croft which does not appear to be a dwelling house – could it be the remains of the "house of brick" which once sheltered the vent (or windpipe) in the Conduit? Historically part of Loxford demesne, the field was therefore in the hospital tithing, and the fourth of the 12 sketches from the 1790s entitled 'Hospital Tithes in Loxford Farm' labels it "Carrot and Conduit Field".[390] So the name was transmitted through the archives of Ilford Hospital, as well as through the manorial archives and title deeds. A deed of 1792 (when part of the field had been leased to Clements Farm) describes it as "Conduit Field being part of Great Loxford".[391] Significantly no.1245 is still in the hospital tithing, like the rest of Loxford, but no.1245a tithes only to the vicar; so the broken line was included on the tithe award map because it showed not merely an old field boundary, but also the ancient boundary between the tithings.[392] The tithe award schedules are not very helpful; no.1243 is there called "Folly House Field", a name not otherwise recorded which appears to have been connected with a house on Green Lane (near the Prince of Wales public house), and no.1245 is called "Sheep Field".

To bring the story up-to-date; the eastern part of no.1243 remained open as a Volunteer (later Territorial Army) drill ground from the 1890s and as playing fields, until it became the site of St Peter and St Paul's Roman Catholic primary school in the 1980s. It appears to have derived the name Gordon Field(s) from Gordon Road, the suburban street adjoining (a name with scant local significance). Part of no.1245 falls within the north-west corner of today's South Park. Thus this field, or parts of a field, has been given six different names over the centuries: one of them revealing an early tenant (Ravening); three pointing to usage (Conduit, Carrot and Sheep); and two more recent of dubious or fortuitous origin (Folly House, Gordon).

Field patterns

The reconstruction of historic landscapes working backwards from tithe award maps has a distinguished ancestry. Howard Levi Gray employed it in his 1915 classic study, *English Field*

Systems, although the official maps were not then so readily available. As early as 1883 Frederic Seebohm in his pioneering work, *The English Village Community*, had used a parish tithe map c.1816 to examine the open field system of Hitchin in Hertfordshire by what has been termed the regressive method.

Gray selected three holdings from the manor of Barking to illustrate his contention that compact virgates were typical of enclosed south-western Essex. He reproduced almost in full the descriptions of these three which he found in the detailed manorial survey of 1609, omitting only previous tenants and rents. All his three examples of copyhold virgates were from the parish of Dagenham to the south of the High Road to Romford, and east of Barking parish. Nor in this instance did Gray attempt to locate them more exactly by using the Dagenham tithe award or other cartographical evidence.[393]

Given that Dagenham does not possess the wealth of tithe documentation available for Barking, this might have presented a lengthy task for Gray. Nevertheless, the present author has succeeded in identifying one of Gray's virgates. The virgate identified is that called 'Longyerd' in the 1609 survey which describes it [Item 467] as "seven acres of arable and seven of woodland abutting upon Blackhethe to the north". This last is, in fact, Chadwell Heath, but the remaining abutments seem a little confused. However, the survey of 1679 (fo.165) reveals that it is "Long Yard alias Purlands, formerly Purlands Grove containing 13 acres… near the Whalebone". The 1726 rental adds that it is "17 acres of arable land lately stubbed and converted into tillage near the Whalebone". When located on the Dagenham tithe award map of 1844, it has become four fields (nos. D399-D402) containing just over 16 acres with the new Eastern Counties railway crossing the southern margin. Forty years later St Chad's church was erected at the northern end where it bordered the original High Road to Romford.[394]

So far it might be argued that Gray could have learnt no more from such identification on the map beyond confirming his belief that the virgate here was a single compact block, although he might also have been interested to find that Long Yard was rectilinear in form. If he had been able to examine further virgates in Barking parish with the resources now available, he would have found still more evidence that the consolidated virgate, sometimes comprising more than one variety of land use, was a customary holding there. Moreover, he would have discovered that the virgate throughout Barking manor had a standard size of 16 acres for which a standard rent of 10s.1d. per annum was commonly demanded (Long Yard was anomalous at four shillings per annum).[395]

The virgates appear to be arranged peripherally to the medieval 'manors', presumably their tenants had once rendered services there (including the collection of tithe). Their form was not always rectilinear, but this field shape occurs frequently to the south of the High Road. Though, somewhat curiously, the grids so formed do not always line up exactly with this Roman road. More irregularity in field boundaries to the north may be associated with clearance of woodland.

The prevalence of rectilinear systems in south Essex and possible clues to their date of origin have been questions formerly much aired in historical landscape studies commencing, so far as Essex is concerned, with the work of Warwick Rodwell in the 1970s. This work has relied heavily for its basic material upon 19th century tithe award maps, supplemented by some earlier estate maps.[396] So far those attempts that have been made to provide direct archaeological confirmation for periods of origin have not met with conspicuous success.[397] It is interesting that Stephen Rippon has now concluded, *contra* Rodwell, that extensive rectilinear landscape features in Essex to the east of Barking are probably Saxon in origin.[398] These enquiries have given little or no attention to southwest Essex.

The regressive, retrogressive, or retrospective mode of historical enquiry – by whatever name we may choose to call it – is really a commonsense procedure for working from the known to the unknown. It should move by stages from a carefully surveyed and well-documented later period into the relative obscurity of earlier times. Barking offers the advantage of being able to regress from a secure vantage point almost 200 years earlier than the tithe award.

The paucity of medieval manorial documentation in Barking has to be set against this advantage. Furthermore, although a decreasing amount of evidence with an increasing problem of interpretation may be unavoidable, perhaps the real danger of the regressive method is that it is liable to encourage too much faith in continuity and gradual change. Thankfully in the last few years historians have become readier to accept discontinuities, including those believed to result from deliberate planning in early periods.

The 1999 overview of an intensive study of the evolution of settlement pattern in the village of Shapwick in Somerset concluded, "it begins to look as if, on selected arable estates, a deliberate decision was made by some large monasteries to re-order both landscape and settlement on an impressive scale... The context for this might be the re-invigoration of monastic life under Dunstan in the 940s and subsequent monastic reforms."[399] Although conducted by a large multidisciplinary team (with an archaeological emphasis), the 'Shapwick Project' also employed the regressive method working back from the local tithe award map of 1839, through 18th century estate maps to a detailed survey of 1515.

Whilst the geographical setting of Shapwick is distinct and its medieval documentation more extensive, there are parallels with the manor of Barking. Shapwick was part of the estates given by King Ine of Wessex to Glastonbury Abbey early in the eighth century and probably reorganised when Dunstan was Abbot in the tenth. Barking was given to Barking Abbey by the East Saxon royal family in the seventh century, and the house was restored after the Danish raids in the tenth to become a nunnery on the Benedictine pattern promoted by Dunstan when he became Archbishop.

In the Barking case, the distribution of consolidated virgates of uniform size also suggests a system engineered at a particular time rather than a gradual and unplanned development. The distinctive 16 acre Barking virgate is not found in adjacent manors (although some examples are known further west in Middlesex and Surrey). It is possible that this reorganisation may have been imposed upon a pattern that already had some coaxial features from an earlier period.

We may never know for certain when this reordering took place, but it could well have been contemporary with the tenth century restoration and so associated with another reorganisation: the introduction of 'radknight' (riding service) tenures into Barking manor. As the *Victoria County History* suggests these tenures were almost certainly introduced at this time since they closely resemble the *lex equitandi* ('riding custom') instituted by Oswald, who succeeded his friend Dunstan as Bishop of Worcester in 961.[400] Such a scheme would be well adapted to a restored nunnery in a time of insecurity. However, as noted above, the uniform rent of 10s.1d per virgate was almost certainly a much later example of planning, dating from the late 14th, or early 15th, centuries.[401]

The 'indelible tithing'

Less hypothetically, the very complexity of the Barking tithings and their relative antiquity can offer a peculiar research facility. The boundaries between tithings persist over the centuries despite changes of tenure and even of field boundaries. This first became apparent to the author in the 1960s when searching for the 'lost' manor of Wyfields.

The disappearance of this ancient Ilford manor in the last decades of the 18th century was mentioned in chapter five. By the beginning of the 19th century the title had been merged and its lands absorbed into five other estates, the chief of which were Cranbrook and Valentines; the house alone remained to be demolished between 1823 and 1825. So by 1839, when Drayson drew up the plan which became the tithe commutation map of Barking in 1846, no obvious traces remained and Wyfields went unrecorded. An illustration of the house survived in the City of London Guildhall library, but in 1899 the schoolmaster and local historian, Edward Tuck, who had known the area well before suburban housing covered all except Valentines Park, could get no closer than to describe it as having been "about half-a-mile north of Ilford".[402]

So in 1960, several years before the rediscovery of the corpus of parish tithe records described in chapter four, a reconstruction of the plan of the manor of Wyfields presented a formidable challenge. The 1846 tithe map was first taken as a convenient base rather than as a source. Fortunately the Essex Record Office had a good copy of a portion of the missing manorial map of 1652/3, made by Edward Sage in the mid-19th century, which showed the houses of Wyfields, Cranbrook and Valentines and some adjoining fields. The attached estates could be distinguished by the names of the tenants – Brewster of Wyfields and Young of Cranbrook – written over the fields. Several unexpected features were immediately apparent. The manor

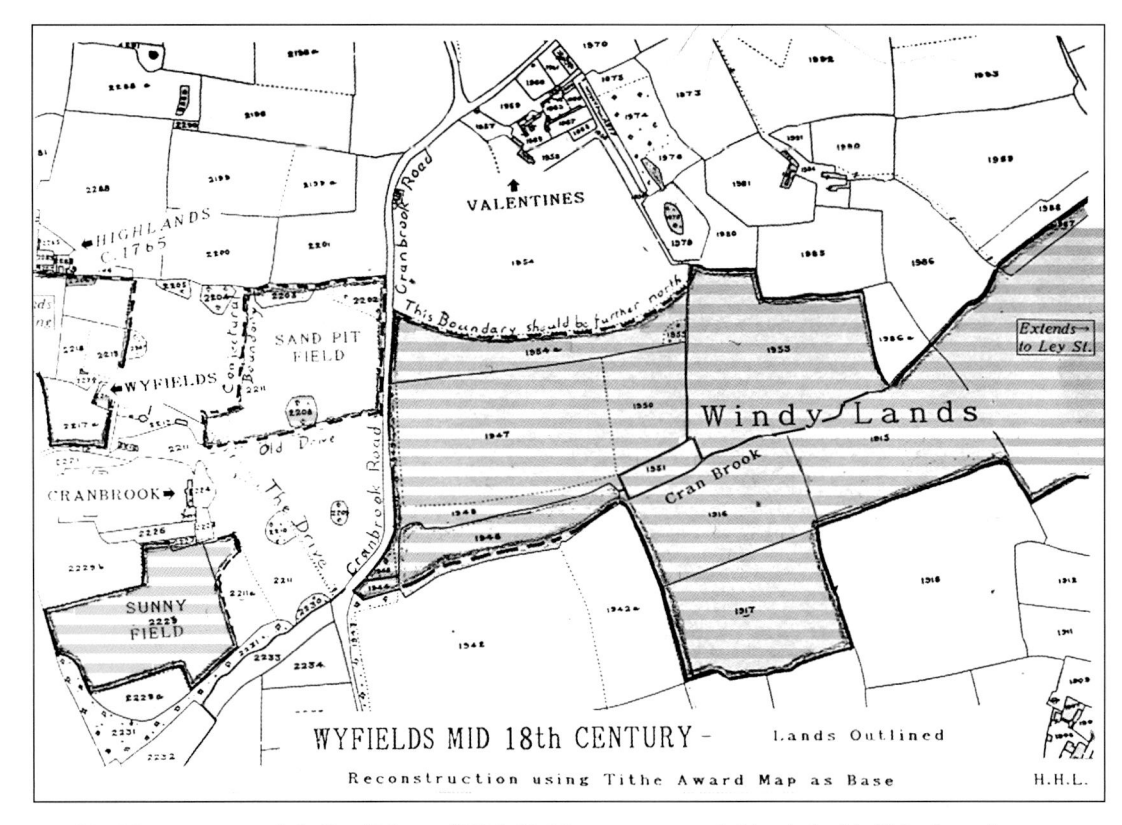

Fig. 21. *A Reconstruction of the 'Lost' Manor of Wyfields. The manor is revealed by the 'indeliable' tithing, despite absorption by adjacent estates in the 18th century.*

house of Wyfields was barely 200 yards north-west of Cranbrook Hall, and their respective lands formed a curious jigsaw. Also the lands of Wyfields extended over the eastern side of Cranbrook Road into the area which was to become the southern half of Valentines Park.

Already aware that the tithes of Wyfields had been granted to the Ilford Hospital in 1219, as soon as a start was made in transferring Brewster's holdings onto the 1846 tithe award map, it became plain that all, except one 16 acre field (Sand Pit Field) between the house and Cranbrook Road, tithed to the Ilford Hospital.[403] More surprising was the revelation that where field boundaries had changed the former boundaries were often indicated on the 1846 map by broken lines.[404]

So the hospital tithing could be used to identify Wyfields' land both east and west of the area covered by the extract from the 1652/3 map. Yet it was evident, even from the limited area, that some adjacent fields tithed to the hospital without being tenanted by Brewster; so some other evidence was required to delimit Wyfields. This was now supplied by a list of fields and their acreages in a private act of parliament obtained in 1767 when Bamber Gascoyne's family sold the manor to Charles Raymond, which also gave its total area as 202 acres. The "Great Field next

106

Ley Street" could easily be identified (no.1914) and the rest ascertained by elimination. The general name of these lands of Wyfields to the east of Cranbrook Road appeared to have been 'Windelands' or 'Windylands'. The name probably derived from 'windel', a winding stream; which could have described the Cran Brook before it was canalised and the lake constructed in what became part of Valentines. The site of Wyfields house was obviously very near no. 2216 (yard and buildings) in 1847.[405]

At the opening of 20th century, Cranbrook Hall was demolished and the whole area submerged by the suburban villas of Peter Grigg's Cranbrook Park Estate. Although the course of The Drive largely preserves the line of the early 19th century drive to the Cranbrook Hall (which had replaced the east-west drive to Cranbrook and Wyfields shown on the 1652/3 map) it is difficult to visualise where the great houses actually stood. However, Seymour Gardens could be said to intersect the site of Wyfields House and De Vere Gardens, the site of Cranbrook Hall.

A year or two after the investigations described above, Dr Stephens' 1750 tithe book and the copy of the vicar's tithe map were found and they amply confirmed previous deductions. Such is the apparent persistence of the tithing boundaries that the area of Wyfields which they delimit may be assumed to be the same as in 1219, when the tithes of this manor were given to the Ilford Hospital. With further assistance from hospital tithe lists and manorial records, the anomalous 16 acre Sand Pit Field turned out to have been a distinct medieval virgate called Walshis or Welchfeild which, though attached to Wyfields, did not render tithe corn to Ilford Hospital. So a 'medieval field map' may now be reconstructed here with a reasonable degree of reliability. Incidentally, the early name of the attached virgate might itself be indicative of local British survival, particularly if Wyfield were in fact the Widmundesfelt of the Hodilred (Oethelred) Charter and a former Romano-British villa estate annexed by the East Saxon monarchy.[406]

This persistence is of wider application. All the tithings of Barking parish have a medieval origin and the hospital tithing in particular lends itself to this mode of investigation because the gifts of tithe to the Ilford Hospital are well documented in the vellum book at Hatfield House and its tithe lists go back to the 14th century. Moreover, lands tithing to the hospital are found in various quarters of the parish interpenetrating other tithings.

The principle again proved useful when applied to Claybury. When the fifth volume of the *Victoria County History of Essex* was published in 1966 it was possible to incorporate the above identification of Wyfields.[407] It was by no means certain then if the 'manor' of Claybury which the Ilford Hospital held in 1401 could be identified with the "120 acres of assart in Estholte" given to the hospital following its foundation c.1145.[408] However, the vellum book made it plain that the additions to the tithes of the hospital made in 1219 included the great and small tithes "of their own lands at the Clay" and the first tithe list of 1384-5 and 1401 included the tithes of "a place called Cleyberye". It followed that the area of land at Claybury tithing to Ilford

Hospital in the 17th century ought to be the same as the original assart, or clearance, in the 12th century. This area measured 176½ statute acres in 1666 whereas the original assart was described as 120 acres, but if the 120 acres had been measured using the larger woodland perch of 20 feet it would, in fact, have been equivalent to 176½ statute acres based upon the standard perch of 16½ feet.

It had now become apparent from archaeological investigation that the straight western boundary of this area of clearance had actually rested on a former Roman road across the forest which, still in use in the early middle ages, had also been adopted as a manorial and parish boundary by the Saxons. The south-east boundary had been a former highway called Clayhooks Lane following the forest fence to Tom-at-Woods.[409]

It is probable that this 'indelibility' could be employed to reconstruct the medieval manor of Fulkes in the south of the parish. The identification of Fulkes' lands and even manor house became increasingly difficult after the Dissolution.[410] Hopefully some reader of these words may accept the challenge!

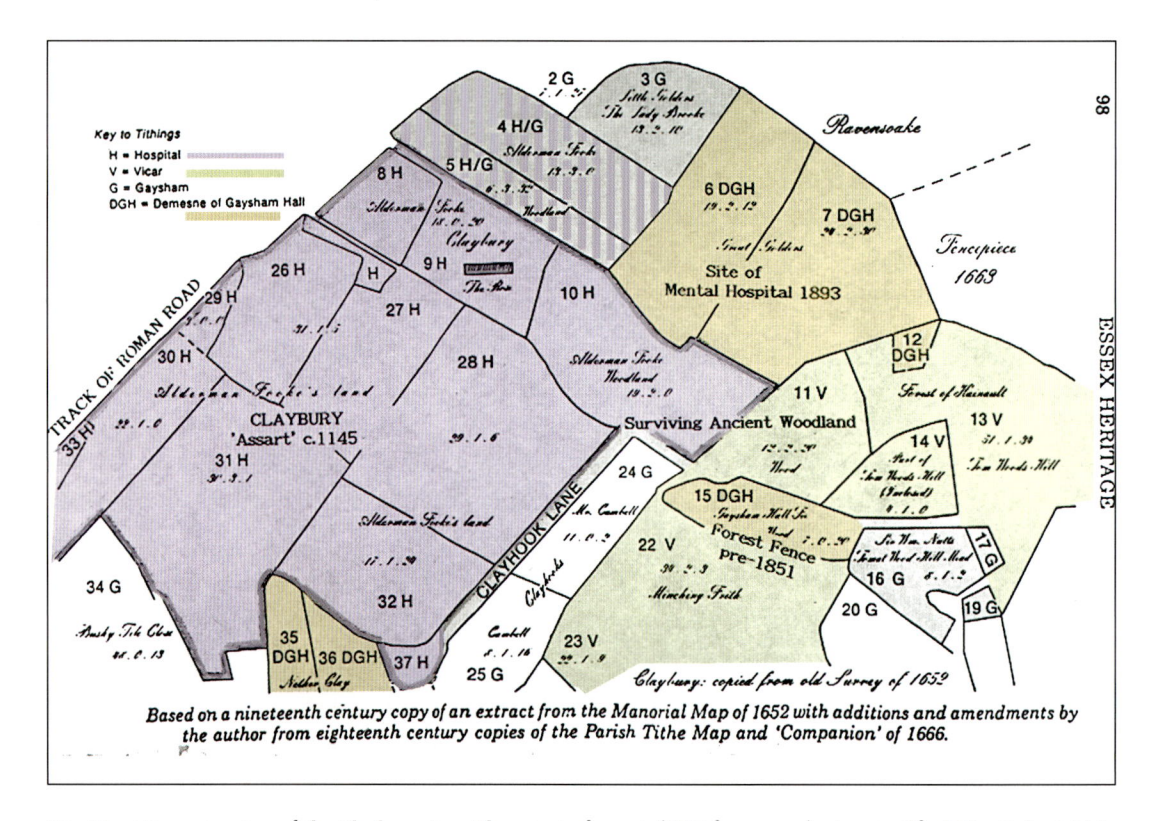

Fig. 22. A Reconstruction of the Claybury Area. The extent of assart (120 forest acres) given to Ilford Hospital c.1145 is outlined; this became the demesne of Claybury, as revealed by the extent of the hospital tithing there (Lockwood, 1992).

The above principle can be used in many parishes with simpler tithe structures than Barking. Opening the first case study of his *Field Systems in Essex*, John Hunter writes "apart from the survival of the two remarkable barns, the great interest of Cressing Temple for the student of landscape lies in the tithe free status of its demesne land, a privilege that survived to be recorded in the tithe award of Cressing and also in adjoining parishes where the Templars held lands. The legal situation was that when ownership changed the status remained with the land, and as a result it is possible to reconstruct the post-Conquest evolution of the manor and parish."[411]

Appendix: notes on the provenance of principal Barking sources

General background

The survival and location of historical documents depends upon historical and personal factors and even upon sheer accident and so may differ markedly from place to place; hence the problem of 'differential survival'. Whilst the Public Record Office had long cared for records of central government, few now realise how inadequate and uneven was the provision for the preservation of local records before the Second World War.[412]

Dr Frederick Emmison, the first county and diocesan archivist of Essex, and Mr John O'Leary, the first librarian of Dagenham, established the Essex Record Office and the Valence Library as the principal repositories for the records of Barking, as well as Dagenham, in the two decades between the ending of the Second World War and 1965 when the boroughs were combined.

Barking, Ilford and Dagenham, like other metropolitan boroughs east of the River Lea were all within the bounds of the historic county of Essex and figured in official series like Quarter Session and archidiaconal records at the base of the Essex Record Office's collection. But from its inception in 1938, Frederick Emmison strove equally to collect parish, manorial and estate documents to ensure their preservation.[413] Amongst early acquisitions were the extensive Petre family records that included material concerning Barking Abbey and its possessions. In 1946 the Essex Record Office acquired the important Sage Collection from the Stoke Newington Library, where it had been deposited by the son of Edward Sage, Deputy Steward of the Manor of Barking for many years during the 19th century. This included two large folio volumes in manuscript for an illustrated 'History of the Manor and Parish of Barking' which Edward Sage had assembled by 1859, as well as a considerable collection of miscellaneous documents, chiefly estate or manorial.[414]

John O'Leary's *Essex and Dagenham Catalogue* of 1961 listed over 2,000 books and documents in Valence Library which related to many places besides Dagenham. Several entries, for example, covered a large collection of Fanshawe family records. The Fanshawes figured prominently in the history of both Barking and Dagenham – O'Leary acquired their family portraits as well! He also sought photocopies of documents and maps in other archive collections such as the Public Record Office, as well as in private ones little explored up to this time.[416] Notably he commissioned photographs from the Hulse family archive at Breamore House in Hampshire of the unpublished manuscript of Smart Lethieullier's 'History of Barking' with an appendix volume of notes.[417] Lethieullier, a scholar of note, was Lord of the Manor of Barking in the first half of the 18th century and his work had been used as a principal source by Daniel Lysons in *Environs of London* (1796-1811) as well as by Edward Sage. His only daughter and heiress married a Hulse. Until O'Leary's investigations it was thought that the manuscript and notes had been destroyed by a fire at Breamore in 1857.

In their respective spheres Emmison and O'Leary were pioneers of what has been justly termed 'the archival revolution'. They were closely allied not only by enthusiasm for collecting documents, but also for stimulating public interest and use. Together they played an active role in the revival of the *Victoria County History of Essex*; O'Leary was County Secretary and Emmison a leading member of the editorial board. Volume five, the second of the new series edited by Raymond Powell and published in 1966, included Dagenham (by O'Leary), Barking and Ilford and provided the foundation for any present-day study of the area.

Prior to amalgamation with Dagenham, Barking Libraries showed relatively little interest in the acquisition of archives, but in 1955 Barking Borough Council financed the publication of *Barking Vestry Minutes and other Parish Documents* by Dr James Oxley. This work of scholarship was based primarily upon a fine series of nine volumes of Barking Vestry minutes from 1694 to 1926 preserved in the strong-room of Barking Town Hall. Fortunately, these minutes had been carefully assembled and bound in vellum with gold lettering at the instigation of Allen Wand, the last of the paid assistant overseers of Barking, before he handed them over to the Borough Council.

In 1965 Barking and Dagenham were absorbed into a single London borough and their library and museum united. Being due for retirement, John O'Leary was replaced by William George Fairchild, the serving borough librarian of Barking. James Howson, who took over at Valence House as curator-archivist, assisted in planning a new muniment room which eventually facilitated the transfer of documents from the Barking strong-room to join the collection inherited from O'Leary.

Barking tithe & other parish documents

A collection of 500 mainly parish documents surfaced in 1963 in response to the author's enquiries. They had been discovered by the Reverend J.D. Wakeling, incumbent of St Margaret's from 1959 to 1965, in a locked container in the back stables of the old vicarage. Apparently, this had been deposited there for safety during the Second World War, but in time the contents were forgotten and the key lost. After this had been forced open by the vicar, the documents were placed in the temporary care of churchwarden, Harold Wand (son of Allen Wand), to await identification. On examination the cache was found to include the dissected 18th century copy of the vicar's tithe map of 1666, the tithe survey of circa 1750, and various tithe accounts from as far back as 1681.[418]

Internal evidence suggested that Vicar Blomfield had sorted out the contents of this 'parish chest' in 1881.[419] Fortunately, he retained much of value to historians amongst the documents that, in his own words, he "selected as examples". Subsequently, later items had been added to this collection. Conjecturally it could always have been stored at the vicarage, but it may equally have been a product of a larger reorganization that is known to have taken place between 1926 and 1927. At this juncture, Allen Wand, who then combined the offices of vestry clerk and vicar's warden with that of assistant overseer (which he had held for around 40 years), endeavoured to separate civil from ecclesiastical documents. The civil, including rate books and surveys, as well as the Barking Vestry minutes mentioned above, were handed over to the borough council in 1927.[420] As explained, these ultimately passed from the strong-room of Barking town-hall into the new muniment store at Valence Library. Those deemed ecclesiastical would have remained in the church with the church registers or been handed over to the vicar. Tithe documents were plainly ecclesiastical, but anomalously Johnson's tithe survey of 1806 was included with other civil documents, possibly because it had provided the base for a rate survey in the following year.

Between 1963 and 1965 the 500 documents rediscovered were sorted and listed and the parish church council agreed to deposition in the Essex Record Office (a copy of the catalogue prepared by the author and David Pryor is on file with the documents).[421] Initial perusal of the tithe documents in this collection revealed there had once been three tithe surveys in the series: Mr Cartwright's book; Mr Fiddes' green book; and Dr Stephens' book. This last had now reappeared; a search was begun for the remaining two.

Cartwright's book was discovered in the possession of the Glenny family of Barking and was given to the Essex Record Office in 1966 by Mr Kenneth Glenny, a leading member of Essex County Council's Records Committee and a supporter of the Essex Record Office. This volume, of course, was the most valuable since it contained the first tithe surveys of 1669 and 1681, as well as the 1617 survey of Barking parish within the forest of Waltham.[422, 423]

Mr Fiddes' green book containing the tithe survey of 1727/8 was discovered around 1974, having been found in an old iron safe at the rear of St Margaret's church. It went missing again for a while, but was eventually sent to join the others in the Essex Record Office in 1988.[424]

Ilford Hospital documents

In 1963 the author, in company with John O'Leary, visited Hatfield House having been alerted to the significance of the collection there by the Reverend Farmiloe, then chaplain of the Ilford Hospital of St Mary and St Thomas of Canterbury. Lord Salisbury, as Master of the Hospital, had inherited a considerable archive. The most interesting individual item proved to be a handwritten volume known for obvious reasons as the 'vellum book'.[425] Much of the content was in Latin and seemed to have been copied from a lost cartulary of Barking Abbey. Apparently the scribe in the late 16th century had been instructed to copy all entries "E magno Registro Barking" which referred to grants to the hospital, but through uncertainty or antiquarian interest included a great deal more. Thus, in addition to copying the earliest hospital tithe list of 1384/5 – 1401 and over 120 more medieval deeds, he reproduced – struggling with unfamiliar orthography – the Latin texts of nine Saxon charters dating from centuries before the foundation of Ilford Hospital.

None of these newly revealed charters concerned lands in Barking or Ilford, although all except one referred to other places in Essex. The two earliest, concerning land at Nazeing were East Saxon and nearly contemporary with the already known foundation charters of Barking Abbey. Moreover, their discovery interlocked remarkably with the archaeological investigation of a Saxon church and burial ground at Nazeingbury in 1975-6: the combined evidence suggesting a dependent cell to Barking.[426] The third charter from King Athelstan, dated 932, referred to land in Bures (or Bowers Gifford), together with four charters from King Eadred, also dating from the tenth century and including lands in Hockley, Tolleshunt, and Wigborough, threw fresh light on the re-founding of Barking Abbey following the Danish incursions, linking with recent archaeology. The remaining two charters from King Aelthelred in the early 11th century referred apparently to Hatfield (Broad Oak) and Horndon.

None of the nine were recorded in P.H. Sawyer's *Anglo-Saxon Charters*, but there can be little doubt now about their authenticity. Actually, Smart Lethieullier did notice them in the early 18th century having recognised this part of the vellum book, then in the hands of the Gascoynes, as a "copy of an ancient MS formerly belonging to the Abbey of Barking".[427]

Tithe disputes

In 1956/7, John O'Leary purchased for the Dagenham Library a late 16th manuscript in Latin and English containing the depositions in two disputes conducted in the Bishop of London's Court concerning tithes claimed by the Ilford Hospital.[428] The first was Fanshawe v. Caroe [Carew] re: tithes of Eastbury commenced in 1586. The second, Fisher v. Wite [Wight] re: tithes of North Grange [marsh] commenced in 1590. Both are full of interesting detail (with legal comments in the margins), but the second includes the deposition of James Armorer, describing how in the 1570s, on the instructions of John Vaughan, former master of the hospital, he copied the earliest hospital tithe list onto parchment "out of a more auncient writing wch was some what defaced" and delivered his "writinges" to Fanshawe (then recently appointed master). Thus he identifies himself as the scribe of the vellum book. Apparently, Vaughan, a Master of Chancery, must have been able to borrow the Abbey cartulary from the Augmentation Office, then a part of the Exchequer, probably with the connivance of the Fanshawes (but where did it go afterwards?)[429]

In 1966, when Jim Howson at Valence Library was preparing an exhibition to commemorate the 1,300th anniversary of the foundation of Barking Abbey, he received from Fairchild a box of several documents which had been in store at the Barking Central Library. These included a manuscript entitled – to gloss the Latin – 'A collection of deeds and evidences to prove that the tithes of Ripple ward belonged to Eastbury and not to the Vicar'. No information was available on the provenance of this MS, but the paper and its watermark, the ink and some of the handwriting suggest it originated from the same 16th century legal source as the above depositions. And, as shown in chapter three, it included valuable information on the management of Abbey demesne in the middle ages and the origins of the Barking tithe-circuits or tithings. The transfer of this document was particularly fortuitous since a few months later, in April 1967, arson completely destroyed Barking Central Library.[430]

Furthermore, as indicated above in chapter two, detailed records of a number of 17th century appeals to the Court of Arches in Barking tithe disputes have been preserved in the Province of Canterbury archives in the Lambeth Palace Library (although in some instances fragility restricts access).

Manorial documents

Notwithstanding the manorial documents and transcripts in the Sage Collection, Dr Oxley complained in 1955, in his introduction to *Barking Vestry Minutes*, "It is unfortunate that the Manorial Rolls of Barking have almost completely disappeared".[431] In fact, probably when he was searching for the Lethieullier manuscripts, John O'Leary became aware that the rolls that belonged to the Hulse family (as lords of the manor) were in store with the family's solicitors in Lincoln Inn Fields. In September 1968, Sir Westrow Hulse granted the author access which revealed a splendid series of rolls from 1679 and many other manorial and estate documents and deeds, generally in fair condition, but in cramped and unsuitable accommodation. By the end of the year, Sir Westrow had agreed to relieve his solicitors of the burden and to loan them to Essex Record Office, where professional cataloguing, conservation and storage could be provided.[432]

Table 3: references for Barking tithe and other selected documents

Numbers bracketed { } refer to MS catalogue by H.H. Lockwood (1963-5), ERO 81/3/84; documents marked with asterisk (*) photocopies or manual transcripts/translations are available for use in Valence House Local Studies Centre (Dagenham).

Tithe awards

ERO D/CT 18A & B	Barking tithe award 1847 & map 1846* Award in two parts in one volume (St Margaret's, Barking & St Mary's, Ilford) Parcel numbers 1 to 2618 keyed to the map (scale of map is $13\frac{3}{8}$" = 1 mile, insets for Barking Town and Ilford, $26\frac{3}{4}$" = 1 mile)
ERO Q/RDC 42B	Plan of the King's Forest… in Hainault 1851 (disafforestation map – T. Thurston. Uses tithe parcel numbers as award above, and also numbers in adjoining parishes, but covers north of Romford Road only)

Tithe surveys, maps & accounts for the parish of Barking, pre-1844

ERO D/P 81/3/16	Dissected copy c.1747 of vicar's tithe map 1666 (based on manorial map 1652/3)* (22 sheets. Parcels numbered 1-1569 woodlands etc. tinted yellow scale c.16"= 1 mile)
Hatfield House Cecil MSS (Ilford Hospital)	1/17 12 sketches from the Vicar of Barking's map copy from above c.1790
Hatfield House Cecil MSS (Ilford Hospital)	1/17A. Partial copy c.1790 of companion to map 1666
ERO D/DSa	'History of Barking' i, 56. Rough outline sketch of vicar's tithe map by Sage(?), pre-1864 no numbers, names or acreage
ERO D/SH 14	Eastbury upland tithing 1735 (numbered as 1666 map)
ERO D/SH 15	Eastbury upland tithing 1742 (numbered as 1666 map)
ERO D/SH 16	Eastbury marshland tithing 1742 (numbered as 1666 map)
ERO D/DSt. F3	Schedule of Eastbury tithing 1775, contains alternative numbering also used on above maps
Lockwood H.H.	'Map of Abbey site [etc] as in the 17th century', *Where was the First Barking Abbey?* (1986), Fig.5, based on Luff's extract from manorial map of Barking town, with many 1666 tithe map numbers added
ERO D/P 81/3/110	[Front] Dr Cartwright's tithe book 1669* Complete survey: field names, acreages, index of occupiers' names at front, of parcel numbers at rear. Numbers refer to above map of 1666
ERO D/P 81/3/11O	Incomplete tithe book (Cartwright) 1680
ERO D/P 81/3/110	Dr Cartwright's tithe book 1681; similar to 1669

	(numbers as 1666 map)*
ERO 81/3/8	Tithe account 1681/82 {51} An account of money received and paid for the Deane of Rippon [Dr Cartwright] for tythes…[etc]
ERO 81/3/9	Tithe account 1684/5 {52}
ERO 81/ Acc. 7648	Tithe accounts (two books) 1690-1711 & 1711-1723
ERO D/P 81 Acc.7648	Mr Fiddes' tithe book 1727/28. Complete survey (index of parcel numbers at rear refer to 1666 map)
ERO 81/3/10	Tithe account 1733 {53}
ERO D/P 81/3/15	Dr Stephens' tithe book c.1750 {15}. Complete survey (Parcel numbers refer to 1666 map; index at rear)
Barking & Dagenham P.L. (Valence Archive Coll.)	Tithe accounts 1763-1778 (Musgrave's 'rental')
ERO 81/3/11	Tithe account (Rashleigh's) c.1781 {54}
	Tithe accounts 1784-87 [included in *Catalogue of Essex Parish Records* 1966, not located]
ERO 81/3/12	Tithe account 1790 {55}
ERO 81/3/13	Tithe account 1792 {56}
ERO 81/3/14	Tithe account 1793 {57}
Barking & Dagenham P.L. (Valence Archive Coll.)	Barking tithe survey (Johnson) 1806 (new system of numbering; map lost, but see rate survey 1829, below)

Selected Barking manorial documents

The manorial map 1652/3 mentioned above as base for tithe map of 1666 survives only in a few extracts in the ERO.*

BM Add.MS 45387	Rental of the Abbey of Barking 1456*
PRO SC 6/964	Ministers' accounts of the dissolved monastery 1540
PRO LR 2/214	Manorial survey 1609*
ERO D/DHs M31	Manorial survey 1679 (English transcript c.1750) * (index of tenants; pencil references to pages in 1726 rental, 'WB')
ERO D/DHs E2	Estate rental of Sir Wm. Humfreys 1726 (includes 'farm rents' i.e. leaseholds; adds names of tenants in the 'survey' i.e. 1679)*
ERO D/DHs M32	Accounts of fines 1705-1741 (gives names of tenants and properties; the actual Manor Court rolls are in Latin before 1733)
ERO D/DHs M27	Index to minute and court books 1764-1856 (index to 10 volumes of Manor Court proceedings working back from 'A' (M23, 1838-56) to 'F' (M16, 1764-82))
ERO D/DHs M34	Schedule of leases of waste land and cottages 1773-1811 (also names tenants of these small properties in 1834)

Other documents complementary to the tithe and manorial records

PRO E 368/449	Inquisition re: possessions of Ilford Hospital 1580
ERO D/P 81/3/110 [rear]	Survey of part of the parish of Barking lying within the forest of Waltham 1617 (parcel numbers added from the 1666 map)
ERO T/A 427/1	Subsidy roll 1522-24
ERO Q/RTh 5	Hearth tax 1671*
Barking & Dagenham	Barking rate survey (Twyford) 1829 (This has two parallel volumes, the Valence archive terrier and the valuation. The second column in the terrier "denotes the collection number upon Mr Johnson's map" [see tithe survey 1806, above]. The number in the first column refers to the valuation which describes its location in words. The terrier has an index of occupiers
Barking & Dagenham	Barking rate books for most years from 1737 and parallel ward books fill gaps (Valence archive coll.) (in 1821, unusually, owners as well as occupiers of cottages were listed)
ERO D/P81/4 Acc.7006	Church rate book 1843 (some properties in this rate book were later identified by the insertion of 1846/7 tithe award numbers)
Redbridge Central Library	Microfilm of tithe award 1847. Local history collection)

Notes

Introduction

1 Nesta Evans, 'Tithe Books as a source for the local historian', The Local Historian, 14, no. 1 (1980): 24-27.
2 Alan Macfarlane, *Reconstructing Historical Communities* (Cambridge: Cambridge University Press, 1977): 37.
3 Pat Hudson, 'A New History from Below' in *The Changing Face of English Local History*, ed. R.C. Richardson (Aldershot: Ashgate, 2000): 177. 'Record linkages' has long been a current term, see, for example, C.D. Rogers & J.H. Smith, *Local Family History in England* (Manchester: Manchester University Press, 1991).
4 Alan Macfarlane, *A Guide to English Historical Records* (Cambridge: Cambridge University Press, 1983): 23; ERO D/P 209/3/1-4.
5 *Essex in London: A guide to the records of the London Boroughs formerly in Essex deposited in the Essex Record Office* (Chelmsford: Essex Record Office, 1992).
6 Eric Evans and Alan Crosby, *Tithes, Maps, Apportionments and the 1836 Act: a guide for local historians*. 3rd ed. (Salisbury: British Association of Local History, 1997).
7 Roger J.P. Kain and Hugh C. Prince, *Tithe Surveys for Historians* (Chichester: Phillimore, 2000).
8 Roger J.P. Kain and Hugh C. Prince, *Tithe Surveys of England and Wales* (Cambridge: Cambridge University Press, 1985).
9 Roger J.P. Kain and Richard Oliver, *The Tithe Maps of England and Wales: a cartographic analysis and county-by-county catalogue* (Cambridge: Cambridge University Press, 1995).
10 Ann Tarver, *Church Court Records: An introduction for family and local historians* (Chichester: Phillimore, 1995).
11 F.G. Emmison, 'Tithes, Perambulations and Sabbath-breach in Elizabethan Essex' in F.G. Emmison and R. Stephens eds., *Tribute to an Antiquary: Essays presented to Marc Fitch* (London: Leopard's Head Press, 1976): 177-216. The essay has no index but some of the places are listed here, p.16; The three volumes of F.G. Emmison, *Elizabethan Life* (Chelmsford: Essex Record Office, 1970, 1973, 1976) were all intended as source books to show the wide variety of evidence obtainable from major classes of materials in the ERO and are fully indexed.

Chapter one

12 Giles Constable, *Monastic Tithes from their Origins to the Twelfth Century*, Cambridge Studies in Medieval Life and Thought (Cambridge: Cambridge University Press, 1964): 2; confirmed by more recent research e.g. E. Le Roy Ladurie, and J. Goy, *Tithe and Agrarian History from the Fourteenth to the Nineteenth Centuries*, trans. by Susan Burke (Paris/Cambridge: Cambridge University Press, 1982).
13 Eric Evans, *The Contentious Tithe* (London: Routledge & Kegan Paul, 1976): 16.
14 J.E. Oxley & W.B. Trigg, 'Tithe rental of Halifax parish', Halifax Antiquarian Society xxxi (1934): 79.
15 R.C. Fowler 'Religious Houses', *Victoria County History* [hereafter VCH] of Essex, ii (1907): 139.
16 Evans, *Contentious Tithe*, 8; Roger J.P. Kain & H.C. Prince, *The Tithe Surveys of England and Wales* (Cambridge: Cambridge University Press, 1985):10. In Elizabethan Essex, "refusal to pay tithe was more prevalent where the holder of a benefice was non-resident" Emmison, "Tithes, Perambulations and Sabbath-breach', 179.
17 Philip Morant, *The History and Antiquities of the County of Essex* (Chelmsford: 1816): i., 42, 45; VCH. Essex, v (1966):157, 170; in fairness it should be added that Edward Denny, Earl of Norwich, voluntarily added an endowment of £100 p.a by his will of 1637, charged on one of his estates, to be administered by a trust.

18 These developments are considered in Margaret James, 'The Political Importance of the Tithes Controversy in the English Revolution, 1640-60', History 26, (1941):1-18.
19 Essex Record Office (hereafter ERO), D/P 214/3/1.
20 The bishops of the established Church of England meeting at the Savoy Palace in London failed to reach agreement with clergy of Presbyterian views on revision of the Prayer Book and around 2,000 clergy, many appointed during the Commonwealth, were expelled by act; the resultant situation is discussed below in chapter four in connection with Barking between 1662 and 1689.
21 C. Hill, *Economic Problems of the Church* (Oxford: Panther, 1971, 1956): 276-285.
22 *VCH Essex*, ii: 76-78; Arthur Brown's 'The Essex Country Parson 1700-1815' in *Essex Heritage*, ed. Kenneth Neale (Oxford: Leopard's Head Press, 1992): 61-81, employs the same source to similar effect; see also Arthur Brown, *Prosperity and Poverty: Rural Essex, 1700-1815* (Chelmsford: Essex Record Office, 1996), chapter five; on the basis of replies to the 1766 pre-visitation questionnaire, Jane Pearson has recently presented a rather more favourable picture in 'Figures in a Landscape: the county of Essex in 1766 through the eyes of its clergy' in *Essex Harvest*, ed. M. Holland & J. Cooper (Chelmsford: Essex Record Office, 2003):1-14.
23 R. Lennard, 'Peasant Tithe Collectors in Norman England', *English Historical Review*, lxix (1954): 586, 590-93.
24 Public Record Office (hereafter PRO) SC6 549/11, 20, 46, 48.
25 ERO D/P 273/3/2.
26 Evans and Crosby, *Tithes, Maps, Apportionments*, 63; John Weller, *Grangia & Orreum The Medieval Barn: a nomenclature* (Bildeston, Suffolk: Bildeston Booklets, 1986): 9, 31.
27 ERO D/P 313/3/1.
28 For example, Rowlandson's 'Tithe Pig' and Cruikshank's 'Clerical Anticipation'.
29 ERO D/P 11/3/7; ERO T/A 433/3; W.F. Quin, *A History of Braintree and Bocking* (Brentwood: 1981): 112.
30 ERO D/DP Q5/3-6 (D/P 50/3/4).
31 ERO D/P 126/3/1; ERO D/P 12/3/1.
32 ERO D/P 184/3/2; ERO D/P 313/3/1.
33 Evans, *Contentious Tithe*, 18.
34 *VCH Essex*, iv, 121.
35 ERO D/Dab Q2,3.
36 ERO D/P 12/3/1.
37 ERO D/P30/3/3.
38 ERO D/P 109/3/2; Morant, *History of Essex*, ii, 580-81.
39 Alan Macfarlane, *The Family Life of Ralph Josselin 1616-1683* (London: Cambridge University Press, 1970): 34-39; the formal grant to the vicar and successors was made in 1673, see Morant, *History of Essex* ii. 214, where the grant is printed.
40 Duffield William Coller, *The People's History of Essex* (Chelmsford: Meggy & Chalk, 1861): 368; *VCH Essex*, iv: 146; ERO D/DU 273 & Draft Cat. D/P 65; *VCH Essex*, v: 224-5.
41 After 1816 such leases could be made binding upon both parties *and* their successors up to 14 years - Kain & Prince, *Tithe Surveys for Historians*, 13.
42 Book of Common Prayer, Ordination of Priests.
43 E.J. Evans, 'English Rural Anti-Clericalism c.1750- c.1820', *Past and Present*, no.66 (1975): 89, 91.
44 ERO D/P 70/3.
45 W.E. Tate, *The Parish Chest* (Cambridge: Cambridge University Press, 1946): 15.
46 ERO T/A 433/2.
47 A. Stokes, *History of East Ham*, (Stratford: Wilson & Whitworth, 1933): 65, see also 98.
48 Richard Burn, *Justice of the Peace* vol. iii (London: Cadell, Davies & Butterworth 1797): 778-779 – lay impropriators and tithe farmers were similarly liable; see below for the conflicts between the Barking Vestry and Vicars Musgrave and Rashleigh during the second half of the 18th century.
49 James Woodforde, *Diary of a Country Parson*, ed. J. Beresford World's Classics ed. (London: Oxford University Press, 1949): 127-8, *passim*.

50 Stokes, *East Ham*, 140.
51 ERO D/P 81/28/8.
52 *VCH Essex*, iv, 32-33.
53 Evans, *Anti-Clericalism*, 106; Evans and Crosby, *Tithes, Maps & Apportionments*, 6.
54 ERO D/P30/3/3.
55 Hill, *Economic Problems*, 81-82; Evans, *Contentious Tithe*, 19; Barking and East Ham provide examples, see below.
56 *VCH Essex*, vi, 25-26.
57 Evans, *Anti-Clericalism*, 86-7; Kain & Prince, *Tithe Surveys of England & Wales*, 18-22, 25-29; Evans and Crosby, *Tithes, Maps & Apportionments*, 9; Kain and Prince, *Tithe Surveys for Historians*, (Chichester: Phillimore, 2000): 13.
58 W. Vamplew, 'Tithes and Agriculture: Some comments on commutation', *Economic History Review*, 2nd series, 34 (1981): 115-6.
59 Evans and Crosby, *Tithes, Maps & Apportionments*, 16; Kain & Prince, *Tithe Surveys of England & Wales*, 51-56, 91-103.
60 Kain & Prince, *Tithe Surveys of England & Wales*, 57-58, 84-66; Kain & Oliver, *Tithe Maps of England & Wales*, 714-717.
61 Kain & Prince, *Tithe Surveys of England & Wales*, 22-25; Evans & Crosby, *Tithes, Maps & Apportionments*, 31. Nearly 80% of the area of England and Wales was covered by tithe award maps; the proportion was obviously greater in Essex where, according to Dr Stuart Mason (ERO T/Z 438/1), only ten parishes were exempt from the 1836 Act as a result of previous Enclosure Acts.
62 Kain & Oliver, *Tithe Maps of England & Wales*, 178, 180 ff.

Chapter two

63 ERO D/Dab Q2,3.
64 ERO D/P273/3/4A.
65 ERO D/P72/8/1.
66 Reproduced in A.F.J. Brown, *Essex People 1750-1900* (Chelmsford: Essex Record Office, 1972): 48.
67 ERO D/P233/3/1-2.
68 ERO D/P94/3/1.
69 ERO 81/ Acc 7648; Tate, *Parish Chest*, 79, notes several similar prescriptions in parish records.
70 ERO D/P30/3/3.
71 ERO D/P268 addl. Acc.9793,'III'.
72 ERO D/P 193/3/1.
73 ERO D/P 193/3/2.
74 ERO D/P 18/3/102; A. Green, *Ashdon: A history of an Essex village* (Aldham, Essex: privately published, 1989): 161-2.
75 ERO D/P18/3/12.
76 ERO D/DMg P15.
77 ERO D/P 166; ERO D/P 244/3. This was accompanied by a map, see below.
78 ERO D/P 212/28/1. Originally accompanied by a map, see below.
79 ERO D/P 212/3.
80 Evans & Crosby, *Tithes, Maps & Apportionments*, 8.
81 Green, *Ashdon*, 16.
82 ERO D/DSm Z2.
83 ERO D/CT 38/1/2; ERO D/Jg/B88; ERO D/Jg/B90; ERO D/DJg B41.
84 ERO D/CT 18
85 ERO D/P 212/28/1; A. Stuart Mason, *Essex on the Map* (Chelmsford: Essex Record Office, 1990): 109, mentions two other maps by John Kingsbury.
86 Mason, *Essex on the Map*, passim.

87 ERO D/DSm P1, the accompanying survey or rental is ERO D/DPr 626. Israel Amyce was agent of the Earl of Oxford who had recently sold the manors of Earls Colne and of Colne Priory to his steward, Richard Harlakeden, together they constituted almost the whole parish, see Alan Macfarlane, ed., *Records of an English Village: Earls Colne 1400-1750*, (Cambridge: Cambridge University Press 1980): 5; also below re: Amyce.
88 The map and text was edited by P.J. Huggins and was accompanied by transcripts of other contemporary documents as part of the Society's 'Millennium Project 3' (1997).
89 *VCH Essex*, v (1966): 157; the Wakes were generally absentee landlords, their principal residence being Courteen Hall in Northamptonshire, the ERO has a copy of the catalogue of the relevant Wake collection in the Northampton Record Office (ERO T/A 395/1).
90 City of London Record Office, M13737, M13738; Eileen Ludgate, *Clavering and Langley 1783-1983* (Clavering, Essex: privately published, 1984): 5-10, 81; Eileen Ludgate, *Clavering and Langley: The First Thousand Years* (Clavering, Essex: privately published, 1996): 10.
91 Mason, *Essex on the Map*, 113-114 and personal communication from Dr Mason; ERO D/P 205/3/1.
92 ERO D/P 85/3/9.
93 Barking & Dagenham public libraries (hereafter B & D PL.) Valence Museum Archive, Barking tithe survey (Johnson) 1806. As will be explained below in chapter five, part II, the Barking survey was paid for jointly by the vicar and a major impropriator.
94 ERO D/CT 149; Mason, *Essex on the Map*, 109.
95 ERO D/DSm Z1 & 2; ERO D/DSm P4, D/DSm P5 (D/CT 61A).
96 ERO D/P 244/3 The map is curiously described as an "Eye Sketch", although both map and terrier appear to be well finished work.
97 ERO D/CT 399.
98 ERO D/P 40/3/2.
99 ERO D/CT 284.
100 ERO D/P 406 addl. Acc.8821.
101 A. Stuart Mason, 'Tithe commutation maps of Essex', *Transactions of the Essex Archaeological & Historical Society* 25 (1994): 222.
102 ERO D/D/St F2.
103 On the evidence of Roger Kain and Richard Oliver, *The Tithe Maps of England and Wales: a cartographic analysis and county-by-county catalogue* (Cambridge: Cambridge University Press, 1995): fig.74, the leading competitor so far identified would appear to be a map of Buslingthorpe, Lincolnshire, 1838 (PRO IR30 20/69), said to be revised from a survey taken in the year 1653, but note the 1598 manorial/parish map of Earls Colne in the ERO mentioned above.
104 See above p.7.
105 ERO D/P 163/3/1.
106 ERO D/P 32/3/3.
107 ERO D/P 210/3. The tithes of this parish were commuted by an Enclosure Act of 1818 under which the rector received 137 acres of land in lieu of tithes. The parish was transferred to Cambridgeshire, but earlier records remain in the ERO.
108 ERO D/P 18/3/81.
109 ERO D/P 18/3/82-87.
110 ERO D/P 360/3/1-3. Tithe cases were often pursued in the Court of Exchequer, see H. Horowitz, *Exchequer Equity Records and Proceedings 1649-1841* (London: Public Record Office, 2001): 38-39, 45.
111 Tate, *Parish Chest*, 136.
112 Jay Pascal Anglin, 'Court of the Archdeacon of Essex 1571-1609' (PhD thesis, University of California, 1965): 223-227.
113 Emmison & Stephens, *Tribute to an Antiquary*, 178-183, 210-215; ERO D/AZ 1; for detailed transcripts of some Barking disputes, see Appendix D below; note that on occasion Browne's translations from the Latin have been found wanting.
114 Jane Houston, *Index of Cases in the Records of the Court of Arches at Lambeth Palace Library 1660-1913* (London:

British Record Society, 1972); for Cartwright see below, p.28.
115 ERO D/P 212/3.
116 See the map of 'Essex Hundreds and Parishes' (John Bartholomew and Sons Ltd.) published with P.H. Reaney, *The Place-Names of Essex* (Cambridge: Cambridge University Press, 1935).
117 ERO D/P 368/3.
118 Reverend W.J. Pressey, 'Beating the Bounds in Essex: As Seen in the Archdeaconry Records', *Essex Review*, xlviii (1939): 84-91.
119 Miller Christy, 'A perambulation of the Parish of Chignal St James in 1797', *Essex Review*, xxxvi (1927): 60-71.
120 Emmison & Stephens, *Tribute to an Antiquary*, 183-193.

Chapter three

121 W. Raymond Powell, 'The Making of Essex Parishes', *Essex Review*, lxii (1953): 6-18.
122 R. Gem, 'Anglo-Saxon Minsters of the Thames Estuary', in *Thames Gateway: Recording Historic Buildings and Landscapes in the Thames Estuary* (Swindon: R.C.H. Monuments of England, 1995).
123 *VCH Essex* v, 190; C.R. Hart, *The Early Charters of Eastern England* (Leicester: Leicester University Press, 1966): 117-135.
124 *VCH Essex*, ii, 344-354; *VCH Essex*, v, 184 ("the largest parish in Essex" requires the qualification made in the present text); *VCH Essex*, vii, 83.
125 *VCH Essex*, v, 190, 267, 276; c.f. Hampshire Record Office (hereafter Hants RO) 17M 55/3 (Map of Marks Manor 1662) with OS 6 inches to mile (1st ed.).
126 *VCH Essex*, v, 182; Marjorie K. McIntosh, *Autonomy and Community: The Royal Manor of Havering, 1200-1500* (Cambridge: Cambridge University Press, 1986): 8; S. Rippon, 'Essex c.700-1066' in *The Archaeology of Essex*, ed. Owen Bedwin (Chelmsford: Essex County Council, 1996): 121-122.
127 Cyril Hart, *The Early Charters of Barking Abbey* (Colchester: Benham & Co., 1953): 6; R. Allison, 'The changing geographical landscape of SW Essex from Saxon times to 1600' (M.A. diss., University of London, 1958): 57; Rippon, 'Essex c.700-1066', 122.
128 Hart, *Early Charters of Barking Abbey*, 10-11; Hart, *Early Charters of Eastern England*, 126, draws attention to the significance of the ordination of priests to serve the monastery.
129 E.A. Loftus & H.F. Chettle, *A History of Barking Abbey* (Barking: Wilson & Whitworth, 1953): 15; H.H. Lockwood, *Where was the First Barking Abbey?* (Barking Historical Society, 1986); Ann Williams, 'The Vikings in Essex 871-917', *Essex Archaeology and History*, 27 (1996): 93.
130 Lockwood, *First Barking Abbey?*, 3, it is now widely accepted that Hatfield House, Essex (Ilford Hospital) 1/6, is largely a copy from a lost cartulary of Barking Abbey, see Appendix C; 'Barking Abbey', *Current Archaeology* 149, xiii (Sept. 1996): 178.
131 Loftus & Chettle, *History*, 53-55.
132 R.C Fowler, *Essex Archaeological Society Transactions*, (n.s.), xviii 1927:15; *VCH Essex*, v, 223.
133 Ibid., 223, 226. Some services involving parishioners were always held in the Abbey church. Winifred M. Sturman, 'Barking Abbey: a study in its external and internal administration from the Conquest to the Dissolution' (Ph.D. thesis, University of London, 1961):130, 135. Sister Sturman agrees there is no record of appropriation and the Abbey church originally "served as the parish church of Barking".
134 PRO E 368/449.
135 Hatfield House, Cecil Papers, Essex (Ilford Hospital) 1/6, 26v-27 [see also note 130 above].
136 *VCH Essex*, v, 203, 224.
137 *VCH. Essex*, v, *passim*.
138 Ibid., 224; The court roll extracts are in PRO SC 2/171/22. Another copy, varying in detail, with an explanatory preface, is contained in the legal reports at Valence House mentioned below, 'Collection … Eastbury', fo.1.

139 B&D PL, Valence Museum MS 'A Collection in which it is proved that the tithes in Ripple Ward belong to the farm of Eastbury and not to the Vicar of Barking'; MS 'Hospital of Ilford: Caroe v. Fanshawe re: tithes of Eastbury [1586], Fisher v Wite re: tithes of North Grange [1590]'; photocopies of both in are held by the ERO T/A 412/ 1; they may be largely in the same hand; see Appendix D.
140 'Collection…Eastbury', fos.1, 2. Incidentally, the 1461 lease of Eastbury contradicts the view held by some local historians that the leasing of the demesne manors was only in anticipation of the Dissolution.
141 Ibid., fo.3.
142 *VCH Essex*, v, 192, 224, 228.
143 Ibid., 224; 'Collection… Eastbury', fos.13v.-16.
144 'Collection… Eastbury', fo.48.
145 *VCH Essex*, v, 216. Evidence from the first two tithe books suggests market gardening was established in Barking earlier than VCH indicates; the tithe book 1750 specifically identifies London butchers holding 137 acres of marsh, but there is little doubt that some other outparish tenants were actually butchers or graziers; see also Daniel Defoe, *Tour through the whole island of Great Britain: 1724-26*, Everyman ed. (London: Dent, 1962): i, 9.
146 Grant of Newbury to Sir Richard Gresham in 1546 (L.& P. Hen. VIII, xxi (1): 529) is typical including, "all tithes of sheaves (garbarum) of grain (granarum) and of hay (feni) relating or pertaining to the said messuage and with the same demised or leased".
147 The tithe survey 1669 (ERO D/P 81/3/110, vii) listed 792 acres of woodland paying tithe to the vicar, which was probably an underestimate.
148 ERO D/P 81/3/16 is a later copy of the tithe map of 1666, see table 2; PRO LR 2/214.
149 *VCH Essex*, v, 206, 224; F.G. Emmison, *Tudor Secretary* (Chichester: Phillimore, 1970): 279.
150 Bodleian Library mss DD, All Souls Coll. c.13, 9.
151 'Charthe to the Cellaress', BM Cotton MS, Julius D. viii; *VCH Essex* v, 200-1, 224; The area of this Downshall demesne may not have been much over 50 acres when separated from the associated estate of Smiths Hall, see the will of John Jeffrey, 1588 (F.G. Emmison, *Essex Wills: Archdeaconry Courts 1583-92* (Chelmsford: Essex Record Office: 1989): 117), but the total estate was almost double that size. It is also to be remembered that the Newbury tithing was sometimes referred to as the Downshall tithing.
152 Here and subsequently in this chapter references to Barking tithe surveys and accounts may be obtained from table 3. Only additional references will be given in the notes.
153 Bodleian Library mss DD. All Souls Coll. c.14.4; the terms by which the executors then conveyed the rectory to All Souls are also printed in Newcourt's *Repertorium* (1710): ii, 34.
154 *VCH Essex*, v, 192; the 'Inquisition Post Mortem' of 1549 on the property of the late Bartholomew Barnes (PRO C 142/86/65) includes "Newbury and the tithes of grain and hay late in the tenure of Laurence Gray [farmer there before the Dissolution]" but does not mention tithes when detailing his possessions in Aldborough Hatch.
155 ERO D/P 81/3/17-61 [61].
156 See the section at the beginning of the 1805-6 survey entitled "Explanation – of the Map".
157 *VCH Essex*, v, 192; Redbridge Public Library (local history collection), abstract of Wm. Lockey Esq. title to lands in Barking, Doc.21.
158 For the mill-ponds see below; ERO D/CT 18; *VCH Essex*, v 192; see also table 2.
159 L.& P. Henry VIII, xx (2), 22; ERO D/DSt T1; ERO D/DCw T7.
160 Stonehall had been attached to the manor of Wanstead since 1578 (*VCH Essex*, v, 210; vi, 323-4).
161 Hill, *Economic Problems*, 106-7; ERO D/DMs E26/6, answers in 'Cartwright v King'; PRO E123/25 fo.48.

Chapter four

162 Gilbert Burnet, Bishop of Salisbury, *History of His Own Times*, Everyman Edition (London: J.M. Dent,

1906): 252; Lord Thomas Babbington Macaulay, *History of England*, Everyman Edition (London: J.M. Dent, 1907): i. 575, 771, 798, ii. 382.
163 *Dictionary of National Biography* (hereafter, DNB); Foster, *Alumni Oxon.* (s.n.). Unless otherwise indicated, details that follow with reference to Cartwright are from these works or from those given in the preceding note.
164 *VCH Essex*, v., 225; Cartwright was inducted at Barking on 11 August 1660.
165 ERO D/P81/1/5, 81/1/6.
166 See chapter two.
167 ERO D/DMs E26/1-7.
168 Margaret James, 'The Political Importance of the Tithes Controversy in the English Revolution, 1640-60', *History* 26 (1941): 6.
169 "I humbly and heartily request him and my brother [-in-law], Henry Wight, after him to be more tender, least the small dues w'ch they detaine from the Church of Barking, and are not parte of that porcon of Tithes granted to Gessames Hall, prove a Canker to their Estate, w'ch blessed be God is soe plentifull as not to need any sacrilegeous addicon." F. Sanders, 'Thomas Cartwright', *Chester Archaeological & Historical Society Journal*, new series iv (1892): 25-26.
170 The diary kept by Cartwright in 1686 and 1687 shows how close his relationship with the Fanshawes of Jenkins and Parsloes eventually became. See J. Hunter, ed., *The Diary of Thomas Cartwright* (London: Camden Society, 1843): passim.
171 *VCH Essex*, v, 192.
172 H.C. Fanshawe, *The History of the Fanshawe Family* (Newcastle: A. Reid & Co, 1927): 237, 239; Cal. Proc. Comm. For Compounding, 1661, (11 Feb., 17 Mar.,1647); Morant, *History of Essex*, i. xxiv.
173 Surviving extracts from this map are listed below under note 175; the most careful sectional copies are D/DSa 146, "The town of Barking and village of Dagenham ... as they appear on a Map of Barking made AD 1653 for Thomas Fanshawe Esq. Traced from the original in the possession of Sir Edward Hulse Bart by George Luff 1861", but the surveyor is identified only by the contemporary Parsloes extract, D/DSa 147 made for John Fanshawe (and the original of this last is no longer extant).
174 Information from Dr Stuart Mason; Felix Hull, 'Aspects of Local Cartography in Kent and Essex 1585-1700' in *An Essex Tribute*, ed. Kenneth Neale (London: Leopard's Head, 1987).
175 See previous note 173. Luff's tracings were made in 1861, so the map was not lost in the fire at Breamore House in 1857; but a letter of 1822 from Sir Charles Hulse (ERO D/DDSa 136) mentions "my Old Large Map of the Manor of Barking... in Rags". It was not in the *Breamore House Records Catalogue* (1985), Hants RO. Extracts are ERO D/DSa 146,148; Sage Collection 'History of Barking': i. 267, ii. 307, 363, 390; D/DSa 147, map of Parsloes. No scale is given on any of the surviving extracts or copies; perhaps it was five chains to the inch.
176 As explained later, this survives only in the dissected copy made presumably for a tithe collector in the 18th century (ERO D/P 81/3/16), see Fig.1.
177 Hatfield House, Cecil Papers (Essex) 1/17A.
178 ERO D/P 81/28/84 [271], the italics are the author's.
179 ERO D/P 81/3/110.
180 ERO T208 1-3 The house was called Jollies, succeeded by Melcombe Lodge in the 19th century, which was absorbed by the Ilford Pioneer Market in the 1920s. In this connection it must be remembered that Barking Town had no direct connection with London prior to the construction of the London Road in 1812 (officially called 'New Road' until 1901!).
181 ERO D/P 81/3/8, *passim*; tithe survey 1669, 42.
182 The Barking registers and his will show that the vicar had at least nine children by Sarah (his second wife) of which seven survived in addition to John, the surviving child of Mary, his first wife. (According to Sanders ('Thomas Cartwright', 23), he married a third wife, Frances Barnard, in 1684).

183 ERO D/P 81/8/1 (Barking Vestry minute book 1666-1694), *passim*. The fabric of the parish church did not benefit from his increasing emoluments, at his visitation in September 1683 (see below), the archdeacon reported "The Chancell belonging to Dr Cartwright is very bad", the pavement "must all be made newe".
184 B & D PL, Valence House, Fanshawe mss, M164: 194-6. Mrs B.M. Ridout (died c.1930) compiled these 'Fanshawe Extracts'.
185 ERO D/P 81/3/8. The tithe account for 1684-5 is D/P 81/3/9
186 *Notes and Queries* Vol. 2, 3rd Series (1st Nov., 1862): 344; also B & D PL, Valence House, Frogley MS, 95.
187 Reverend H. Smith, 'Some Essex Parliamentarians 1642-1653', *Essex Review*, 33 (1924): 149-155; in 1654 John Brewster was made a commissioner for ejecting "scandalous, ignorant and inefficient ministers", H. Smith, *Ecclesiastical History of Essex* (Colchester: Benham & Co. 1931): 336.
188 *VCH Essex*, ii, 63-64; VCH Essex, v., 228; *Acts & Ordinances of the Interregnum*, ii. 812; *Cal. S.P. Dom.* (1547-1775), Vol. 7, 557; PRO LRRO 198; see also pp.34, 71-72.
189 E. Calamy, *The Nonconformist Memorial*, revised edition (London, 1802): iii, 478. See also note 20.
190 Foster, *Alumni Oxon.*; margin of Barking marriage register 2 July, 1668 (ERO D/P 81/1/6).
191 ERO D/P 81/8/1, *passim*; church rates, levied specifically to pay for repairs to the parish church, were resented by some dissenters more than tithe.
192 Reverend W.J. Pressey, 'Visitations held in the Archdeaconry of Essex in 1683', *Transactions of the Essex Archaeological Society* new series xix (1929): 264. He could well be the only tithe collector named in the visitations.
193 ERO D/AEV 11 (archdeacon's visitation, 7 July, 1683).
194 Alexander Gordon, *Freedom after Ejection* (Manchester: Victoria University Publications, 1917): 38, 365; VCH Essex, v., 231.
195 Valence House Library, Frogley MS, 95; Taylor's ledger stone is now hidden beneath choir stalls, but see the list of monuments in ERO D/P 81 addl., Acc.7648. Here, and in the church registers, he is described as 'clerk(e)'- it is probable he regarded himself to the last as a minister of the national church.
196 G.V. Bennett, 'Conflict in the Church' in *Britain after the Glorious Revolution*, ed. G. Holmes (London: Macmillan, 1969): 158.
197 Cartwright was now an outspoken advocate of 'divine right' and inclined to religious toleration providing the position of the Church of England was assured, see his *An Answer of a Minister of the Church of England, etc.*, 1687 (B.L. 108 c.50)
198 Anne Whiteman, 'The Compton Census of 1676' in Surveying the People K. Schurer & T. Arkell eds. (Oxford: Leopard's Head Press, 1992): 96; see also her own *The Compton Census of 1676: A Critical Edition* (London, Oxford University Press, 1986): xxxvii-lxi; it may or may not be significant that there are no returns for Barking in the Compton census (*idem* 61).
199 Sanders, 'Thomas Cartwright', 21-23. It is interesting to note that, despite close connections developed latterly with Roman Catholics and the possibility of pleasing James even further, Cartwright resisted conversion to the end.
200 Foster, *Alumni Oxon.*, Leopold Finch; Venn, *Alumni Cantab.*, John Chisenhall; (in the Barking Vestry minute book he generally signs 'Chisenhale'); *VCH Essex*, v, 226.
201 ERO D/P 81 addl., Acc.7648.

Chapter five: part I

202 Foster, *Alumni Oxon.*; ERO D/AEV M6; ERO D/P 81 addl., Acc.7648.
203 ERO D/P 81/3/10.
204 Morant, History of Essex, i. 9; Foster, *Alumni Oxon.*, William Stevens, probably refers to the same person but concludes with B.A. in 1744 - if so, Barking must have been his first incumbency and obtained shortly after his doctorate.

205 ERO D/P 81/3/15.
206 ERO D/P 81/3/16; see also the description in F.G Emmison, ed., *Third Supplement to Catalogue of Maps* (Chelmsford: Essex Record Office, 1968): 33.
207 ERO Q/RHi 1/4; see above, p.34, but the New Chapel was probably not ready before completion of the Manorial Map in 1653. The correct position is discussed in chapter eight.
208 For an example see Lockwood, *First Barking Abbey?*, 27 & Fig.5.
209 ERO D/P 81/28/76 [255].
210 DNB, Musgrave, Sir Christopher.
211 J.E. Oxley, *Barking Vestry Minutes & other Parish Documents*, (Colchester: Benham & Co., 1955): 76.
212 (Sir) Crisp Gascoyne bought the hospital by 1730. His son, the first Bamber Gascoyne, inherited on his death in 1761. The letter (Hatfield House, Cecil Papers, Essex (Ilford Hospital) 1/5) was obviously not sent to him and probably found its way into the Gascoyne archives (together with the following memo) when the second Bamber Gascoyne allied himself with Vicar Rashleigh (see below).
213 DNB, Gascoyne, Sir Crisp.
214 Such a change is marked by the licence to clear 30 acres of Bunting Bridge Coppice in July 1733, followed by 40 acres of Sparkes Wood (near Clayhall) in September 1744 (City of London Guildhall library, Doyley ms 1377).
215 See above for the vicar's claim to take tithes of wood. It was generally held that new enclosures converted to arable or meadow were tithe-free for at least seven years (see Hill, *Economic Problems*, 106), but even after that period an impropriator like the landlord of Gaysham or the Master of the Ilford Hospital might have a better claim than the vicar. The complaint continued to be made until the tithe award.
216 'Memorandum from Dr Musgrave's little book No.1', Cecil Papers, Essex (Ilford Hospital) 1/5.
217 ERO C/P 81/3 /17-61 [63].
218 ERO D/P 81/3/17-61 [64--69].
219 B & D PL., Valence Archive Collection, tithe accounts 1763-1788 (Musgrave's Rental No.1).
220 See p.18; *VCH Essex*, ii, 474-5.
221 Oxley, *Barking Vestry Minutes*, 51-52; ERO D/P 81/5/1; ERO D/P 81/8/3; ERO Q/SBb 279-281.
222 Sir L. Namier & J. Brooke, *The House of Commons 1754-1790* (London: HMSO, 1964): ii, 486, 488, 491.
223 Oxley, *Barking Vestry Minutes*, 76-81; ERO D/P 81 addl. Acc.7648.
224 Nancy Briggs, 'The evolution of the office of county surveyor in Essex 1700-1816', *Architectural History*, 27 (1984): 301; ERO T/B 251/7; ERO D/P 81/5/28.
225 Oxley, *Barking Vestry Minutes*, 33-36; H.H. Lockwood, 'The Barking Vicarages and Jeremy Bentham', *Essex Journal* xxvii, (Summer 1992): 43-44; H.H. Lockwood, 'The Chaplain Trail and the Lodge Connexion', *Ilford Historical Society Newsletter* 46, (September 1995); DNB (Sir) Oliver Joseph Lodge [a grandson].
226 Oxley, *Barking Vestry Minutes*, 52.
227 ERO C/P 81/28/9 [321].
228 ERO C/P 81/3/11.

Chapter five: part II

229 ERO D/P 81/3/12, /13, /14; *VCH Essex*, v. 198, 211-212, 213-214; this 'rearrangement' is examined further below pp.107-8.
230 See above for the agreement of 1219; Oxley, *Barking Vestry Minutes*, 52-53 (the dispute of 1793-4 was settled by agreement).
231 For documents relating to tithes of Ilford Hospital from the 14th century onwards see below.
232 Hatfield House, Cecil Papers, Essex (Ilford Hospital) 1/5, 1/17, 1/17A; in 1797 Bamber Gascoyne Jnr. also paid more than £70 to the vicar to clear the arrears of tithe and offerings which his father had not paid during the last ten years of his life.
233 ERO D/P 81/3/17-61 [74, 75].

234 Mason, *Essex on the Map*, 109; also see above chapter two.
235 B & D P.L., Valence Archive Collection, Barking tithe survey (Johnson) 1806; Hatfield House, Cecil Papers, Gascoyne bills and receipts, 1806; ERO Sage Collection ms 'History of Barking', ii. 395; 'Extract from a map of Barking'.
236 ERO D/P 81/3/17-61 [79, 80].
237 Ibid, [81].
238 Oxley, *Barking Vestry Minutes*, 46-47.
239 ERO D/P 81/28/53 [281-284] – the final letter [287] was more diplomatically phrased.
240 Order in Council 7 April 1830 (quoted N. Jackson, *St. Mary's Church* (1983): 15-16); the ancient ward boundaries can be seen in Oxley, *Barking Vestry Minutes*, plate 2.
241 Oxley, *Barking Vestry Minutes*, 48; ERO G/RM 1 & 2; A. Stuart Mason, 'Tithe commutation maps of Essex', *Transactions of the Essex Archaeological & Historical Society*, 25 (1994): 222 (but it will be seen below that the author comes to a different conclusion in regard to the use of Drayson's plan).
242 Drayson's 'No.2 Plan... containing Barking and Rippleside Wards and part of Chadwell Ward' was only rediscovered recently in the muniment room of Valence House; the great size of the map and the imminent need for conservation have restricted examination, but the author is grateful to Mark Watson, heritage officer, for his assistance; 'No.1 Plan' is still missing.
243 Kain and Oliver, *The Tithe Maps of England and Wales*, 178, table 12/2; ERO G/RM 1-3; PRO IR 18/2204; ERO D/DOp B10/3.
244 ERO G/RM 3, pp. 114, 117; PRO IR 18/2204; Obituary of James Paulin, *Essex Times*, 20 February. 1869.
245 For the origin of this example, see below pp.107-108. In most tithe maps dotted lines denote the boundaries of unenclosed parcels in open field (Kain and Prince, *Tithe Surveys for Historians*, 19).
246 ERO D/CT 18.
247 Hatfield House, Cecil Papers, Essex (Ilford Hospital) 1/3.
248 ERO D/DSa 151 (Estate Map of William Lockey, c.1725); ERO D/P 81/3/110.
249 Ibid., the eastern part of Lessons Grove [Levesons Grove, see below, p.71]; PRO 191 MPE 444 (Map 1781, with notes added); Perkins sublet to Gosling for a nursery, now the site of Canon Palmer's High School.
250 The previous descent of Whites Farm is not known. Whitings tithes were claimed by Lockey as part of his Aldborough Hatch estate in 1725, but a different view may have prevailed in 1847.
251 The Aldborough estate owned by the Barnes family had been split into two during the 17th century. The crown eventually bought one portion called the Aldborough House estate in 1828. The other portion, which was bought by the Stevens family at the beginning of the 19th century, was usually referred to as the Aldborough *Hatch* estate (VCH *Essex*, v, 192-3).

Chapter six

252 Hatfield House, Cecil Papers, Essex (Ilford Hospital) 1/6.
253 Valence Ho. MS. Fisher v. Wite fos.31v., 37.
254 The discovery and provenance of the Hatfield House, MS Ilford Hospital 1/6 (the vellum book) is described more fully in the appendix (C and D) below.
255 PRO SC.2/171/22; VCH *Essex*, v. 203, 224; p.20 above.
256 Valence House MS. 'Fisher v Wite' fo.43-44v. There is a difficulty with dating - fo.43 gives 5th October in 'ninth yere' of Henry 7 viz. 1493, but fo. 37 gives 'decimo nono' which is the 19th year viz. 1503. VCH *Essex*, ii, 187 seems to refer to another copy of the same survey giving the date 1504.
257 Ibid., ii.286-7; PRO E301/20/46.
258 VCH *Essex*, ii, 187 (Godfrey Fanshawe, master from 1578 to his death in 1588, followed by Dr William Fisher); Fisher v. Wite, fos. 27-29.
259 The early evidence for this is circumstantial though persuasive. Later pages of Hatfield House, MS Ilford Hospital 1/6 (the vellum book) were used as a register during the time of Fisher (who seems to have been chaplain as well as master) and his successor, recording four baptisms, two marriages and five burials. Earlier, William Squire asked to be buried there in his will of 1588 (Emmison, *Essex*

Wills 1583-92), as was the priestly master 'Sir' John Smythe in 1475. Several clauses in the will of Dame Alice Wyche in 1474 suggest the chapel was already used for public worship. (P.E. Jones, *Calendar of Pleas & Memorandum Rolls of the City of London 1458-82* (Cambridge: Cambridge University Press, 1961): 101-104).
260 See chapter four.
261 Fanshawe, *History of the Fanshawe Family*, 13; *VCH Essex*, ii, 187.
262 PRO E368/449.
263 Hatfield House, Cecil Papers, Essex (Ilford Hospital), 1/1, 1/2.
264 This allegation was obviously part of an attempt to discredit the enquiry itself but several witnesses, including Allen, testified to a dispute though not to a threat of violence. Nevertheless, Godfrey Fanshawe does seem to have been an unstable character.
265 See above, p14; Edwards, A.C., & K.C. Newton. *The Walkers of Hanningfield*. (London: Buckland, 1984): 24; S. Bendall ed., *Dictionary of Land Surveyors and Local Mapmakers* (London: British Library, 1997): i, 23; *VCH Essex v.*, 197 & ERO D/DCw T46A show Israel Amyce (steward to de Vere, Earl of Oxford) resident at Cranbrook in the period 1572-1586. Indexer's Note: Bert Lockwood attended the exhibition on Estate Maps at the Guildhall Library, London, in late October 2004. To his suprise, the earliest map on display there was one of the Manor of Belchamp St Paul in Essex, by Israel Amyce. Bert had not heard of this map before. It is part of the St Paul's Cathedral Archive. What most excited him about it was not just its birds-eye detail but its date: 1576. He had been aware of the 1599 Amyce map of Edmonton/Enfield for Sir Robert Cecil, but the importance to him of the 1576 map and its written schedule was that it showed that Amyce was the formative surveyor, not the follower, of late Tudor map-makers.
266 See note 258; Hatfield House, Cecil Papers, Essex (Ilford Hospital) 2/28.
267 Ibid., 1/5.
268 ERO D/P 81/8/1; *VCH Essex v.*, 229.
269 Hatfield House, Cecil Papers, Essex (Ilford Hospital), 2/28; ERO D/DSa 58.
270 Ibid., 2/25; other evidence is given in 1/3 & 4, 1/22-24, 2/26-28.
271 Quoted *Encyclopaedia Britannica*, 9th ed (London: 1875): i, 299.
272 Hatfield House, Cecil Papers, Essex (Ilford Hospital), 1/5, 2/32; D. Lysons, *Environs of London*, Vol. iv., (London, 1796):109.
273 See chapter five, part II.
274 ERO D/SH 14.
275 ERO D/SH 15.
276 ERO D/SH 16; James Bermingham's plans of Westbury, Eastbury & Ripple Levels (ERO D/SH 19 & 21) made for the commisioners in 1740 appear, in contrast, to have been based on a new survey.
277 ERO D/DSt F3.
278 ERO D/DSt F1, draft bill in Court of Exchequer.
279 ERO D/SH 17.
280 PRO E134 39 Eliz. Easter 25.
281 ERO D/P81/3/110 rear; another copy ERO D/DHs M29a, though found amongst the manorial records, appears to be later, c.1730.
282 H.H. Lockwood, 'Those Greedy Hunters after Concealed Lands' in *An Essex Tribute*, 165.
283 Ibid, 164; PRO SP 39/6.
284 PRO SP 14/104/49; ERO D/DHS M29; the Essex Record Office has now completed the conservation of this original document.

Chapter seven

285 See above, pp.17-19.
286 The attention given by past historical research to open-field systems and subsequent enclosure may have tended to divert attention away from the persistence of other field patterns.

287 About a quarter of Essex tithe maps are on this scale. Drayson had originally used construction lines to produce an accurate survey, but the Barking map would have had to use a larger scale, at least four chains to the inch (approximately 20 inches to the mile), to be even considered for the small elite category designated 'First Class Maps'; see Kain and Prince, *Tithe Surveys for Historians*, 38.

288 The second edition of the 25 inch, or more properly the 'First Revision', began the practice of putting the area underneath the parcel number on the map itself.

289 D. Hall, *Medieval Fields* (Aylesbury: Shire, 1982): 26 ff.

290 Field boundaries are shown on the unpublished surveyors' drawings for the First Edition of the OS one inch map 1805 (now in the British Library). Barking: no.132 at 3" to mile, 138 at 2" to mile, but their reliability is doubtful; Kain and Prince, *Tithe Surveys of England and Wales*, 186-8.

291 There is a useful summary of evidence regarding the prevalence of subletting in the section on leaseholding in P. Edwards, *Farming: Sources for Local Historians* (London: Batsford, 1991): 126-135.

292 ERO 1671: Tax is Q/R Th5; 1662 Tax is Q/R Th1; Valence House has photocopies; drafts for 1664 and 65 are in the Mildmay archive held by the ERO.

293 The general rate books for the parish of Barking and most of the overseer's copies for individual wards are in the Valence House archive; Oxley, *Barking Vestry Minutes*, appendix 1, 285ff is a useful guide. Note also that odd copies for wards have found their way into other collections such as the ERO and the local history collection at the Redbridge Central Library.

294 Oxley, *Barking Vestry Minutes*, 38, 47, 56-61; *Essex Standard*, 28 September 1833, 21 August 1835.

295 ERO D/P 81/4, Acc.7006.

296 A. Henstock, 'House Repopulation from the CEBs of 1841 and 1851' in *Local Communities in the Victorian Census Enumerators' Books* eds. D. Mills & K. Schurer (Oxford: Leopard's Head Press, 1996): 367.

297 ERO D/DMs 027/4.

298 ERO D/DMs 023/14, /7, /2, 020, 021; J.A. Sharpe, *William Holcroft His Booke* (Chelmsford: Essex Record Office, 1986): 5-6, 11-12.

299 PRO E179/141/150 (ERO T/A 427/1). For an examination of the procedures and reliability of these assessments see Richard Hoyle, *Tudor Taxation Records: A Guide for Users* (London: Public Record Office, 1994). The PRO is currently developing an E179 Database of all lay subsidy returns; it will include a place-name search facility.

300 In the ERO (D/P 81) most have been microfilmed; copies are held in the Valence library.

301 1666-94 is ERO D/P81/8/1; the remaining nine volumes are in the Valence House Museum collection. When Dr Oxley wrote his valuable *Barking Vestry Minutes* in 1955 he was not aware of the first volume, then at Hatfield House.

302 Oxley, *Barking Vestry Minutes*, 6-7 for annual totals for Barking baptisms and burials from 1694-1812. For further comment see *VCH Essex*, v, 185.

303 *An Index of Testamentary Records in the Commissary Court of London*, vols.1 (1374-1488), 2 (1489-1570), 3 (1571-1625), ed. M. Fitch [British Record Society Index Library, nos.82 (1969), 86 (1974), 97 (1985).

304 A good many books have been published to assist the student and amateur historian in the use of manorial records: see Mary Ellis, *Using Manorial Records*, PRO Readers' Guides, (London: Public Record Office in association with the Royal Commission on Historical Manuscripts, 1994), for clear directions without over-simplification.

305 See chapter three.

306 See above, chapter four and notes 173 & 175.

307 ERO Sage Collection no.274.

308 ERO D/DHs M31.

309 See chapter four.

310 This can be deduced from the manorial surveys and rentals and corroborated from the tithe books and map; the Barking virgate will be examined further in chapter eight.

311 The attribution is doubtful but cf. virgate in R.E. Zupko, *A Dictionary of English Weights and Measures from Anglo-Saxon times to the Nineteenth Century* (Madison etc.: University of Wisconsin Press, 1968).

312 M.K. McIntosh, 'Land, tenure and population in the royal manor of Havering, Essex, 1251-1352/3' *Economic History Review*, 2nd series, xxxiii (1980): 26, n.1.

313 Such facetiousness would be in line with several touches of vulgar wit in the transcript itself.

314 ERO D/DHs E2 (a bound photocopy is also available in the Valence library); similar information is contained in E1, but that lacks an appendix with details of farms.

315 *VCH Essex*, v, 192.

316 The advantage to the lord was obvious, though difficult to achieve with copyholds of inheritance. The [private] Act for the Sale of Certain Lands... of the late Sir Orlando Humfreys, May 1748 (21 Geo. II, c.12) includes lands in the Goodmayes area "which were formerly copyhold land, and held of the Manor of Barking and surrendered to the said Sir William Humfreys" and as a result many interesting customary names like 'Old Moggs by Heavywaters' vanished into limbo.

317 ERO D/DHs M32, 'fines' were payments made to the lord, principally on admission of new tenants to a copyhold (or leasehold); they were valuable because a lord could, within certain limits, increase a fine even where the rent was fixed by custom. According to a calculation made in 1728 the annual yield from fines in Barking manor averaged almost two and a half times that from quit-rents (ERO Sage Collection 'History of Barking', i. 182).

318 *VCH Essex*, v, 192; ERO D/DHs M42, 44, 46, & M47-69, the last going down to 1912.

319 The first Barking court recorded in English took place on 5 April 1733 (ERO D/DHs M10); the index is ERO D/DHs M27; see the D/DHs catalogue in the ERO for dates and catalogue marks of the other court and minute books.

320 M.K. McIntosh, 'Land, tenure, and population', 17-31; *Autonomy and Community: The Royal Manor of Havering 1200-1500* (Cambridge: Cambridge University Press, 1986); *A Community Transformed: The Manor and Liberty of Havering 1500-1620* (Cambridge: Cambridge University Press, 1991). In these cases, 'extent' is a technical term for a type of medieval manorial survey which began with a detailed description and valuation of the lord's demesne.

321 McIntosh, 'Land tenure and population', 21.

322 ERO D/DP M187.

323 PRO SC6 849/11.

324 Sturman, 'Barking Abbey', 13; the Barking Abbey cartulary disappeared after it had been partly copied into the vellum book of Ilford Hospital (see pp.46, 93-94); the 1440-1 roll was preserved in the Petre archive; the 1456 Rental reappeared in a 20th century auction; PRO E112/80/87; PRO E123/26/91; jurors in 1609 (see below) saw rolls from the time of Henry VIII.

325 ERO D/DHs M1 fo.70.

326 PRO LR.2/214.

327 *Essex and Dagenham Catalogue* (Borough of Dagenham Public Libraries, 1961): 96 (no.1098).

328 PRO S.C.6/964; Smart Lethieullier, 'History of Barking' (MS):131.

329 Some corrections have been made by the present author in the margins of the translation.

330 British Museum Add. MS 45387 (purchased by F.J. Brand at Sotheby's in 1923 and subsequently donated to the British Museum); *Essex Review* xxxii 1923: 122, xxxiii 1924: 138; *Transactions of the Barking and District Archaeological Society* (1936): 'North part' (1937) 'South part'.

331 Accounts of the office of the cellaress exist for 1535-39 see PRO SC/929/1, photocopy in the Valence Library. This has been translated in part by Dr Oxley in *Transactions of the Barking and District Archaeological Society*, 1957.

332 See chapter three.

333 ERO D/DP M187; typescript copies of a translation of this by the late Hilda Grieve are to be found in both the Valence and in ERO libraries.

334 PRO SC6 849/11, typescript transcript and translation in both the Valence and in ERO libraries; Sturman, 'Barking Abbey', *passim*; *VCH Essex*, v, 215-6.

335 Jennifer C. Ward, ed., *The Medieval Essex Community: The Lay Subsidy of 1327* (Chelmsford: Essex Record

Office, 1983).
336 W.C. Waller, 'The Foresters Walks in Waltham Forest', *Essex Review* xiv (1915); PRO MPE 130, this map (c.1640) shows the boundary between the 'walks' running up Aldborough Road. The name 'chapel' is unconnected with Barkingside New Chapel, instead it derives from a medieval hermitage in the forest near Dagenham on the site of Chapel Lodge, see *VCH Essex*, v, 230.
337 PRO C99/144, 145; E32/21.
338 ERO D/DMs 049, 050; J.A. Sharpe, ed., *"William Holcroft*, 24ff. Information about the duties of regarders and verderers and the operation of forest courts can be found in Sharpe's introduction to the same.
339 Bodleian Lib., MS rolls Essex box 2 (12) 'Curia Swainmote, 1594'; ERO D/DU 403/19, 403/22.
340 For evidence of conflict between manor and forest courts in the early 19th century see ERO D/DSa 39.

Chapter eight

341 Ward, *The Medieval Essex Community*; C.D. Rogers, *The Surname Detective* (Manchester: Manchester University Press, 1995):148-9, 161; the 14th century is no doubt a formative period in the development of surnames, but in the case of minor place names when does a family derive its name from the place and when does the opposite occur?
342 F.G. Emmison, 'Essex Genealogical Indexes: A million references to personal names', *Genealogists' Magazine* 20, no. 2 (London: Society of Genealogists, 1983):55-59. Subsequently reprinted as a pamphlet for the Essex Record Office by the Friends of Historic Essex.
343 ERO D/P 81/3/110. The larger holding, previously tenanted by Robert Cawdle, was probably called Kennites, and the house, Sprotly; ERO D/P 81/3/9.
344 Arthur Young, *Survey of Essex* (1807).
345 An agreement including the livestock was added into the 1669 survey.
346 *VCH Essex*, v, 215, 216.
347 C.f. R. Allison, 'The changing landscape of south-west Essex, 1600-1850', (Ph.D. thesis, University of London, 1966): ii. 304-5; the name Ripple must have particular reference to this marsh-edge zone and derive from the Saxon period, for *rippel*, 'a strip of land' is cognate with *rip(p)*, 'an edge, a shore, a slope', see A.H. Smith, *English Place Name Elements* (Cambridge: Cambridge University Press, 1987): ii. 84, c.f. Reaney, *Place-Names of Essex*, 89.
348 ERO D/SH 17.
349 ERO D/P 81/3/15.
350 Cecil Papers, Essex (Ilford Hospital) 1/6, fo.7v, it seems to suggest that six acres of marshland were then under the plough, not improbable at this date; 'hawe' was used locally (as in Kent) to denote 'houseground'.
351 ERO Sage sale catalogues: 12/26, 'Plan of an estate in Barking and Dagenham 14 July 1894, (another copy is to be found in the Valence Library local studies collection, land sale catalogues); *VCH Essex*, v., 215.
352 Comparatively little research has been done on the Thames-side marshes, but note W. W. Glenny, 'The Dykes of the Thames', *The Essex Review*, x (1901): part 1, 149-162 and part 2, 218-230; D.W. Gramolt, 'The Coastal Marshlands of East Essex between the Seventeenth and mid-Nineteenth Centuries' (MA dissertation, University of London, 1960) (a copy is held by the ERO library; Hilda Grieve, *The Great Tide* (Chelmsford: Essex Record Office, 1959): 1-34.
353 PRO E 178/821; ERO D/P 81/3/16 [sheet 18]. It is uncertain whether the 1582 enquiry resulted in any royal help; in the mid-century the crown had loaned £600 for drainage in Barking, but that may have been spent on another 'New Inned Marsh' west of the Roding (*Acts of P.C. 1654-56*, 10 Jan. 1555). In regard to 'ague' in Essex marshes, see Defoe, *Tour*, i, 9, 13-14, and the recent extensive study by Dr Mary Dobson, *Contours of Death and Disease in Early Modern England*, Cambridge studies in population,

economy, and society in past time, (Cambridge: Cambridge University Press, 1997).

354 For the Rant and its drainage see figure 18. The 'contour drainage channel' on sheet 18 of ERO D/P 81/3/16 was probably added onto the 1666 map and copied by Wyeth in 1742 (ERO D/SH 16); but new plans of the levels made by James Bermingham for the Commissioners of Sewers in 1740 (D/SH 19 & 21) appear to show the Mayesbrook streams back in their natural confluent courses into the Roding at Kings Bridge. See also Cecil Papers, Essex (Ilford Hospital), 1/17, sketch 9, for outlet of drainage channel.

355 ERO D/SH 21: F.Z. Claro & J. Howson, 'Barking Memories'; *The Barking Record*, 82 (1972): 12-14.

356 ERO D/P 81/3/16; above, pp.50-51; compare list of tithable woods in 1750 at rear of D/P 81/3/15.

357 Reaney *Place-Names of Essex*, 588.

358 ERO D/DHS M29 [items 166, 330]; this does not necessarily imply that the colliers were themselves the cause of clearance, cord-wood for burning became available after routine felling as well as after 'stubbing'.

359 *Historic Manuscripts Commission, 6th Report*, (1877): appendix, 539.

360 Levesons Grove, nos. 1635-7, 1640-41, in the triangle formed by Aldborough and Cameron Roads and the High Road; see also Fig. 18, & note 250. It is highly probable that Dunshall Ridden was so named in the early 13th century since Dunshall took its name from the Dun family during that period.

361 ERO D/DP M187.

362 PRO LRRO 19 (1544-45).

363 See below, p.117.

364 ERO D/CT 18; PRO C99/144; W.R. Fisher *The Forest of Essex: its history, laws, administration and ancient custom, etc.* (London: Butterworths, 1887): 324.

365 Fisher, *Forest of Essex*, 324; ERO D/P 81/3/110 rear, 7; Hampshire Record Office, Breamore House Records Catalogue (1985) no.1413; The present, so-called Old Maypole public house in Fencepiece Road, opposite New North Road, Hainault, was only built after WWII. Until then, the genuinely old Maypole public house was immediately south of the junction between Tomswood Hill and Fencepiece Road, on the west side where the position of its forecourt can still be observed.

366 ERO D/CT 18; see above, pp.31, 34. Probably by coincidence, a mission room was built on, or very near, the former site of the New Chapel in modern times and, more recently, a public lavatory.

367 Oxley, *Barking Vestry Minutes*, 131-4; Barking Vestry minutes, 5 December 1839, includes a nominal list of tenants.

368 W. Addison, *Essex Worthies* (Chichester: Phillimore, 1973): 32; *Essex Herald*, 21 April 1818; *Essex Standard*, 8 October 1831; for 'home colonisation' see J. Burchardt, *The Allotment Movement in England, 1793-1873* (Woodbridge: Boydell & Brewer, 2002.): 12, 52, 85.

369 Oxley, *Barking Vestry Minutes*, 246; Reaney, *English Place Names*, 221; A.D. Law and S. Barry, *The Forest in Walthamstow and Chingford*. ed. W.G.S. Tonkin (London: Walthamstow Antiquarian Society, 1978): 14 and personal information; G.F. Tasker, *Ilford Past and Present* (Ilford: S.W. Hayden, 1901): 118; recently the former 'Lower Canada' became the site of King Solomon High School.

370 *VCH Essex*, v, 216; ERO D/DQs 74/4. (Order to reeves re: Right of Common in Forest from Court of Attachments. 2 August 1790); PRO LRRO 198; PRO C 99/129 (Claims of Forest 1630); Act 21 & 22 Vict. c.37 (Schedule of Claims of Common of Estovers, 1858); poor widows received a special allotment.

371 Tasker, *Ilford Past and Present*: the petition for a parish church at Barkingside calls the local inhabitants "very destitute and degraded" (*VCH Essex*, v, 258); in the last 30 years the literature touching this subject has been extensive but diffused, see, for example, J. Neeson, *Commoners, Common Rights, Enclosure and Social Change* (Cambridge: Cambridge University Press, 1993).

372 Eliot Howard, 'Some Reminiscences of an Essex Police Court', *Essex Review* xxiv (1915): 190. Of Quaker extraction, Howard probably took a more liberal view than some of his fellow JPs.

373 A police report of 1869 suggested that the Barkingside police station had proved a "great deterrent on the numerous pig and straw jobbers… who resided there."; James Gott, was so described in the 1851 census, the year after George was born.

374 VCH Essex, v, 241; ERO D/P 81/3/110. (1669), 17, 36; ibid (1681), 6; lease 1726 (renewed 1774) in ERO D/DH/S E2; tithe account 1781 in ERO C/P 81/3/11.
375 ERO D/P 81/3/110 rear (1617), 15; ibid (1669) 41, (1681) 25, 33; ERO D/P 81 addl., Acc.7648 (1727/8), 37; B & D P.L. (Valence archive collection), Barking tithe survey 1806 (Johnson), 19; ERO D/DCT 18; Tasker Ilford Past and Present, 115, his remark "the edge of a forest seems an odd place for such a business" suggests he was not perhaps well informed; Essex Herald, 18 May 1813, 4 June 1816, 4 May 1819.
376 ERO D/P 81 addl., Acc.7648 (1727/8), 85; ERO D/DU 520/2 & 3.
377 Emmison, Essex Wills, vol.6 (1591-97), No.458; ERO D/DHs M29, fo.81; ERO D/P 81/3/110 rear (1617), 15; ERO D/P 81/3/16 sheets 5, 7; ERO D/P 81/3/110 (1669) 29; ibid (1681), 28; ERO D/P 81/3/9; ERO D/DSa 151; Sage 'History of Barking', ii. 395.
378 Sage, 'History of Barking', i, 44.
379 VCH Essex, v, 208.
380 Morant, History of Essex (1768), i, 5; Morant concludes by confusing it with another smaller estate in Gale Street called Hedgemans; Lysons, Environs, iv., 33-34.
381 ERO D/P 81/3/110. (1669), fo.47; ERO Sage collection no.276; ERO D/DHs M31, fo.46; PRO PCC 24 Cobham (will of Stephen Porter 1597); ERO D/DAER 21/124 (will of Stephen Porter 1665); VCH Essex, v, 209.
382 ERO D/P 81/3/110. (1669), fo.18; ERO D/P 81 addl., Acc. 7648; ERO D/DHs E2 (rear); ERO D/DSH 15.
383 ERO D/DHs M29, fo.206, 203; see also extracts from the manorial map of 1653 showing Jenkins and Parsloes (Sage, 'History of Barking', i, 207; D/DB P2). Neither copy includes the house shown on the 1666 Tithe Map; 'from Porters Lodge' may have been added later in the lane to copy, the Porter family holdings in Gale Street are distinguished by their name.
384 VCH Essex, v, 206; Act for the Sale of the Estate of Francis Osbaldeston, 4 & 5 William. & Mary, c.14 (private Act); ERO D/DCw T7.
385 Reaney Place-Names of Essex, xi-xii.
386 E.P. Murphy, 'Essex Tithe Apportionment Maps: their research value', Essex Review, lii (1943):135-6.
387 'Notes for completing Tithe Map and Award recording forms', no.6 (c.1997).
388 Lethieullier, 'History of Barking', 162-167; Lysons, Environs, iv. 72-73; where Lethieullier found the register and what happened to it subsequently remains a mystery.
389 One 'John Ravenyng' occurs in the 1327 lay subsidy rolls (the family name was preserved into the 20th century by a farm in Goodmayes).
390 Hatfield House, Cecil Papers, (Ilford Hospital) 1/17; across Conduit Field the ground level rises approximately five feet, but the flow could have been maintained by deeper trenching and a siphon effect – there were no air vents indicated between the 'brick house' and over Loxford Bridge.
391 ERO T208/38.
392 ERO D/DCT 18; the earlier identity of field no.1245a requires further investigation, the name Huntings Farm adopted at the beginning of the 20th century by the farmhouse built in Green Lane on its northern edge could be misleading. In the 1609 survey it seems to be part of a copyholding called Stonehalls [Item 370], Hobses in the 1669 tithe survey [fo.59], and possibly Hicks or Hudsons Farm in the 18th century. Huntings was the name of field no.1244 further south (now the southern half of South Park) which was Abbey demesne at the Dissolution and so tithe-free (though the vicar made a claim to the small tithe).
393 Howard Levi Gray, English Field Systems (Cambridge, Massachusetts: Harvard University Press, 1915): 392-400.
394 PRO LR.2/214 [467]; ERO D/DHs M31, 164; ERO D/DHs E2, 139, 201; ERO D/CT 110 (Valence Library has a MS copy); J. O'Leary, Dagenham Place Names (Dagenham: Borough of Dagenham, 1957): 78 was also helpful; it must be realised that the original High Road through Chadwell Heath towards Romford (the former Roman road) followed the course of Back Lane, as shown by the southern boundary of the forest down to 1851 (PRO MR 801, m.3), the present course began as a diversion across the open heath.

395 See chapter seven, above. Quarter (four acre), half (eight acre) and three-quarter (12 acre) divisions also appear; the occasional anomalies are survivals of more ancient customary rents; examples of changeovers can be found in the 1440 court roll (ERO D/DP M187), for example, Old Geryes, Rollersyerd.
396 Warwick J. Rodwell, 'Relict landscapes in Essex' in *Early Land Allotments*, eds. H.C. Bowen & P.J. Fowler, (Oxford: British Archaeological Reports, 1978): 89-98; P.J. Drury & W.J. Rodwell, 'Settlement in Later Iron Age and Roman Britain' in *Archaeology in Essex to AD 1500*, ed. D.G. Buckley (London: Council for British Archaeology, 1980): 59-95. None of these studies specifically included Barking or Dagenham.
397 S. Rippon, 'Early Planned Landscapes in South-East Essex', *Essex Archaeology and History*, 22 (1991): 46-60; C.J. Going, 'The Roman Countryside' in *The Archaeology of Essex* ed. O. Bedwin, (Chelmsford: Essex County Council, 1996): 100-101.
398 Rippon, 'Early Planned Landscapes' 54-55; as Going, 'Roman Countryside', 100-101, suggests, earlier studies were influenced by a hope of finding traces of Roman 'centuriation'; for more recently published comments, see Hunter, 'Regions and sub-regions of Essex' and Rippon, 'The Rayleigh Hills: patterns in the exploitation of a woodland landscape' both in L.S. Green, ed. *The Essex Landscape: in search of its history* (Chelmsford: Essex County Council, 199): 7-8, 20-25.
399 Michael Aston & Christopher Gerrard, 'The Shapwick Project', *The Antiquarian Journal*, vol.79 (1999): 1, 3, 29, 46
400 See above p.19.; VCH Essex, v., 190-1; Dunstan, then Abbot of Glastonbury, was a witness to King Eadred's charter to Barking Abbey in 950 (Hatfield House, Essex (Ilford Hospital) 1/6 fos 17v-18r; Sawyer, P.H. *Anglo-Saxon Charters: an Annotated List and Bibliography* (London: Royal Historical Society, 1968): no.552a. It is not intended to imply here that the radknight tenures were equivalent to virgate holdings – these latter were manorial copyholds whereas the former, though paying quit-rent to the lord, would evolve into freehold tenures – so it is more likely that the systems were complementary.
401 See note 394; the 1456 Abbey rental (B.M. Add. MS 45387) shows that this plan was successful in standardising virgate rents but if it was intended to substitute leases for lives for copyholds of inheritance, as the 1456 formula *pro firme* ('for farm of') might suggest, it did not succeed and by the Dissolution these newer rents had become the customary rents.
402 E. Tuck, *A Sketch of Ancient Barking Its Abbey and Ilford* (Barking & Ilford: Wilson & Whitworth, 1899): 42, and even this may only be a quotation borrowed from Lysons' *Environs*, 79.
403 Hatfield House, Essex (Ilford Hospital) 1/6 (the vellum book).
404 The 16 acre Sand Pit Field became part of no.2211 when the area became part of the park of Cranbrook and the old drive to Wyfields and Cranbrook was replaced. No broken lines show the former field boundaries here, but around no.2229 and between nos.1954 and 1954a they attempt to show the old boundaries between tithings.
405 An Act for the sale of divers messuages, farms, lands & tenements in Co. Essex, 7 Geo.III, cap.103. Reconstruction: see Fig.19.
406 Reaney, *Place-Names of Essex*, 100; VCH Essex, v, 190,213; Sawyer, *Anglo-Saxon Charters*, no.1171. The balance of probability seems to support at least part of this proposition, despite the doubts of Reaney and the hesitation of the VCH; BM Add. MS 45387 North fo.i; PRO LTR E368/449 rot.v [Tithes item 3].
407 *VCH Essex*, v, 213-4.
408 Ibid. 194.
409 H.H. Lockwood, 'Claybury and the Golden Woods' in *Essex Heritage*, ed. K. Neale (Oxford: Leopard's Head Press, 1992): 83-117.
410 VCH Essex, v, 203, but also see H.H. Lockwood, 'Those Greedy Hunters', 162; according to the Inquisition of 1580 all the tithes of Fulkes belonged to Ilford Hospital.
411 John Hunter, *Field Systems in Essex* (Colchester: Essex Society for Archaeology and History, 2003): 15.

Appendix

412 Tate, *Parish Chest*, 5-9; V.W. Gray 'The County Record Office: the unfolding of an idea' in *Essex Tribute* ed. K. Neale (London: Leopard's Head, 1987):11-25; F.G. Emmison, 'Early years in county record offices' *Journal of the Society of Archivists*, 7 (October 1988): 534-536.

413 The eventual extent of the acquisitions from metropolitan Essex can be judged from the Essex Record Office's *Essex in London*.

414 Documents in the ERO Sage Collection (D/DSa) are fully listed in a duplicated foolscap bound catalogue (1952) in the ERO Library. Some of the more significant are listed in *Essex in London*, List 23

415 The Fanshawe collection includes the notes compiled by H.C. Fanshawe for his *History of the Fanshawe Family*, his ms, and a great deal more material.

416 These included full-length copies of the 1540 ministers accounts and the 1609 survey of the manor of Barking which he had bound. Assisted by Dr C.J.R. Hart, then a Dagenham medical student, he also made hand-written translations. For the many further contributions of Cyril Hart see *An Autobiography and Personal Philosophy of a Retired Physician* (Lampeter etc. Edwin Mellon Press, 1997):60-61, 64-65, 97-109.

417 Copies in the ERO are indexed under T/P 93/1-4.

418 See above pp.49-50.

419 Reverend Alfred Blomfield was the son and biographer of Charles. J. Blomfield, the famous reforming Bishop of London. He himself became suffragan Bishop of Colchester in 1882.

420 A minute of the Barking Overseers in 1926 (Valence Library microfilm) reads "decided that the Assistant Overseer employ assistance in the removing of the old Rate Books from the Store Room and cleaning same, in readiness to hand them over to the Barking Council at the close of the year at a cost of £1.10.0." Harold Wand recollected being paid 25 shillings for assisting his father, Allen Wand, to carry a large collection of old papers and books to his father's new office in Clock House Chambers at Blakes Corner from a locker in the church vestry (personal communication).

421 ERO D/P 81/28/84.

422 See above pp.45-46.

423 See above pp.70-71.

424 See above p.50

425 H.H. Lockwood, 'One Thing Leads to Another: the discovery of additional charters of Barking Abbey', *Essex Journal*, 25, (1990): 11-13; the name vellum book was given to Cecil ms, Essex (Ilford Hospital) 1/6 by a 19th century Hatfield Librarian.

426 Foundation charters, the so-called 'Erkenwald' and 'Hodilred' charters, Sawyer, *Additional Charters*, nos.1246 & 1171, see also Hart, *Early Charters of Barking Abbey*; K.N. Bascombe, 'Two Charters of King Suebred of Essex' in *Essex Tribute* ed. Kenneth Neale (London: Leopard's Head, 1987): 85-96.

427 ERO T/P 93/4; so far only the first two charters have appeared in print and it is uncertain if and when the promised definitive edition of all the charters of Barking Abbey by Dr Cyril Hart will appear in the British Academy series, although the provisional text of the rediscovered charters has now been placed on their Anglo Saxon charters website (www.trin.cam.ac.uk/chartwww/barking.html).

428 The document was offered for sale in 1956 by S. Crowe, Bloomsbury (Catalogue 49).

429 Fisher versus Wite, fos.31v & 37.

430 The Essex Record Office now has copies of the above documents held in the Valence Library indexed T/A 412.

431 Oxley, *Barking Vestry Minutes*, 2.

432 ERO D/DHs: see above pp.80-81.

Bibliography

A

Addison, Sir William. *Essex Worthies*. Chichester: Phillimore, 1973.

Aston, M., & C. Gerrard. 'The Shapwick Project.' *The Antiquarian Journal*, 79, (1999): 1-46.

B

Bascombe, K.N. 'Two Charters of King Suebred of Essex' in *Essex Tribute* edited by Kenneth Neale, 85-96. London: Leopard's Head, 1987.

Bendall, S., ed. *Dictionary of Land Surveyors and Local Mapmakers*. London: British Library, 1997.

Bennett, G.V. 'Conflict in the Church' in *Britain After the Glorious Revolution* edited by G. Holmes insert page nos. London: Macmillan, 1969.

Briggs, Nancy. 'The evolution of the office of county surveyor in Essex 1700-1816'. *Architectural History*, 27, (1984).

Brown, A.F.J. *Essex People 1750-1900*. Chelmsford: Essex Record Office, 1972.

Brown, A.F.J. 'The Essex Country Parson 1700-1815' in *Essex Heritage*, edited by Kenneth Neale, 61-81. Oxford: Leopard's Head Press, 1992.

Brown, A.F.J. *Prosperity and Poverty: Rural Essex, 1700-1815*. Chelmsford: Essex Record Office, 1996.

Burchardt, J. *The Allotment Movement in England, 1793-1873*. Woodbridge: Boydell & Brewer, 2002.

Burn, R. *Justice of the Peace*. London, 1797.

Burnet, Gilbert, Bishop of Salisbury. *History of His Own Times*. Everyman Edition. London: J.M. Dent, 1906.

C

Calamy, E. *The Nonconformist Memorial*. Revised edition, three volumes. London, 1802.

Camp, A. *Wills and their Whereabouts*. Chichester: Phillimore, 1974.

Cartwright, Thomas. *An Answer of a Minister of the Church of England*, etc., London: 1687 [British Library, L.108 c.50.]

Christy, M. 'A Perambulation of the Parish of Chignal St James in 1797.' *Essex Review* xxxvi (1927): 60-71.

Claro, F.Z. & J. Howson. 'Barking Memories.' *The Barking Record*, 82 (1972): 12-14.

Coller, Duffield William. *The People's History of Essex*. Chelmsford: Meggy & Chalk, 1861.

Constable, Giles. *Monastic Tithes from Their Origins to the Twelfth Century*. Cambridge Studies in Medieval Life and Thought. Cambridge: Cambridge University Press, 1964.

D

Defoe, Daniel. *Tour through the Whole Island of Great Britain, 1724-26*. Everyman edition. London: Dent, 1962.

Dobson, Mary. *Contours of Death and Disease in Early Modern England*. Cambridge studies in population, economy and society in past time. Cambridge: Cambridge University Press, 1997.

Drury, P.J., & W.J. Rodwell. 'Settlement in Later Iron Age and Roman Britain' in *Archaeology in Essex to AD 1500*, edited by D.G. Buckley, 59-75. London: Council for British Archaeology, 1980.

E

Edwards, A.C., & K.C. Newton. *The Walkers of Hanningfield*. London: Buckland, 1984.

Edwards, P. *Farming: Sources for local historians*. London: Batsford, 1991.

Ellis, Mary. *Using Manorial Records*. Public Record Office Readers' Guide. London: Public Record Office in association with the Royal Commission on Historical Manuscripts, 1994.

Emmison, F.G. *Wills at Chelmsford*. Volume 1, 1400-1619. Chelmsford: Essex Record Office, 1958.

Emmison, F.G. *Wills at Chelmsford*. Volume 2, 1620-1720. Chelmsford: Essex Record Office, 1961.

Emmison, F.G., ed. *Third Supplement to Catalogue of Maps*. Chelmsford: Essex Record Office, 1968.

Emmison, F.G. *Wills at Chelmsford*. Volume 3, 1721-1858. Chelmsford: Essex Record Office, 1969.

Emmison, F.G. *Tudor Secretary*. Chichester: Phillimore, 1970.

Emmison, F.G. *Elizabethan Life*. Volume 1, *Disorder*. Chelmsford: Essex Record Office, 1970.

Emmison, F.G. *Elizabethan Life*. Volume 2, *Morals and the Church Courts*. Chelmsford: Essex Record Office, 1973.

Emmison, F.G. *Elizabethan Life*. Volume 3, *Home, Work and Land*. Chelmsford: Essex Record Office, 1976.

Emmison, F.G. 'Essex Genealogical Indexes: A million references to personal names.' *Genealogists' Magazine* 21, no.2 (1983): 55-59.

Emmison, F.G. 'Early years in county record offices.' *Journal of the Society of Archivists* 7, no.8 (Oct. 1988): 534-536.

Emmison, F.G. *Essex Wills: The Archdeaconry Court*. Volume 5, 1583-92. Chelmsford: Essex Record Office, 1989.

Emmison, F.G. *Essex Wills: The Archdeaconry Court*. Volume 6, 1591-97. Chelmsford: Essex Record Office, 1991.

Emmison, F.G., and R. Stephens eds. *Tribute to an Antiquary: Essays presented to Marc Fitch*. London: Leopard's Head Press, 1976.

Essex in London: A guide to the records of the London Boroughs formerly in Essex deposited in the Essex Record Office. Chelmsford: Essex Record Office, 1992.

Essex Trades and Professional Directory. Kellys, 1906.

Evans, E.J. 'English Rural Anti-Clericalism c.1750- c.1820.' *Past and Present* 66 (1975): 84-109.

Evans, Eric. *The Contentious Tithe*. London: Routledge & Kegan Paul, 1976.

Evans, Eric, and Alan Crosby. *Tithes, Maps, Apportionments and the 1836 Act: a guide for local historians*. Third edition. Salisbury: British Association of Local History, 1997.

Evans, Nesta. 'Tithe Books as a source for the local historian.' *The Local Historian* 14, no.1 (1980): 24-27.

F

Fanshawe, H.C. *The History of the Fanshawe Family*. Newcastle: A. Reid & Co., 1927.

Fisher, William Richard. *The Forest of Essex: its history, laws, administration and ancient custom, etc*. London: Butterworths, 1887.

Fitch, M., ed. *An Index of Testamentary Records in the Commissary Court of London*. Vol.1, 1374-1488. British Record Society Series. London: H.M.S.O, 1969.

Fitch, M., ed. *An Index of Testamentary Records in the Commissary Court of London*. Volume 2, 1489-1570. British Record Society Series. London: H.M.S.O, 1974.

Fitch, M., ed. *An Index of Testamentary Records in the Commissary Court of London*. Volume 3, 1571-1625. British Record Society Series. London: H.M.S.O, 1985.

Foster, J. *Alumni Oxonienses*. Four volumes. Oxford: Oxford University Press, 1968.

Fowler, R.C. 'Religious Houses' in *Victoria County History of Essex*. Volume ii. London: 1907.
Fowler, R.C. 'Fulk Basset's register and the Norwich taxation.' *Essex Archaeological Society Transactions* xviii (1928): 15-26.

G

Gem, R. 'Anglo-Saxon Minsters of the Thames Estuary', in *Thames Gateway: Recording Historic Buildings and Landscapes in the Thames Estuary*. Swindon: Royal Commission on the Historical Monuments of England, 1995.
Glenny, W.W. 'The Dykes of the Thames.' *The Essex Review* x (1901): 149-162.
Going, C.J. 'The Roman Countryside' in *The Archaeology of Essex*, edited by Owen Bedwin, 100-1. Chelmsford: Essex County Council, 1996.
Gordon, Alexander. *Freedom after Ejection*. Manchester: Victoria University. Publications, 1917.
Gray, Howard Levi, *English Field Systems*. Cambridge, Massachusetts: Harvard University Press, 1915.
Gray, V.W. 'The County Record Office: the unfolding of an idea' in *Essex Tribute* edited by Kenneth Neale, 11-25. London: Leopard's Head, 1987.
Green, A. *Ashdon: A History of an Essex Village*. Aldham, Essex: privately published by the author, 1989.
Grieve, Hilda. *The Great Tide*. Chelmsford: Essex County Council, 1959.

H

Hall, D. *Medieval Fields*. Aylesbury: Shire, 1982.
Hanson, T.W. *The Story of Old Halifax*. Halifax: F. King & Sons, 1920.
Hart, C.R. *The Early Charters of Barking Abbey*. Colchester: Benham & Co, 1953.
Hart, C.R. *The Early Charters of Eastern England*. Leicester: Leicester University Press, 1966.
Hart, C.R. *An Autobiography and Personal Philosophy of a Retired Physician*. Lampeter etc: Edwin Mellon Press, 1997.
Hayns, David. 'SOS for MSS.' *Local History* 73 (1999).
Henstock, A. 'House Repopulation from the CEBs of 1841 and 1851' in *Local Communities in the Victorian Census Enumerators' Books* edited by D. Mills & K. Schurer. Oxford: Leopard's Head Press, 1996.
Hill, C. *Economic Problems of the Church*. Oxford: Panther, 1971.
Horowitz, H. *Exchequer Equity Records and Proceedings 1649-1841*. London: Public Record Office, 2001.
Hoskins, W.G. *The Making of the English Landscape*. London: Hodder & Stoughton, 1955.
Houston, Jane. *Index of Cases in the Records of the Court of Arches at Lambeth Palace Library 1660-1913*. London: British Record Society, 1972.
Howard, Eliot. 'Some Reminiscences of an Essex Police Court.' *Essex Review* xxiv (1915): 190-2.
Hoyle, Richard. *Tudor Taxation Records: a guide for users*. London: Public Record Office, 1994.
Huggins, P.J., ed. *Millennium Project 3*. Waltham Historical Society, 1997.
Hull, Felix. 'Aspects of Local Cartography in Kent and Essex 1585-1700', in *Essex Tribute* edited by Kenneth Neale, 241-252. London: Leopard's Head, 1987.
Hunter, J., ed. *The Diary of Thomas Cartwright*. London: Camden Society, 1843.
Hunter, John. 'Regions and sub-regions of Essex' in *The Essex Landscape: in search of its history* edited by L.S. Green. Chelmsford: Essex County Council, 1999.
Hunter, John. *Field Systems in Essex*. Colchester: Essex Society for Archaeology and History, 2003.

I & J

James, Margaret. 'The Political Importance of the Tithes Controversy in the English Revolution, 1640-60.' *History* 26, (1941): 1-18.

Jones, P.E. *Calendar of Pleas & Memorandum Rolls of the City of London 1458-82*. Cambridge: Cambridge University Press, 1961.

K

Kain, Roger, and Richard Oliver. *The Tithe Maps of England and Wales: a cartographic analysis and county-by-county catalogue*. Cambridge: Cambridge University Press, 1995.

Kain, Roger J.P., and Hugh C. Prince. *The Tithe Surveys of England and Wales*. Cambridge: Cambridge University Press, 1985.

Kain, Roger J.P., and Hugh C. Prince. *Tithe Surveys for Historians*. Chichester: Phillimore, 2000.

L

Ladurie, E. Le Roy, and J. Goy. *Tithe and Agrarian History from the Fourteenth to the Nineteenth Centuries*. Translated by Susan Burke. Paris/Cambridge: Cambridge University Press, 1982.

Law, A.D., and S. Barry. *The Forest in Walthamstow and Chingford*. Edited by W.G.S. Tonkin. London: Walthamstow Antiquarian Society, 1978.

Lennard, R. 'Peasant Tithe Collectors in Norman England.' *English Historical Review*, lxix (1954).

Lockwood, H.H. *Where Was the First Barking Abbey?* Trans. n.s.1??, Barking Historical Society, 1986.

Lockwood, H.H. 'Those Greedy Hunters after Concealed Lands' in *Essex Tribute* edited by Kenneth Neale, 153-170. London: Leopard's Head, 1987.

Lockwood, H.H. 'One Thing Leads to Another: The discovery of additional charters of Barking Abbey.' *Essex Journal*, 25, no.1 (1990): 11-13.

Lockwood, H.H. 'Claybury and the Golden Woods', in *Essex Heritage*, ed. K. Neale (Oxford: Leopard's Head Press, 1992).

Lockwood, H.H. 'The Barking Vicarages and Jeremy Bentham.' *Essex Journal* xxvii, (Summer 1992): 43-7.

Lockwood, H.H. 'The Chaplain Trail and the Lodge Connexion.' *Ilford Historical Society Newsletter* 46, (September 1995).

Loftus, E.A., & H.F. Chettle. *A History of Barking Abbey*. Barking: Wilson & Whitworth, 1953.

Ludgate, Eileen. *Clavering and Langley 1783-1983*. Clavering, Essex: privately published by author, 1984.

Ludgate, Eileen. *Clavering and Langley: The first thousand years*. Clavering, Essex: privately published by author, 1996.

Lysons, D. *Environs of London*. Vol. iv. London, 1796. Supplementary volume, London, 1811.

M

Macaulay, Lord Thomas Babington. *History of England*. Everyman edition in 3 volumes. London: Dent, 1906.

Macfarlane, A. *The Family Life of Ralph Josselin 1616-1683*. London: Cambridge University Press, 1970.

Macfarlane, A. *Reconstructing Historical Communities*. Cambridge: Cambridge University Press, 1977.

Macfarlane, A., ed. *Records of an English Village: Earls Colne 1400-1750*. Cambridge: Cambridge University Press, 1980.

Macfarlane, A. *A Guide to English Historical Records*. Cambridge: Cambridge University Press, 1983.

[MacGowan, K.] 'Barking Abbey.' *Current Archaeology* 149, no. xiii (Sept. 1996).

McIntosh, M.K. 'Land, tenure and population.' *Economic History Review*, second series, xxxiii (1980): 17-31.

McIntosh, M.K. *Autonomy and Community: The Royal Manor of Havering 1200-1500*. Cambridge: Cambridge University Press, 1986.

McIntosh, M.K. *A Community Transformed: The Manor and Liberty of Havering 1500-1620*. Cambridge: Cambridge University Press, 1991.

Mason, A. Stuart. *Essex on the Map*. Chelmsford: Essex Record Office, 1990.

Mason, A. Stuart. 'Tithe commutation maps of Essex', *Transactions of Essex Archaeological & Historical Society* third series 25, (1994): 219-225.

Morant, Philip. *The History and Antiquities of the County of Essex*. Two volumes. Chelmsford, 1816.

Murphy, E.P. 'Essex Tithe Apportionment Maps: their research value.' *Essex Review*, iii, (1943): 135-6.

N

Namier, Sir L., & J. Brooke. *The House of Commons 1754-1790*. Three volumes. London: H.M.S.O. 1964.

Neale, Ken, ed. *Essex Heritage*. Oxford: Leopard's Head Press, 1992.

Neeson, J. *Commoners, Common Rights, Enclosure and Social Change*. Cambridge: Cambridge University Press, 1993.

Newcourt, R. *Repertorium Ecclesiasticum Parochiale*. Two volumes. London: C. Bateman, 1708-10.

Notes and Queries. London: Oxford University Press, 1849- .

O

[O'Leary, J., ed.] *Essex and Dagenham Catalogue*. Dagenham: Borough of Dagenham Public Library, 1957. 2nd edition 1961.

O'Leary, J. *Dagenham Place Names*. Dagenham: Borough of Dagenham, 1957.

Oliver, R. *Ordnance Survey Maps: a concise guide for historians*. London: Charles Close Society, 1993.

Owen, T., and E. Pilbeam. *Ordnance Survey: Map Makers to Britain since 1791*. London: H.M.S.O., 1992.

Oxley, J. E., ed., 'Barking Abbey Rental 1456.' *Transactions of Barking and District Archaeological. Society* (1936-37); two parts.

Oxley, J.E. *Barking Vestry Minutes and other Parish Documents*. Colchester: Benham & Co., 1955.

Oxley, J.E. 'Accounts of the office of the Cellaress, 1535-9.' *Transactions of Barking and District Archaeological. Society* (1957).

Oxley, J.E., & W.B. Trigg, 'Tithe rental of Halifax parish.' *Halifax Antiquarian Society* xxxi (1934): 77-111.

P

Page, W., & J.H. Round. *Victoria County History of Essex*. Volume 2 London, 1907.

Pearson Jane. 'Figures in a Landscape: the County of Essex in 1766 through the eyes of its clergy', in *Essex Harvest*, edited by Michael Holland & Jacqueline Cooper. Chelmsford: Essex Record Office, 2003.

Powell, W.R. 'The Making of Essex Parishes.' *Essex Review*, lxii (1953): 6-17.

Powell, W.R. *Victoria County History of Essex*. Volume 4 London, 1956; Volume 5 London, 1966; Volume 6 London, 1973; Volume 7 London, 1978.

Powell, W.R. 'Essex' in *English County Histories: A Guide*. Stroud: Alan Sutton, 1994.

Pressey, Reverend W.J. 'Visitations held in the Archdeaconry of Essex in 1683.' *Transactions of the Essex Archaeological Society*, new series, xix (1929): 260-276.

Pressey, Reverend W.J. 'Beating the Bounds in Essex: As seen in the Archdeaconry records.' *Essex Review*, xlviii (1939): 84-91.

Q & R

Quin, W.F. *A History of Braintree and Bocking.* Brentwood, 1981.

Reaney, P.H. *The Place-Names of Essex.* Cambridge: Cambridge University Press, 1935.

Reaney, P.H. *The Origin of English Place Names.* London: Routledge & Kegan Paul, 1964.

Richardson, R.C., ed. *The Changing Face of English Local History.* Aldershot: Ashgate, 2000.

Rippon, S. 'Early Planned Landscapes in South-East Essex.' *Essex Archaeology and History*, 22 (1991): 46-60

Rippon, S. 'Essex c.700-1066' in *The Archaeology of Essex* edited by Owen Bedwin. Chelmsford: Essex County Council, 1996.

Rippon, S. 'The Rayleigh Hills: patterns in the exploitation of a woodland landscape' in *The Essex Landscape: in Search of its History* edited by L.S. Green. Chelmsford: Essex County Council, 1999.

Rodwell, Warwick J. 'Relict landscapes in Essex' in *Early Land Allotment* edited by H.C. Bowen & P.J. Fowler. Oxford: British Archaeological Reports, 1978.

Rogers, C.D. *The Surname Detective.* Manchester: Manchester University Press, 1995.

Rogers, C.D., & J.H. Smith. *Local Family History in England.* Manchester: Manchester University Press, 1991.

S

Sanders, F. 'Thomas Cartwright.' *Chester Archaeological & Historical Society Journal*, new series. iv (1892).

Sawyer, P.H. *Anglo-Saxon Charters: An Annotated List and Bibliography.* London: Royal Historical Society, 1968. Note: 'Electronic Sawyer', a revised, augmented & updated version is now available online at 'www.trin.cam.ac.uk/chartwww/'

Schurer, K. *Local Communities in the Victorian Census Enumerators' Books.* Oxford: Leopard's Head Press, 1996.

Seebohm, Frederic. *The English Village Community.* London: Longmans Green & Co. 1883.

Sharpe, J.A. *"William Holcroft His Booke."* Chelmsford: Essex Record Office, 1986.

Smith, A.H. *English Place Name Elements.* Two volumes. Cambridge: Cambridge University Press, 1987).

Smith, H. 'Some Essex Parliamentarians 1642-1653.' *Essex Review* 33 (1924): 149-155.

Smith, H. *Ecclesiastical History of Essex.* Colchester: Benham & Co., 1931.

Stephen, L., & S. Lee, eds. *Dictionary of National Biography.* London: Smith Elder, 1885-1909. (Later editions and supplements: Oxford University Press.)

Stokes, A. *History of East Ham.* Stratford: Wilson & Whitworth, 1933.

T

Tarver, Ann. *Church Court Records: An introduction for family and local historians.* Chichester: Phillimore, 1995.

Tasker, G.F. *Ilford Past and Present.* Ilford: S.W. Hayden, 1901.

Tate, W.E. *The Parish Chest.* Cambridge: Cambridge University Press, 1946.

Tuck, E. *A Sketch of Ancient Barking, its Abbey and Ilford.* Barking & Ilford: Wilson & Whitworth, 1899.

U & V

Vamplew, W. 'Tithes and Agriculture: Some Comments on Commutation.' *Economic History Review*, second series, 34 (1981).

Venn, J., & J.A. *Alumni Cantabrigienses*. 10 volumes. Cambridge: Cambridge University Press, 1922-54)

W

Waller, W.C., 'Essex Field Names [Tithe Award].' *Essex Archaeological Society Transactions*, new series, v – ix (1895-1906).

Waller, W.C. 'The Foresters Walks in Waltham Forest.' *Essex Review* xiv, (1905): 193-203.

Ward, Jennifer C., ed. *The Medieval Essex Community: The Lay Subsidy of 1327*. Chelmsford: Essex Reocrd Office, 1983.

Weller, John. *Grangia & Orreum. The Medieval Barn: A nomenclature*. Bildeston, Suffolk: Bildeston Booklets, 1986.

Whiteman, Anne, ed. *The Compton Census of 1676: A critical edition*. London: Oxford University Press on behalf of the British Academy, 1986.

Whiteman, Anne. 'The Compton Census of 1676', in *Surveying the People* edited by K. Schurer & T. Arkell. Oxford: Leopard's Head Press, 1992.

Williams, Ann. 'The Vikings in Essex 871-917.' *Essex Archaeology and History* 27 (1996): 92-101.

Wood, Hutton. *A Collection of Decrees by the Court of Exchequer in Tithe-Causes, from the Usurpation to the Present time*. Four volumes. London, 1798/99.

Woodforde, James. *Diary of a Country Parson*. Edited by J. Beresford. World's Classics edition. Oxford: Oxford University Press, 1949.

X, Y & Z

Young, Arthur. *Survey of Essex*. London, 1807.

Zupko, R.E. *A Dictionary of English Weights and Measures from Anglo-Saxon times to the Nineteenth Century*. Madison etc.: University of Wisconsin Press, 1968.

Newspapers referred to

The earliest form of the title is given; dates given are total periods of publication, not all numbers issued within these dates may be available. Copies are normally on microfilm.
Essex Herald   1800 – 1903   (Essex Record Office)
Essex Standard   1831 – 1964   (Essex Record Office)
Essex Times   1866 – 1937   (Havering Central Library, Romford)

Unpublished dissertations and theses

Allison, R. 'The changing geographical landscape of SW Essex from Saxon times to 1600.' (M.A. dissertation, University of London, 1958).

Allison, R. 'The changing landscape of south-west Essex, 1600-1850.' (Ph.D. thesis, University of London, 1966).

Anglin, J.P. 'Court of the Archdeacon of Essex 1571-1609'. (Ph.d. thesis, University of California, 1965).

Gramolt, D.W. 'The Coastal Marshlands of East Essex between the Seventeenth and mid-Nineteenth Centuries' (M.A. dissertation, University of London, 1960).

Sturman, M. 'Barking abbey: a study in its external and internal administration from the Conquest to the Dissolution' (Ph.D. thesis, University of London, 1961).

Unpublished histories of Barking

Lethieullier, Smart. 'History of Barking', c.1750. MS in Hulse family collection at Breamore House, Hants. [see p.89] Photocopies at Essex Record Office (T/P 93/1-3); documentary Appendix (T/P 93/4). Photocopies, microfilm and typed transcript at Valence House Local Studies Centre (Dagenham).

Sage, Edward. '(Collection for the) History of Barking' 2 vols. c.1859. Essex Record Office Sage Collection. Microfilm at Valence House Local Studies Centre (Dagenham).

Frogley, (William Holmes). 'History of Barking', c. 1900-1911 MS loaned by Essex Society for Archaeology and History to London Borough of Barking and Dagenham at Valence House. Photocopies at Essex Record Office (T/A 333), Valence House Local Studies Centre (Dagenham) & Redbridge Central Library Local History Room. A major portion recently published as Mr Frogley's Barking: *A First Selection* (2002), *A Second Selection* (2003) and *A Third Selection* (2004), edited by Tony Clifford & H.H. Lockwood, published by London Borough of Barking & Dagenham, fully illustrated and annotated.

General Index

Acts of Parliament: 19, 45, 70, 98-99, 106, 121; Act of Uniformity (1662); 10, 46; Sturges Bourne Acts (1818-9): 73-74; Tithe Commutation Act (1836): 6, 7, 17-19, 23, 54, 58, 95, 120; *see also Court*
Advowsons: 34
Agistments: 35
Agricultural improvements: 17-18, 51-53
Allotments: 86, 92-93
Appropriation of tithe: *see tithe appropriators*
Assarts: 91, 107

Barking Abbey: Augmentation office: 113; Cartulary ('vellum book'): 62, 107, 112-13, 122, 127, 130; Dissolution of: 9, 14, 23, 31, 33-35, 37, 39, 50, 63, 80, 91, 96; Foundation & charters: 28, 107, 113; Precinct: 30, 39, 61, 69; Stewards: 33-36, 82; *see also subject index*
Barking account book (1690): 21
Barking, manor of: Charters: 28, 77, 92, 107, 122; Court: 31, 33, 76-77, 84: Court records: 80, 114, 130, 134; Lordship of: 29, 77-79, 81
Barking maps & surveys: Abbey rental of 1456: 80, 82-83, 101, 116, 130, 134; Court of Survey (1609): 77, 81-82, 98; Court roll (1440): 80, 83, 91, 130; Manorial map (1652-3): 50, 76; **Manorial survey (1609):** 35, 80-82, 102-103, 116, 113; Manorial survey (1663): 41, 77, 97; **Manorial survey (1679):** 77-79, 96-97, 103, 114, 116; Minister's accounts (1540): 75, 81-82, 100, 116; Part-survey (1617): 45, 67-69, 80-81, 83, 90, 95-96, 112; Reeve's account for Westbury (1321): 80, 83
Barking rate surveys and valuations: 1807: 55, 57, 73; 1829: 57, 73-74, 80, 116-117
Barking tithe maps and surveys: Eastbury tithing maps (1735 and 1742): 66, 98, 115; Eastbury tithe map (1831): 66, 87; Rate survey (1807): 55, 57, 73; Tithe accounts (1681-2): 45; Tithe accounts (1690-1723): 21; Tithe commutation & award map (1846-7): 38, 58, 70, 71, 73, 92, 102, 105-106, 115, 117; Tithe survey (1669): 37-38, 41, 43-44, 46, 67, 72, 85, 87, 95, 97-98, 100, 112, 115, 124, 131, 133; Tithe survey (1681): 43-45, 47, 77, 95-96, 111-112, 115; Tithe survey (1690): 47; Tithe survey (1727-8): 38, 48, 79, 95, 112, 116, 133; Tithe survey (1750): 39, 49, 73, 79, 87, 101, 107, 111, 116, 123; Tithe survey map & terrier (1805-6): 37, 55, 58, 66, 73, 80, 116, 123; Vicar's tithe map (1666): 25, 41-42, 49-50, 54-55, 59, 66-67, 69, 71, 79, 81, 87, 89, 102, 111, 115, 117, 123, 132-133; Westbury tithe circuit (1596): 67
Barking Vestry (inc. minutes): 43-44, 46-47, 50-53, 57-58, 65, 73-75, 93, 111, 112, 114, 119, 126, 129
Black mutton: 94
Bridge repair: 91
Butchers: 35, 85, 123

Cartage: 11, 33
Census (1841, 1851): 74, 95, 132; Compton 'Census' (1676): 125

Charcoal burners (Colliers): 91, 94, 132
Church rates: *see Rates*
Commissioners of Sewers: 66, 87, 132
Commons: 19, 25, 39, 66, 68, 88, 132
Commutation: *see Tithe commutation*
Compositions: 12, 14, 16, 20-21, 33-34, 36-39, 44, 47, 51, 53, 55, 59, 65, 77; Composition book: 21
Conduit: 100-102
Court: Arches: 26, 41, 114, 121; Assize: 118; Attachment: 84, 132; Barking Court of Survey (1609): 81-82, 98; Chancery: 65, 113; Commissary: 26; Ecclesiastical: 26, 42, 64; Exchequer: 25, 33, 51, 62, 67, 89, 113; Kings Bench: 25; Quarter Session Appeals: 17, 51, 110; Manor: 33; Swainmote: 84, 131
Crops: Acreages under cultivation: 14, 20-21, 25, 37, 42-44, 51, 55, 63-66, 69, 73-79, 106, 115; Animals: 12, 14, 25, 49, 65, 87-89, 93-94; Arable: 14, 16, 18, 21, 25, 53, 65, 71, 86-88, 102-103; Cattle & horse feed: 18, 35, 87, 43; Charges per acre: 14, 51, 53, 68; Fishermens' boats: 35; Honey: 49; Hops & hop grounds: 12, 14, 16-17, 21; Market gardens & orchards: 18, 31, 35, 37, 39, 51, 53, 61, 66, 68, 86, 88, 94, 123; Meadow & pasture: 19, 21, 25, 35, 59, 63, 68, 71, 85, 87-90, 93-94, 100, 126; Milk: 12, 26; Price: 14, 18, 51, 53, 86; Wood: 11, 14, 16, 21, 35, 43, 84, 123, 126, 132; Wool: 12, 14, 25; *see also Great tithe*
Crown exemption: 59

Dagenham tithe maps and surveys (1609 + 1679): 103; Tithe award map (1844): 103
Demesne lands: 14, 16, 24, 31, 33-37, 39, 61, 63, 79-80, 82-83, 96, 98, 101-102, 114, 123, 130, 133
Dissent: 10, 11, 17, 45-47, 52, 125
Dissolution of the monasteries: 9, 14, 23, 28, 31, 33-35, 37, 39, 50, 63, 80, 91, 96, 108, 122-123, 133
Donative curates: 10
Drovers: 21

Enclosures: 19, 70, 91, 121, 127
***Essex Place Names* (Reaney):** 99, 132
Estovers: 94, 132

Farming practices: 83, 88, 91
Field name origins: 20-21, 42, 48-49, 57, 66, 73, 80, 82, 85, 91, 99-100, 115
Fields named: 45, 80, 87-88, 91-92, 95, 98-102, 106-107, 133
Forests of Waltham & Hainault: Clearances and assarts: 51, 70, 90-92, 94, 103, 107-108, 115, 132-133; Dealers and jobbers: 11, 94, 132-133; Courts: 84, 131; Documents: 83; Forest-edge & inhabitants: 45, 50, 83, 93-96; Laws: 35, 83, 132-133; Wastes: 35, 39, 83, 87, 90-93, 96;

Foresters' walks: 130; Stubbing and Grubbing: 35, 83, 91, 132; Royal Forests: 51, 60, 91-2; Timber for Royal Navy: 91; *see also Clearances and Index of place names*

Glebe lands: 17, 21, 23, 25
Great (rectorial) tithe: 10-12, 14, 16, 31, 33-39, 57, 59, 92; *see also Crops*

Havering, extent of (1352-3): 80
Hop grounds: *see Crops*

Ilford Hospital tithe: 54, 63-65, 67, 82-83, 91, 102, 106, 113; *see also Index of place names*
Impropriators: *see Tithe impropriators*
Irrigation: 89

Lay rectors and impropriators: 10, 16, 23, 25, 34, 59, 119; *see also Tithe impropriators*
Lay subsidy list (1327): 83, 85

Manors: 31
Maps: used for Tithe: 23-25, 35, 124, 126-129; Companions to maps: 42-43, 50, 54, 66; Cost of making: 20, 24, 25, 55, 58; Estate maps: 23-24, 104; Land uses noted on: 24, 66, 68, 71, 103; Occupiers noted on: 21, 23-24, 44, 59, 71, 73-74, 76, 79, 81, 115-116; Ordnance Survey: 54, 70, 97, 99-100, 129; Parish tithe maps: 24-25, 35, 41-42, 49-50, 54, 76, 80, 90, 103, 126; Tithe award maps: 19, 24, 70, 74, 100, 102-104, 106, 120; Tithe maps and surveys: 7, 18, 20-21, 23-25, 38-39, 41-44, 55, 128-129; *see also Barking maps and surveys and Surveyors*
Market gardens: *see Crops*
Marsh: 31, 35, 37, 39, 61, 66, 85-90, 93-4, 97, 113, 115, 123, 131
Marsh-edge settlement: 93, 131
Mills (wind and water): 16, 21, 38, 59, 91, 95, 123
Moduses: *see Compositions*
Monasteries: *see Dissolution of*

Non-Conformity: 10, 11, 17, 45-47, 52, 125
Norwich Valuation (1254): 30

Open Field: *see Commons*
Orchards: *see Crops*
Overseers: 10, 16, 46, 72, 92-3, 111, 112, 129

Parish Chest: 25, 110, 111, 120
Parishioners meetings: 16, 25-26, 41, 46, 50, 52-53, 75, 122; *see also Barking Vestry*
Perambulations (beating the bounds): 8, 10, 26-27, 118

Personal tithe: 11, 35, 72
Poor Law: 25, 58

Quakers: 11
Quitclaim: 59
Quitrents: 82, 130

Radknight tenures: 105, 134
Rates: Church: 46, 74; Highway: 52; Poor: 16, 17, 21, 52, 54, 72-74; Rate Books: 49, 72-74, 80, 112, 117, 129; Rating of tithe owners: 57, 72; *see also Barking rate surveys and taxes*
Reeves: 33
Riding collectors: *see Tithe collection*
Ryden (and similar field names): 91, 101; *see also Forest clearances*

Savoy Conference (1662): 10, 119
Small tithe: 9-12, 14, 16, 21, 23, 34-39, 46, 51, 59, 107
Surveyors: 21, 23-24, 42-43, 45, 52, 55, 57-58, 64, 66, 68-69, 73, 93, 112, 124-125, 127-128

Tanning: 95
Taxes: Hearth (1671): 72, 74, 86, 117; Land: 21, 72, 74; Subsidy rolls: 82, 117, 133
Tenants & occupiers name indexes: 44, 49, 64, 66, 69, 73-74, 77-80, 82, 85, 116-117, 132
Tenter fields: 21
Terriers (field books): 14, 18, 21, 44, 50, 55, 66, 69, 73, 117, 121; *see also Maps*
Timber: *see Crops*

Tithe: Accounts: 20-21, 25-26, 45, 47-51, 53-54, 73, 86, 96-98, 111, 115-116, 125, 132; Agreements: 12, 14, 16, 18, 25, 31, 44, 52, 63, 65; Appropriators & impropriators: 10, 11, 17, 23-25, 30, 33-35, 38, 41-42, 51, 59, 62, 72, 119, 126; Annual rent-charge in lieu of: 14, 18, 21, 36, 43, 121; Audit dinners: 17; Awards: 19, 23-25, 39, 55, 57, 59, 70-74, 86, 91-92, 95-96, 99-100, 102-104, 106, 115, 117, 120, 126, *see also Maps*; Barns: 11, 33-34; Cartage: 11, 33; Case law: 9; Circuits: 23, 35, 37, 42, 44, 49, 54-55, 59, 61, 66, 96, 102, 105, 107, 114, 134; Collection: 9-11, 23, 31, 33, 36, 45, 49, 54, 63-65, 83, 103; Commissioners for: 38, 59, 64, 128; Commutation, Award & map: 6-7, 17-19, 24-25, 58, 70, 85, 95, 100, 105, 121, 127, *see also Acts of Parliament*; Defined: 9; Disputes: 9, 13, 16, 25-26, 33-34, 43, 53, 63-66, 113-114, 118, 128; Evasion & exemptions: 35, 37-39, 59, 61, 65, 120; Farming: 9, 17; Inducements to pay: 9-11, 17-18 Impropriators: *see appropriators*; Paid in kind: 4, 11-12, 14, 18, 20-21, 31, 33-35, 43, 49, 63; Rent-charge: 14, 18, 23; Riding collectors: 33; Valuations & apportionments: 18, 23, 55, 57, 70-71, 99-100, 133;
Tithings: *see Tithe circuits*

Valuers, use of: 18
Vellum Book: *see Barking Abbey, Cartulary*
Verderers: 83, 91-92, 94
Virgates: 77, 86, 103, 105, 107, 129, 134

Water supply: *see Conduits*
Waste land: 35, 39, 79, 83-84, 87, 91-95; *see also Forest wastes*
Woodland: 21, 35, 38, 54, 83-84, 90-91, 103, 108, 115, 123; *see also Crops*

Yard-lands: *see Virgates*

Index of personal names

Addison, W: 132
Adelicia, Abbess: 31 & fig.13
Aethelred, King: 113
Allen, John: 64, 128
Allis: 53
Amyce, Israel: 24, 64, 121, 128
André, Peter: 93, 96
Armorer, James: 113
Athelstan, King: 113

Bamber, Dr John: 99
Barnes: 36, 96, 127
Barnes, Bart: 36, 123
Barnes, Isabel: 38
Barnes (aka Baron), Thomas: 34, 36, 38, 96
Barry, S: 132
Beacon, Thomas: fig.14
Bede: 29-30
Belgrave, William: 42-43
Bertie family: 46
Bird, Rev: 10
Bladen, Col: 49
Blomfield, Rev: 112, 135
Boards: 58
Bourne: 95
Bowen, H.C: 134
Bracton: 77, 130
Brand, Fred: 130
Brewer, Thomas: 89
Brewster, Augustine: 45
Brewster, Elizabeth: 45
Brewster, John: 45, 125
Browne, R.H: 26
Brushfield, Thomas: fig.12
Burgoyne, Montague: 92, 94

Cambell, Lady: 43
Cambell, Sir Thomas: 43
Camp, Anthony: 75
Caroe (Carew): 113, 123

Carter, Dr Thomas: 12
Cartwright, Frances: 124
Cartwright, John: 124
Cartwright, Mary: 41, 124
Cartwright, Sara: 41, 124
Cartwright, Rev Thomas: 26, 40-49, 51, 53, 67-69, 77, 112, 115-16, 121-125
Cawdle, Robert: 87, 131
Cecil family: 115, 122, 125-28, 131-33
Cedd, Bishop: 28
Chapman, John: 93, 95-6
Chisenhall (Chisenhale), John: 46-8, 75, 125
Chisnell, Richard: 20
Clark, Richard: 86
Cole, William: 24
Colyer, Thomas: 91
Cordell: see Cawdle
Cowper, William: 5
Cox: fig.16
Crawter, Henry: 58
Cromwell, Thomas: 9
Cuff, James: 61
Cuffley, Rev: 20
Curwen, J.C: 23

Dapifer, Eudo: 11
de Beauvoir, R.B: 61
de la Pole, Abbess Katherine: 101
Denham, Sir William: 38
Denny family: 10, 23-4, 118
Dodson, Joseph: 95
Downer, John: 97
Downes, William: 23, 26
Doyly, John: 24, 126
Drayson, Frederick: 58, 105, 127, 129
Drury, William: 86-7
Dunstan: 30, 104-5, 134
Durham, Lord: 93

Eadred, King: 113, 134

Emmison, Dr F: 8, 26-7, 75, 85, 110-11, 118, 121-3, 127, 133
Erkenwald: 28, 29-30
Ethelburga, Abbess: 30
Evans, Eric: 7, 9, 118-120

Fairchild, William: 111, 114
Fanshawe family: 33, 42-3, 63-4, 96, 110, 113, 123-4, 127-8
Fanshawe, G: 64, 127
Fanshawe, Henry: 63-4
Fanshawe, Thomas: 39, 42, 62, 64, 67-9, 77-8, 89, 97-8, 124
Fanshawe, Thomasina: 63
Farmiloe, Rev: 112
Fiddes, Thomas: 48-49, 112, 116
Finch, Rev Leopold: 47, 125
Fisher, Dr William: 34, 62-4, 113, 123, 127
Fitch, Marc: 8, 76, 121, 129
Frogley, William: 46, 125
Fuller: 68

Gascoyne family: 55, 65, 106, 113, 126
Gascoyne, Bamber: 50-52. 54-5, 65, 106, 125-6
Gascoyne, Joseph: 65
Gascoyne, Sir Crisp: 50, 54, 65, 125-6
Gem, Richard: 28, 30, 122
Gennynges, Nicholas: 82
Glenny family: 112
Glenny, Kenneth: 112
Gott, George: 94
Gott, Jason: 95
Gray, Howard Levi: 102, 133
Gray, Laurence: 123
Gray, Rev Robert: 23
Green, Angela 23, 120
Grigg, Peter: 107

Hall, David: 71, 129

Hardwicke, Justice: 14
Harlakenden, R: 16, 121
Hart, Cyril: 81, 122, 135
Hartley, F.D: 71
Harvey, Eliab: 92
Harvey-Mildmay family: 74
Hennynges: see Gennynges
Henry VIII, King: 9-10, 130
Henstock, Adrian: 74, 129
Hiett, Elizabeth: 46
Hildelitha, Abbess: 30
Hill, Nathaniel: 66
Hillyer, William: 52
Holcroft, William: 74, 83, 129-131
Hopkins, Thomas: 64
Houghton: 65
Houston, Jane: 26, 121
Hudson, Pat: 6
Hughes, Rev Charles: 24
Hull, Felix: 42, 124
Hulse family: 76, 79, 86, 110
Hulse, Sir Charles: 91
Humfreys, Sir Orlando: 79, 99, 130
Humfreys, Sir William: 78, 116, 130
Hunt, William: 92
Hunter, John: 109, 124, 134
Hutchinson, Henry: 86, 96

Ine, King: 104
Isham, Edmund: 52

James I, King: 42
James II, King: 40, 46, 125
Jennings: see Gennynges
Johnson, Isaac: 24, 55-59, 73, 112, 116-7, 121, 127
Jolley, John: 96
Josselin, Ralph: 16, 119
Kain, Prof Roger: 7, 19, 118, 120, 121-7, 129

Kemble, James: 100
Keniston: fig.16
Kingsbury, John: 23, 120

Lennard, R: 11, 119
Lethieullier, John: 99
Lethieullier, Smart: 79, 99, 101, 110, 113-4, 122, 130, 133
Liddell, Rev Robert: 58
Linton: 51
Lockey: 38, 96
Lockey, Abigail: 38
Lockwood, H.H: 108, 116, 122, 126, 128, 134-5
Lodge, Oliver: 52, 126
Lucas, Thomas: 98
Luff, George: 50, 115, 124 & fig.8
Lugar: 57, 73
Lysons, Daniel: 50, 97, 101, 111, 133

Macaulay, Lord: 46, 123
Macfarlane, Alan: 6, 85, 119, 121, 131
Mason, Dr Stuart: 7, 25, 120-1, 124, 127
Maud, Abbess: 31
Maynard, Lord: 23
McIntosh, Prof Marjorie: 80, 122, 130
Mead, Nicholas: 95
Middleton, Thomas: 16
Mildmay, Carew: 83, 129
Morant, Philip: 97, 119, 124-5, 133
Mornington, Lord: 39
Murphy, Patricia: 99, 123
Murray, Lord George: 20
Murray, William: 61
Musgrave, Rev Dr Christoher: 38, 50-4, 116, 119, 126
Musgrave, Sir Christopher Sr: 50

Neale, Kenneth: 108, 119, 124, 128, 134
Newcourt: 103

Newman, Robert: 97
Nichols, Thomas: 95
Nicholson, Otto: 68
Nixon, Richard: 61
Noel, Susan: 78
North, Henry: 43
North, Rev John: 23
Northey, Edward: 77

O'Leary, John: 81-2, 110, 112-4, 123, 133
Oliver, Richard: 7, 19, 71, 120-1, 127
Osbaldeston (aka Osbaston), Francis: 99, 133
Osbaldeston (aka Osbaston), Mary: 99, 133
Osekyn, Alice: 88
Osekyn, John: 88
Oswald, Bishop: 105
Owen, Leslie: 49
Owen, T: 71
Owens: 51
Oxley, Dr J.E: 50, 82, 111, 114, 118, 126-7, 129-30, 132, 135

Pallavicino, Sir Toby: fig.14
Pamphlin family: 87-8
Paulin, James: 58, 127
Pearson, Rev Robert: 27
Pedley, Samuel: 61
Peel, Sir Robert: 17
Penn, William: 47
Perkins, Joseph: 38, 59, 61, 127
Perry, John: 14, 25
Petre family: 110, 130
Petre, Sir William: 36
Pilbeam: 71
Poole, Rev Robert: 16
Porter family: 97-8, 133
Porter, Stephen: 98
Porter, William: 97
Powell, W. Raymond: 28, 31, 33, 97, 111, 122

Powle, Thomas: 36
Pownsett family (inc. Thomas + William): 34-6, 82
Pownsett, Henry: 102
Pryor, David: 112

Quin, W.F: 119

Raikes, Robert: 55
Rashleigh Rev P: 38, 52-4, 57, 65, 116, 119, 126
Raymond, Charles: 106
Reaney, P.H: 91, 93, 99, 122, 131-4
Rigby, Joan: 101
Rigby, John: 101
Rippon, Stephen: 104, 122, 134
Rodwell, Warwick: 104, 134
Rowlandson: 119 & fig.2
Sage, Edward: 45-6, 76, 96, 105, 110-111, 114-5, 124, 127, 129-131, 133, 135 & fig.17
Salisbury, Marquis of: 61, 112
Salter, Andrew: 34
Savill, John: 20
Sawyer, P.H: 113, 134-5
Scratton, James: 87-8
Seebohm, Frederic: 102-3
Sharp, James: 59, 61
Shelley, John: 98
Skingle, Rev: 20
Skinner, John: 55, 57, 73
Skinner, Stephen: 65
Skinner, William: fig.3
Spencer, Chris: 95
Stephens, Hester: 38
Stephens, R: 8, 118, 121-2
Stephens, Rev Dr William: 49-50, 107, 112, 116, 125
Sterry family: 61, 66
Stevens, Francis: 38, 61
Stevens, Samuel: 38, 61
Stoddard, Thomas: 64
Sturman, M: 83, 122, 130
Swan, Edward: 21
Swan, Owen: 21

Tarver, Ann: 8
Tasker, G.F: 95, 132
Taylor, Elizabeth: 46
Taylor, Richard: 45-6, 53, 75, 125
Taylor, William: 46
Thomas, Robert: 34
Thompson, J.S: 61
Tresswell, Robert: 68-9
Tuck, Edward: 105, 134
Tuggell, Andrew: 92
Twyford: 57, 73, 117
Tyndall, Savage: 50
Tyser, Thomas: 52

Unwin, W.C: 5

Vaughan: 64
Vaughan, John: 113
Waddington, B: 24
Wake, Sir William: 24-25
Wakefield, Gibbon: 93
Wake-Jones family: 24, 121
Wakeling, Rev J.D: 111
Waller, William: 99, 100, 130
Walter, H: 66
Wand, Allen: 111-12, 135
Wand, Harold: 111, 135
Warner, Rev William: 24
Warren, William, Earl of: 9
Weldale, Mary: 66
Wellesley, Viscount: 61
Whiteman, Ann: 47, 125
Wight, Henry: 41, 124
Wight, John: 61

Wight, Sarah: 41
Wignall, Richard: 34, 36, 67
William I, King: 30
Wite: 62-3, 113, 123-4, 127, 135
Wood, Hutton: 25
Wood, Robert: 21
Woodforde, Rev J: 17, 119
Woodward, Godfrey: 97
Wright, H.C: 24
Wulfhilda, Abbess: 30
Wyeth, Wm: 66

Young, Arthur: 87-8
Young Thomas: 105

Index of place names
The county is Essex unless otherwise noted

Aldborough Hatch: estate, mill & millponds: 38, 59, 61, 96, 127; other: 38, 49, 59, 61, 86-87, 92-93, 123
Aldborough Road: 131-132
Aldersbrook: 99
Appletons & close: 98
Ashdon: 23, 25-26, 120
Astley, Cambs: 93
Aveley: 26

Barking & Dagenham LB: 7, 33, 76, 78, 87-88, 97, 110-112, 116-117, 121, 131
Barking & Barking parish: 6-129
Barking Lane (Ilford Lane): 43
Barking Mill & Mill Meadows: 59
Barking Rectory: 30, 36
Barking Town & Town Ward: 46, 50, 57, 63, 74-75, 95, 111-112, 115, 124
Barking Uplands: 87
Barking Vicarage: 30-31, 36, 43, 46, 52, 82, 111-112, 126
Barking Abbey: *see Index*
Barking Manor: *see Index*
Barkingside, Ilford: 45, 49-50, 91-96, 99, 131-132
Barley Lane: 50
Baronesredene: 91
Bartlow & Bartlow End, Cambs: 23, 26
Becontree Estate, Dagenham: 98
Becontree Hundred: 29, 74
Beehive Lane, Ilford: 46, 50, 68, 99
Belchamp Otten: 10, 16, 20
Bifrons, Barking: 52
Bocking: 12, 16-17, 20-21, 119
Boreham: 27
Bowers Gifford: 113
Boxted: 26
Bradwell Minster church: 28
Braintree: 21, 119
Breamore House: 111

Brentwood: 41
Bunting Bridge & Estate: 61, 126
Buntons Brook (Cranbrook): 95
Bures, Suffolk: 113
Bures Hamlet: 23-24
Buslingthorpe, Lincs: 121

Cameron Road: 132
Canada Allotments: 92-93, 132
Canterbury, Kent: 26, 28, 75, 9.
Chadwell Heath (Blackhethe), Dagenham: 68, 83, 103, 133
Chadwell St Mary: 27
Chadwell Ward, Barking: 34, 50, 57, 68, 74-75, 83, 127
Chafford Hundred: 74
Chapel Field & Piece, Barkingside: 45, 92
Chapel Lodge, site of: 131
Chase Lane & Gate, Barkingside: 95-96
Chelmsford: 7, 20
Chigwell: 17, 23, 25, 75
Chingford: 132
Clavering & Langley: 9, 24, 121
Clay, The (Cleyberye): 107
Claybury & Manor & Hall: 31, 37, 49, 65, 87, 91-92, 107, 134
ClayHall: 43, 126
Clayhooks Lane: 108
Clements Estate: 43, 99, 102
Colchester: 11, 26, 124
Cold Norton: 27
Collier Row, Romford: 93
Colne Engaine: 21, 23 & *see also Earls Colne*
Combecroft: 101
Conduit Field, Ilford: 100-102, 133
Courteen Hall, Northants: 121
Cranbrook Hall & Estate, Ilford: 54-55, 64, 95, 100, 105-107, 128
Cranbrook Road, Ilford: 50, 106-107
Cressing Temple: 109

Cricklefields: 39, 91, 101-102

Dagenham Parish & Vicarage: 28, 30, 42, 68, 76, 88, 103, 124
Dagenham: 70, 75-76, 78, 80, 82-83, 87-88, 93, 97, 110-111, 130, 131, 133
Dagenhams (Jenkins): 98
De Vere Gardens, Ilford: 107 & 128
Debden: 14, 17, 20
Deptford, Kent: 59
Downham: 26
Downshall Manor (Dunshall): 31, 34, 36, 91, 101, 123
Dunmow: 12
Drive, The, Ilford: 107

Earls Colne: 6-7, 16, 20, 24, 85, 121 & see also Colne Engaine
East (Chapel) Hainault Walk: 83
East Ham Level (Westmarsh): 37
East Ham: 16-18, 35, 53, 75, 119-20
East Street, Barking: 82
Eastbury Common Field: 87
Eastbury Level & Marshland & Upland: 66, 87, 113, 115, 128
Eastbury Manor & Farm, Barking: 31, 33-35, 37-38, 59, 61, 64-66, 87, 90, 98, 113-115, 123, 128
Emelingbury Manor, Ilford: 33, 63
Epping Forest: 83-84, 92-94
Essex: 6, 9-11, 18, 44-45, 55, 65, 70, 104, 113, 119-127, 130
Essex, ancient kingdom of: 28

Fairlop Fair: 94
Faversham, Kent: 58
Fencepiece: 45, 92, 132.
Folly House & Field, Green Lane: 102
Forest Fence & Gate: 92-94
Foxearth: 26

Fulks (Fulkes): 79, 82, 108, 134
Fullwell, Barkingside: 45, 49, 92-93, 99

Gale Street: 89, 97, 133
Gaysham Hall: 31, 33, 37-39, 41, 50, 54, 59, 61, 63, 82, 126
Gearies (Little): 50, 99
Gessames Hall: 34, 124
Gestingthorpe: 24, 55
Glastonbury Abbey, Somerset: 104, 134
Golden Woods: 134
Goodmayes: 57, 66, 86, 130, 133
Gordon Fields & Road: 102
Great Baddow: 16
Great ChisHall: 25
Great Dunmow: 12
Great Horkesley: 24, 26
Great Ilford & Ward: 57, 62, 68, 83
Great Loxford: see Loxford
Great Parndon: 14
Great Porters, Gale Street: 97-98, 133
Great Tey: 24
Great Wakering: 25
Great Wigborough: 113
Green Lane or Way (Green Streate): 57, 66, 100, 102, 133

Hainault Forest: 35, 83, 87, 91, 115, 132-133
Hainault Road, Little Heath: 93
Halfpenny Marsh: 87
Halifax, Yorks: 9, 17, 118
Hanningfield: 128
Harlow: 25
Hatfield Broad Oak, Herts: 113
Hatfield House, Herts: 54, 62, 64-66, 88, 107, 112, 122, 126-129, 134
Havering-atte-Bower: 28, 77, 80, 93, 122, 130
Heavywaters: 130

Hedgmans Estate, Gale Street: 133
Heybridge: 27
High Road to Romford: 35, 68, 83, 91, 101, 103, 108, 115, 132-133
Highlands: 54
Hitchin, Herts: 103
Hobses (StoneHalls Farm/Hudsons/Hicks): 133
Hockley: 113
Hornchurch: 28
Horndon (on-the-Hill): 26, 128
Huntings Farm, Green Lane: 133
Hunts Hall (Maypole Inn): 92

Ilford High Road: *see High Road to Romford*
Ilford Hospital & Chapel: 31-35, 37, 42, 50, 54-55, 59, 61-67, 82-83, 87, 91-92, 102, 106-107, 115, 122-123, 126-128, 130-132, 134
Ilford Hospital Almshouses: 65
Ilford Lane (Barking Lane): 43
Ilford Pioneer Market: 124
Ilford Ward, Barking Parish: 74
Ilford: 6, 7, 31, 43, 45-46, 53-54, 57-59, 61-62, 68, 74-75, 91, 94-95, 99-100, 105, 110-111, 113, 115, 124, 127, 132-134

Jenkins (Dagenhams): 31, 35, 37, 42, 65, 78, 98, 124, 133
Jollies (Melcombe Lodge): 124

Kelvedon: 26.
Kennedy Allots, Walthamstow: 93
Kennites Farm: 86-87, 131
Kent, county of: 28, 42, 124, 131
King Solomon High School: 132
Kings Bridge, Barking: 13
Kirkby Lonsdale, Westmoreland: 6

Lambourne: 26

Langley: 9, 24, 121
Lawford: 55
Lea & Bridge & Mill: see Stratford
Levesons (Lessons Grove): 91, 127, 132
Lewes Abbey, Sussex: 9
Lexden: 11, 20-21
Ley Street, Ilford: 106
Little Beagles (Beehive): 68
Little Heath: 50, 92-93, 95
Little Horkesley: 26
Lodge Avenue & Porters Lodge Lane: 88, 98
London: 7, 11, 35, 46, 50, 96, 111, 123
London Road, Barking: 124
Long Yard (Purlands): 103
Longbridge Farm & Road: 80, 82
Loughton & Hall & Manor: 14, 20, 99
Loxford Bridge &Brook: 95, 133
Loxford Manor & Farm: 34, 80, 102
Loxford, Ilford: 33-35, 65, 87, 99, 101-102
Loxfordbury: 31, 33, 37

Magdalen Laver: 26
Malmaynes & Farm: 88
Marks Hall &Gate: 83, 93, 122
Marsh Way (Mogges Lane): 90
Mayes Brook & Park: 90, 98, 132
Maypole Inn (Hunts Hall): 92-93, 95, 132
Melcombe Lodge (Jollies): 124.
Middlesex: 50, 105
Mill Mead, Barking: 59, 61
Mistley: 47
Mogges Farm & Lane: 88, 90, 130
Moreton: 20
Mossford Green: 50
Mount Bures: 24

Navestock: 16
Nazeing & Nazeingbury: 113
New Chapel, Barkingside: 45, 92, 126, 131-132

New Inned Marsh & Gate: 131
New North Road, Hainault: 132
Newbury & Manor & Ward: 31, 33-34, 36-37, 61, 92, 101, 123
Newport: 16
Norfolk, county of: 6, 17
North Grange & Marsh: 113, 123
Northstrete: 30

Oaks Lane, Aldborough Hatch: 49
Old Geryes: 134
Old Moggs: 130

Padnall Corner: 50, 93, 95
Parsloes, Dagenham: 124, 133
Perrymans & Shonks: 61
Pooles Cottages & Court: 86
Porters Manor, & Lodge & Lane Goodmayes: 97-98, 133
Priests Marsh/ Prestemede: 87
Prince of Wales, Green Lane: 102
Prittlewell Priory, Southend: 9
Purlands or Longyerd: 103.
Purpenfield: 101

Ramsden Bellhouse: 26
Rant flood lake, Ripple: 88-89, 131
Ravenynefield/Conduit Field: 102
Rawreth: 24
Rayleigh Hills: 134
Rayne: 14
Red Rose Farm (Tanyard): 95
Redbridge: 3, 7, 17
Renwick Road, Barking: 90
Ripple Levels (Marsh): 87-88, 128
Ripple or Rippel: 131
Ripple Road & Rippleside Farms: 66, 87-88
Ripple Ward: 34, 114, 123, 127
Ripple, Barking: 34, 45, 57, 66, 74-75, 87-88, 93, 97, 131

Rippledown: 87-88
Roding, River: 90, 100, 131
Romford: 45, 58, 133
Romford Road: see High Road to Romford
Rose Lane: 93
Royal Forest: 39, 45, 51, 68, 91-95 & *see also Waltham, Great Forest.*

Scrattons Farm: 88
Serlis Croft: 101
Seven Kings: 60
Sewardstone(bury): 23-24
Seymour Gardens: 107
Shapwick, Somerset: 104, 134
Sheppey, Kent: 28
Ship and Shovel Public House: 90
Smiths Hall Estate: 123
South Park & StoneHall Ilford: 102,133.
Southend: 9
Southfleet, Kent: 52, 55
Southminster: 24
South Park, Ilford: 102, 133
Sparkes Wood, ClayHall: 126
Spittle Grove, Ilford: 91
Spratly (Sprotly) Hall: 86, 131
St Chad's, Chadwell Heath: 103
St Margaret's Parish Church, Barking: 30, 46, 52, 57-58, 63, 74-75, 111-112, 115, 122, 124-125
St Mary's Church, Ilford: 57, 115, 127
St Peter's & Paul's Roman Catholic School: 102
Stanstead Mountfitchet: 16
Stepney, London: 53
Stock: 5
Stonehall Manor & Farm: 37, 39, 51, 61, 123
Stratford: 91, 110
Sturmer: 24
Suffolk, county of: 6
Surrey, county of: 105

Tanner Street, Barking: 95
Tannery related names: 94-95
Thanet, Kent: 28
Thames Gateway: 122
Tilbury: 27, 28
Tolleshunt: 113
Tomswood & Hill: 93, 132
Toppesfield: 25
Trumpete(e)rs: 92
Tuggalls Hall: 92-93
Twinstead: 23-24, 26

Uphall, Ilford: 31, 36-37, 61, 100
Upminster: 26

Valentines, Ilford: 54, 59, 99, 105-106
Volunteer Drill Ground: 102

Wakefield & Manor, Yorks: 9
Waltham Abbey & Holy Cross: 10, 14, 23-24, 28
Waltham, Great Forest of: 35, 68, 83-84, 87, 91-95, 108, 112, 117, 130-132 & *see also Royal Forest; Index*
Walthamstow: 41, 83, 93, 108, 132
Wangey Estate, Goodmayes: 31, 36-37, 61, 80, 99
Wanstead: 39, 123
Warley: 31, 65
West Hainault Walk: 83
West Ham: 75
West Tilbury: 27
Westbury, Barking: 31, 33-35, 37-38, 45-46, 59, 65-67, 80, 83, 87, 128
Westmarsh, East Ham: 37
Westmoreland: 6
Whalebone, Dagenham: 103
Whites (Whitings) Farm: 38, 59, 127
Wickford: 16-17
Widdington: 14, 17

Widford & its mill: 21, 24
Wigborough: 113
Wimbish: 11, 14, 16, 21
Wimbledon: 77
Windelands, Ilford: 107
Witham: 16-17, 21
Woodbridge, Suffolk: 24, 55.
Woodford: 26
Writtle & Vicarage: 12
Wyfields Manor & House: 31, 37, 45, 54, 59, 65, 99, 105, 107